D0081258

PARTY SYSTEM CHANGE

Party System Change

Approaches and Interpretations

PETER MAIR

CLARENDON PRESS · OXFORD

1997

Tennessee Tech Library
Cookeville, TN

Oxford University Press, Great Clarendon Street, Oxford OX2 6DP
Oxford New York
Athens Auckland Bangkok Bogota Bombay
Buenos Aires Calcutta Cape Town Dar es Salaam
Delhi Florence Hong Kong Istanbul Karachi
Kuala Lumpur Madras Madrid Melbourne
Mexico City Nairobi Paris Singapore
Taipei Tokyo Toronto
and associated companies in
Berlin Ibadan

Oxford is a trade mark of Oxford University Press

Published in the United States
by Oxford University Press Inc., New York

© Peter Mair 1997

All rights reserved. No part of this publication may be reproduced,
stored in a retrieval system, or transmitted, in any form or by any means,
without the prior permission in writing of Oxford University Press.
Within the UK, exceptions are allowed in respect of any fair dealing for the
purpose of research or private study, or criticism or review, as permitted
under the Copyright, Designs and Patents Act, 1988, or in the case of
reprographic reproduction in accordance with the terms of the licences
issued by the Copyright Licensing Agency. Enquiries concerning
reproduction outside these terms and in other countries should be
sent to the Rights Department, Oxford University Press,
at the address above

British Library Cataloguing in Publication Data
Data available

Library of Congress Cataloging in Publication Data
Data available
ISBN 0–19–829235–X

1 3 5 7 9 10 8 6 4 2

Typeset by Hope Services (Abingdon) Ltd.
Printed in Great Britain
on acid-free paper by
Biddles Ltd., Guildford & King's Lynn

For Cathleen, 'brave new world . . .'

PREFACE

Parties and party systems form a popular theme in comparative political science. At one time or another, most of us in the profession have written on the subject. More often than not, however, it's a somewhat peripatetic interest, and, with time, though not in my case, the concerns of the individual scholar tend to move on to other themes and problems. More general engagement with the study of parties and party systems has also tended to ebb and flow in the profession as a whole, being very prominent in the 1960s and 1970s, when many of the now classic works were first published, and then fading into unfashionability in the 1980s, when alternative modes of political representation and intermediation grabbed attention. More recently, and not least as a result of the prominence accorded to the role of parties in the 'third wave' of democratization in the 1990s, the study has once more come back into favour, and this time with renewed vigour. This is especially true in Europe. In 1995, for example, the first ever major journal to be devoted entirely to the comparative study of parties and party systems, *Party Politics*, was launched from the University of Manchester, while in 1996, during the annual Joint Sessions of the European Consortium of Political Research in Oslo, as many as five of the twenty-three workshops dealt exclusively with party themes. Little more than a decade ago, students of party politics were often accused of being engaged in a somewhat *passé* branch of the discipline; today it is a field of study which is brimming with health and promise.

Such renewal is especially welcome for people like myself, who have tended to stay in the same sub-disciplinary rut over the years. I first began to study parties in the mid-1970s, focusing initially on the Irish case alone, and later broadening out to comparative analyses in Western Europe and occasionally further afield. This present volume is now intended to reflect those more recent and broader interests. At one level, spending two decades within more or less the same sub-field of the discipline is limiting. You develop a sort of expertise, but it is confined. At another level, however, and this probably also explains the attested attraction of the study of parties and party systems to so many political scientists, it is also almost limitless, being a field of study which affords access to, and is touched by, an extraordinarily wide range of concerns running from political culture to voting behaviour, from theories of competition to the study of coalition formation, from policy analysis to political performance, and so on, and with little in the way of insight being achieved without a least some reasonable grasp of how institutions work, how values develop, and how ideologies are constructed. If parties and party systems remain a popular theme then, it is at least partly because they embrace so much of the real core of traditional political science.

This book is not about parties and party systems as such. Rather, it is about party and party system *change*, with the focus resting primarily on how this question can be approached and interpreted. In this sense, it is also, and perhaps even more so, a book about party and party system *stability*. In common with most party scholars of my generation, I grew into the study at a time when most of the talk was of crisis and transformation, and of how old orders were crumbling. Caught up in the excitement generated by the varieties of post-1968 alternative political movements, and by the various shocks suffered by otherwise stable and persistent party systems in the 1970s, much of the most interesting literature on parties, party systems, and electoral behaviour then chose to focus on the extent to which things were changing, and on how much of the recognizable past was being left behind.

But although some of this thinking also suffuses part of the discussions in the earlier chapters of this book, the more general and consistent emphasis is on persistence and survival: the persistence and survival of parties, and the persistence and survival of party systems. For, in the end, and despite the appeal of the new, it is the sheer staying power of traditional patterns which still remains the most striking feature of contemporary party alignments. That said, my primary purpose is not one of marshalling the various arguments which might show that the long-established parties and party systems still continue to hold sway—although that is certainly one of the intentions here, as can be seen in Chapters 2, 3 and 4. Rather, and more fundamentally, this book is primarily about *how* survival is effected, and about how change, when it does occur, may be analysed and understood. It is about processes of party adaptation and control, and processes of party system adaptation and control. It is about how parties and party systems 'freeze' themselves into place.

Because this is also primarily a book devoted to approaches and interpretations, it tries to avoid being tied down to specific events, places, and times. In this sense, and perhaps more accurately, it is less about persistence and change as such, and rather more about how we are to begin to understand these crucial processes. Thus, for example, a lot of the attention in this book is devoted to the question of party organization (see especially Chapters 5 and 6), and to the ways in which parties increasingly come to invade the state and how they find there a new means of ensuring their survival. A lot of attention is also given to party strategies and structures of competition (see Chapters 7, 8, and 9), and to the idea that established party systems as such may generate their own momentum, a feature which, almost by definition, has yet to be crystallized in the newly emerging party systems of post-Communist Europe (Chapter 8). Indeed, I would contend that it is only by comparing established party systems with those which are still in their infancy that we can really begin to understand the basis of the freezing process.

The various essays included in this volume reflect work which has been carried out since the late 1980s, and in the course of that work, and also earlier, I have incurred many debts to friends and colleagues in the field. The biggest of these is to my various collaborators and co-authors over the years, especially since I have been fortunate enough to have worked closely with some of the very best scholars in the field. These include Hans Daalder, who first guided my interest in the comparative study of West European parties and party systems, and Gordon Smith, with whom I once directed an invaluable workshop on parties in the ECPR Joint Sessions in Rimini, and whose knowledge of this field is immense. I have also benefited from and learned more than I can say from my long-standing collaboration with Stefano Bartolini, who is a wonderful political scientist, as well as from my more recent collaboration with Dick Katz, an excellent and clear-thinking colleague with whom I have been engaged in work on party organizations, and who is co-author of the paper which now reappears as

Chapter 5 of this volume. I am also indebted to my Irish colleagues and collaborators Michael Gallagher and especially Michael Laver, as well as to the various members of the party organization project which Dick Katz and I originally developed, and with whom it was always a delight to work: Luciano Bardi, Lars Bille, Kris Deschouwer, David Farrell, Ruud Koole, Leonardo Morlino, Wolfgang Müller, Jon Pierre, Thomas Poguntke, Jan Sundberg, Lars Svåsand, Hella van de Velde, Paul Webb, and Anders Widfeldt. That project was supported by the American National Science Foundation, as well as by the ECPR and, in various guises, the late Rudold Wildenmann, and to these thanks are also due. Finally, I would like to acknowledge the support and assistance afforded by the networks of colleagues and the facilities made available to me in the Department of Government in the University of Manchester and the Department of Political Science in the University of Leiden, as well as in the Netherlands Institute for Advanced Study in Wassenaar, where some of these ideas were initially drafted.

Less directly, and as is more than evident from the recurring citations in this book, I owe a great deal to the insights of an earlier generation of scholars, and in particular to Giovanni Sartori, whose understanding of parties and party systems remains unrivalled, and the late Stein Rokkan, with two of the chapters (4 and 8) in this volume first taking shape in the form of two Stein Rokkan memorial lectures, one during the ECPR Joint Sessions in the University of Limerick in 1992 and the other in the University of Bergen in 1995. Here in the Netherlands, I have benefited particularly from the advice, feedback, and insights of a most impressive bunch of Ph.D. students, some of whom are already beginning to make their mark in the discipline, including Ingrid van Biezen, Petr Kopecky, André Krouwel, Anya van der Meer, Cas Mudde, and Marc van den Muyzenberg. Various undergraduate students, in Leiden and earlier in Manchester, have also proved a great source of feedback and, as always, have tried to push me towards more clear-headedness.

Most of the chapters in this book have already been published in various forms in journals or edited collections over the past few years, and I am grateful to the various publishers for permission to reproduce them here, whether in whole or in part. Although sometimes modified, combined, and restructured to avoid too much repetition, as well as for reasons of clarity, I have largely refrained from attempting to update them or to recast them in the light of developments subsequent to their publication. The arguments are as they are. Chapter 2 is a merger of parts of two earlier pieces, one of which was first published in the journal *West European Politics*, vol. 12, no. 4, 1989, with the other being first published as my introduction to Peter Mair (ed.), *The West European Party System* (Oxford University Press, 1990). Chapter 3 was first published in the *Journal of Theoretical Politics*, vol. 1, no. 3, 1989. Chapter 4 was originally delivered as the Stein Rokkan lecture during the ECPR Joint Sessions in the University of Limerick in 1992, and was subsequently published in the *European Journal of Political Research*, vol. 24, no. 2, 1993. Chapter 5 was co-authored with Richard S. Katz and was first published in the journal *Party Politics*, vol. 1, no. 1, 1995. Chapter 6 is a merger of parts of two earlier pieces, one of which was first published as my Introduction to Richard S. Katz and Peter Mair (eds.), *How Parties Organize*: *Change and Adaptation in Party Organizations in Western Democracies* (Sage, 1994), with the other being first published in the journal *West European Politics*, vol. 18, no. 3, 1995, both of which drew on my inaugural lecture here at the University of Leiden. Chapter 7 was first published as a chapter in Michael Moran and Maurice Wright (eds.), *The Market and the State*: *Studies in Interdependence* (Macmillan, 1991), and Chapter 9 was first published as a chapter in Lawrence LeDuc, Richard G. Niemi, and Pippa Norris (eds.), *Comparing Democracies* (Sage, 1996).

This book would probably never have seen the light of day without the active and enthusiastic encouragement of two OUP editors, Tim Barton and especially Dominic Byatt, both of whom have the marvellous capacity of instilling confidence in their authors. Confidence and encouragement, and more, were also generated in immeasurable quantities by Karin Tilmans, to whom I, and Cathleen and John, owe so much. She is really great!

Peter Mair
Leiden
Summer, 1996

CONTENTS

Part III Party Organizations and Party Systems

Part IV Party Systems and Structures of Competition

FIGURES

TABLES

PART I

Introduction

1

On the Freezing of Party Systems

In late 1995 I was invited to present a short paper to an occasional seminar series in the University of Bergen.[1] The theme of the series was 'Law and Structure', and those presenting papers were asked to summarize some particular classic law in the social sciences, to review its background and development, and then to discuss the question of its current validity and viability. In my case, the 'law' on which I was asked to contribute was 'the freezing of party systems', which had first been promulgated, as it were, by S. M. Lipset and Stein Rokkan almost thirty years before, and which, even now, continues to be one of the most familiar and most frequently cited theses within the field of comparative party studies: 'The party systems of the 1960s,' wrote Lipset and Rokkan (1967: 50), 'reflect, with few but significant exceptions, the cleavage structures of the 1920s . . . [T]he party alternatives, and in remarkably many cases the party organizations, are older than the majorities of the national electorates.' This thesis also recurs frequently in the subsequent chapters of this book, with the burden of most of the chapters in Part 2 being devoted to its defence. In brief, and particularly in those first chapters, I contend that the freezing hypothesis remains largely valid, at least up to now, with the evidence of long-term continuities in party systems far outweighing the ostensibly more striking and more immediate evidence of change. In other words, and some three decades later, the long-standing party alternatives which had been instanced by Lipset and Rokkan are now even older still (see especially Chapter 4 below).

---

[1] Some of the ideas presented in the chapter were first stimulated by the discussion in the Bergen seminar, and for this I would like to thank the convenor, Stein Ugelvik Larsen, and the various participants. I would also like to thank my Leiden colleagues, Huib Pellikaan and Herman van Gunsteren, for guiding me to some valuable literature.

LAWS AND STRUCTURES

Although the continuities which I emphasize in the early chapters of this volume do not simply derive from chance, it is also important to recognize that no actual 'law' is involved here, and in this sense the freezing hypothesis did not really fall within the remit of the Bergen seminar series. Strictly speaking, of course, there are no real laws at all within political science, or even within the social sciences more generally, but only probabilities and standard expectations.[2] Even within these limits, however, and especially when measured against the potential predictions which might be derived from analyses in related fields, such as, for example, the relationship between electoral systems and party systems, or the theory of coalition formation, the freezing hypothesis fails to convince. In fact, not only does it not enjoy a law-like status, but it was hardly even a real hypothesis. Rather, and more simply, it was an empirical observation: the party systems of the 1960s had more or less frozen into place by the 1920s, and the party alternatives had more or less tended to survive. To be sure, Lipset and Rokkan had devoted considerable effort to explaining why the various constellations which had settled into place in the 1920s had taken the particular form which they did, and they had also outlined a variety of general patterns and conjunctures which made sense of both the diversity and the commonalities which were then apparent across the Western European party mosaic. Evidence of the subsequent continuities was presented almost incidentally, however, and what we now tend to read as the principal message of that path-breaking analysis—the freezing of party systems into the 1960s and beyond—was actually not much more than a coda to an otherwise differently directed analysis, with little effort being made to elaborate an argument as to how this bias towards stability was realized in practice.

Subsequent discussions of the freezing hypothesis have also taken a lot for granted. Since no 'freezing law' had ever really been elaborated, and since there was no actual theory which could be formally tested and/or challenged, much of the discussion of the original Lipset and Rokkan analysis has tended instead to revolve

---

[2] See the illuminating discussion in Sartori (1986), and his treatment of conditionality and 'tendency laws' (49–52, 52–5).

around questions of its continued empirical validity. How and why party systems freeze into place is therefore seen as less important than the question of whether they still continue to be frozen today. Nor is this simply the particular bias of a new generation of party scholars, for, with the exception of the occasional clues offered by Lipset and Rokkan themselves at the end of their original essay,[3] and the more extensive and insightful elaboration of the argument by Sartori (1969), little attention has ever really been paid to the actual 'mechanics' of the freezing process. Stability is assumed, and only change tends to be explained.

It has always proved possible, of course, to turn the various explanations of change on their heads, and thereby to transform them into explanations of stability. For example, the (sometimes gradual) readjustments which occur in party systems in the wake of institutional changes (such as changes in the electoral system or in the structure of the executive) clearly underline the importance of institutional continuity for party system stability (see also below). The impact of socio-economic changes on voting behaviour, and the way in which these can then feed through into electoral realignment or dealignment, also serves to emphasize how the long-term survival of individual parties may be dependent upon stable social relations. Finally, the apparent linkage between party organizational change on the one hand and party vulnerability on the other (see especially Chapter 2 below) helps to indicate that the stabilization of party alignments rests partly on how the parties themselves link into the wider community. In all three circumstances, the understanding of how change occurs may also be seen to cast some light on the factors which promote stability and inertia, and, in this sense at least, may afford some degree of insight into the mechanics of the freezing process itself.

But there is often something missing here. For when we associate the freezing process with the stabilization of a particular social structure, for example, or with the consolidation of a particular type of organizational intervention, we risk dissolving the problem of the freezing of party *systems* into that of the freezing of individual parties or groups of parties. In other words, we risk forgetting about the system as such, and devote most of our effort instead to

---

[3] Lipset and Rokkan (1967: 51–6), where, among other factors, they refer to the importance of organizational intervention and the notion of parties 'narrowing the "support market" '.

an understanding of its component parts. To offer a very concrete example, we tend to explain the survival and consolidation of, say, the British Conservative and Labour parties, rather than the survival and consolidation of the British two-party system as such. And while the long-term survival of the Conservatives and Labour certainly helps to ensure that the two-party system remains intact, it might also be argued that it is the survival of the two-party system which guarantees the dominant position of both individual parties. In this sense it is the system which makes for the parties as much as it is the parties which make for the system. This argument can also be extended even further, suggesting that a particular party system may survive even when some or all of its components have changed quite substantially (the United States offers a very obvious example of what is arguably a much more generalized phenomenon); conversely, a particular system may change even when some or all of its components prove relatively persistent (as has been amply illustrated by recent developments in the Irish case—see also Chapter 9 below).

Since parties and party systems offer two quite distinct foci of analysis (Bartolini, 1986; Sartori, 1976: 42–7; Ware, 1996: 6–7), it also follows that we should distinguish the freezing and unfreezing of parties on the one hand from that of party systems on the other (see also Chapter 3 below). With few exceptions, however, an independent sense of the latter has often been missing from the now voluminous and still growing literature on persistence and change. How individual parties or even groups of parties survive, and how they change, is certainly well documented and discussed. Continuities and shifts in the patterns of alignment between voters and parties have also been widely recorded and analysed. The processes which may either freeze or undermine a particular party system have received much less attention, however, in that the stabilization or destabilization of a particular form of interaction between parties—the stabilization or destabilization of a party system as such—has usually been assumed to follow from, or even to be dependent upon, the prior performance of the individual parties involved.[4]

---

[4] Indeed, this sense of the system as being little more than the sum of its parts is also implicit in the relative amount of attention devoted to the discussion of individual party organizations in Lipset and Rokkan's (1967: 51–6) own brief discussion of the freezing process.

Among the exceptions to this otherwise generalized sense of neglect is, of course, the attention which is paid to the institutional conditions of persistence or change. Institutions are precisely trans-partisan in their impact, and while not all parties will be affected in the same way by a particular social-structural balance, for example, or by the preference for a particular organizational form, all parties are equally subject to the same set of institutional conditions. From this, then, it is just a small step to trace a linkage between particular institutions on the one hand and particular types of party system on the other, a linkage that can be seen most obviously in the literature dealing with the political consequences of electoral laws. This was also one of the only systemic factors emphasized by Rokkan (1970: 90, 160–1), who cited the adoption of systems of proportional representation as one of the key elements accounting for the long-term stabilization of the balance of forces between the parties. 'Institutions reflect the interests of those who devise them' (Geddes, 1995: 239) and the particular institutional structures which were devised in the early twentieth century to accommodate the representation of fully mobilized electorates have clearly helped to maintain the then newly emergent party systems thereafter. Notwithstanding subsequent changes at the level of the electorate and at the level of party organization, the freezing of institutions has therefore facilitated the freezing of party systems.

In other respects, however, the neglect of a systemic reference may well be justified. Intriguing as the freezing of individual parties or groups of parties may be, for example—and in this regard the existing literature continues to debate the relative importance of the influences of social structure, organizational effort, and the strength of collective identities and ideological predispositions—the freezing of party systems may be, in the end, simply not problematic. Indeed, among the reasons why Lipset and Rokkan devoted so little effort to the mechanics of the freezing process is possibly that they could take persistence more or less for granted. 'Stasis is the norm for complex systems,' notes Gould (1991: 69), and it may well be that party systems simply have an inherent bias towards stability. In other words, once electorates had become fully mobilized, and once the institutional structures of mass democracy had become consolidated, a crude equilibrium became established; thereafter, the laws of inertia—and more—took over (Sartori, 1969: 90).

It goes almost without saying that the establishment of an equilibrium, however rough round the edges, would have been virtually impossible prior to full electoral mobilization. New actors—new parties—then hovered in the wings, awaiting the full recognition of their rights of incorporation and representation (Rokkan, 1970: 79 ff.), and until the point was reached when they would become wholly legitimate players, any equilibrium would be necessarily unstable and short-lived. Once the cast of characters was more or less complete, however, and once the rules of the game had been established, equilibrium could be achieved and a party system could become consolidated. This is why Lipset and Rokkan could afford 'to stop' more or less in the 1920s; and this is why, with few exceptions, the party systems of the 1960s and thereafter could continue to reflect the patterns of the 1920s. It was then that the first real (national) equilibria were defined.[5]

Two points follow from this. First, as indicated, it is then not really surprising or intriguing that party systems should persist. Once an equilibrium had been established, however crudely defined, the system could simply generate its own momentum: the structure of competition was more or less defined (see also Chapter 9 below), the terms of reference were given, and there ensued what Schattschneider (1960) once defined as 'the mobilization of bias'. The party system 'freezes' itself, as it were.

Second, this also indicates that despite their evident longevity, and perhaps paradoxically, party systems were also to prove quite vulnerable phenomena. The fact that an equilibrium could be actually maintained in the long term should not therefore cloud our awareness that equilibria in general, and party systems in particular, are susceptible—and hence vulnerable—to dramatic change. In this sense, the long-term development of party systems, and the moments when they change, can be seen perhaps as reflective of the dynamics in Gould's (e.g. 1985: 241–2) notion of 'punctuated equilibrium', a biological model which has already been most usefully adapted elsewhere in political science to offer insights into the 'evolution' of the international system,[6] and in which change, by definition, though rare, can prove both sudden and substantial; hence the

[5] For a discussion of the more general logic of the equilibrium, see Pellikaan (1994: 95–119), and the literature cited therein.

[6] See Spruyt (1994: 22–33), as well as Krasner (1984: 240–4), who makes explicit reference to the Lipset–Rokkan thesis in the context of his discussion.

sense of vulnerability. But it is also important to recognize that this logic does not necessarily hold true for individual parties, which cannot be construed in the same sense as party systems: as equilibria, party systems can experience fundamental changes almost overnight; as organizations—as organisms—fundamental change in parties takes time.[7]

CONSTRAINTS, CONTROL, AND ADAPTATION

Given their potential vulnerability, the fact that fundamental transformations in party systems are actually quite infrequent therefore tells us more about the capacity of those party systems to constrain voter choice than it does about any inherent integrity of the equilibria themselves. The notion of constraint is crucial here, in that it is the constraints which are 'imposed' on voters by the party system *and* by the parties as individual actors which constitute the real motor of persistence. Thus, while parties and party systems may generate their own momentum, they do not do so just by accident, but rather because of their own independent capacities to limit both choice and change. To put it another way, and again to echo Sartori (1969), parties and party systems are not simply objects, but also subjects. It is they who ultimately set the agenda, and it is they who ultimately determine the terms of reference through which we, as voters and as citizens, understand and interpret the political world.

To be sure, parties and party systems are not the only agenda-setters, and their role in this regard is certainly far from exclusive. In contemporary Western societies, for example, it would be difficult to overestimate the role of private business and the market in determining the parameters within which party policy is unfolded, and in this sense the party system suffers from constraints as well as imposing them. Interest organizations, whether private or (semi)-public, have also long enjoyed an agenda-setting role, cited most dramatically in recent years in the once voluminous, but now ebbing literature on neo-corporatism (e.g. Scholten, 1987;

---

[7] For some revealing insights derived from the application of evolutionary models to the development of individual party organizations, where long-term adaption rather than punctuated equilibrium would seem the more appropriate metaphor, see Deschouwer (1992).

Williamson, 1989). The power and influence of the new social movements (e.g. Kriesi *et al.*, 1995), as well as the ever-growing importance of the new mass media (Kleinnijenhuis and Rietberg, 1995), have also won considerable attention in contemporary studies of mass politics and electoral behaviour, with various authors imbuing both with a capacity for political influence which is often quite independent of party and which, in functional terms, might even seem to afford them the status of alternatives to party.

But even if parties and the party system do not stand alone, they do stand apart—and above. Despite many assertions to the contrary, for example, it is difficult to see the influence of neo-corporatism as being really other than something which ultimately developed under the licence and authority of party, with the conditions of successful modes of neo-corporatist intermediation being closely linked to the success of particular parties and to the existence of particular party systems (see, for example, Lehmbruch, 1977). Moreover, despite their apparent challenges, it is striking to note how the very success of the new social movements appears to impel them so often in the direction of party formation, a translation which is most obviously seen in the development of Green parties, and in their eventual drift towards a more conventional organizational style. Finally, while the importance of the independent agenda-setting role of the new mass media is incontrovertible, the net result, and inevitably so, is simply to push voters in one partisan direction rather than another. That the media can influence the preferences of citizens is beyond doubt; what is often forgotten, however, is that it is at the level of electoral behaviour that this influence ultimately finds expression, and it is here, of course, that the parties come back in.

The constraints imposed by parties and the party systems, and their continuing ability to frame the terms of reference through which we filter politics, reflect two important and related capacities, *adaptation* and *control* (see also Mair, 1983, as well as Chapters 5 and 6 below), and it is the loss or even erosion of these capacities which is what places parties at risk. Most crucially, however, when we look at experiences over the postwar years, it would seem that both capacities have actually become enhanced with time.

On the one hand, as individual parties have moved from being relatively closed communities to more open, catch-all, and professionally driven structures, they have proved better equipped, at least in principle, to respond to shifts within the wider society. No longer obliged to listen almost exclusively to their own distinct clienteles, and no longer burdened with the particularistic demands associated with those clienteles, the parties have become more flexible and more adaptable. Having acquired a new legitimacy as the potential managers of government and the state, and having therefore begun to eschew the limits and potential hostility associated with the status of the party 'as part' (see Daalder, 1992), the parties now find themselves more capable of fine-tuning their appeals. Indeed, for all the criticisms that may be levelled against the banalities involved in the emergence of the catch-all party (Kirchheimer, 1966), and in the adoption of 'electoral-professional' organizational structures (Panebianco, 1988), it should not be forgotten that these were the modes adopted precisely in order to afford political leaderships more room for manoeuvre and, eventually, greater success. In other words, as the age of the amateur democrat has waned, and as the less grounded and more capital-intensive party organizations have come increasingly under the sway of professional consultants, marketing experts, and campaigners, they have clearly improved both the pace and the extent to which they can adapt to changes in their external environments. These may not be attractive parties, especially in the eyes of those who mourn the passing of the golden age of the mass party; they may even be seen as quite unrepresentative parties (see also Chapter 6 below); but, in these terms at least, they are certainly more effective.

On the other hand, the control capacity of party has also been enhanced. No matter that it is now sometimes difficult to perceive the differential benefits which might be associated with one particular party or coalition of parties coming to office in place of another; no matter that parties may sometimes be accused of existing in their own world, at one remove from the immediate concerns and dilemmas of citizens; and no matter that the ostensibly competing political leaderships appear to have more in common with one another than with those who are asked to turn out and vote them into office. Instead, what does matter in the end is that in *none* of the contemporary Western democracies, including the United States, which has often been too easily dismissed as effectively party-less,[8] does

[8] For two valuable accounts which highlight the importance of parties as organizing mechanisms in the American political process, see Katz and Kolodny (1994) and Cox and McCubbins (1993).

government now evade the principle of party. Indeed, despite the apparent erosion of differences *between* parties, both the steady growth of government over the postwar period and the steady accretion of responsibilities and capabilities accruing to public office clearly suggest that the potential control capacity of parties as organizations and agenda-setters has actually increased. To adopt the somewhat awkward but nevertheless invaluable terminology promoted in the multi-volume *Future of Party Government* project, directed by the late Rudolf Wildenmann, we have seen in the postwar period a growth of both the 'partyness of government' and 'party governmentness' (Katz, 1986: 42–6), with their combined effect perhaps even leading to a growth in the 'partyness of society' (Sjöblom, 1987: 156–9). Parties still matter, and it is somewhat ironic, at a time when much of the contemporary literature is awash with references to their decline, that we have never seen so great and so widespread an effort on the part of citizens and aspiring political leaders to form new parties and to win representation in parliaments. If the ship of party really is sinking, then it is difficult to understand why so many new bodies are still frantically in search of embarkation cards.[9]

The control capacity of parties has also been strengthened through what Richard Katz and I have referred to as their recent 'invasion' of the state (see Chapter 5 below), which has now made available to the parties a substantial fount of new resources. Better and more fully staffed, richer in terms of personnel and material resources, and with increased access to widespread appointment and patronage facilities, parties now enjoy a 'reach' within state institutions which far outweighs that of their early postwar predecessors. Elsewhere in this volume (see Chapter 6 below) it is argued that the combination of these new privileges of party with their declining representative capacities may well serve to promote a new hostility to party within the wider society. Be that as it may, however, these privileges also indicate that parties may now be in a better position to control the public agenda than at any time in their recent past. Being now less engaged on the ground, not least as a result of the erosion of the party-movement symbiosis,[10] parties

[9] Figures on the emergence of new parties in west European democracies are reported in Gallagher *et al.* (1995: 231–3).

[10] For an earlier consideration of this theme, see Mair (1984: 179–83), where some of the implications of the changing nature of the linkages between interest groups

have tended to compensate for their waning social presence by enhancing their grip on the state. And while the resulting imbalance may serve in certain circumstances to undermine their more generalized legitimacy, it is nevertheless also effective—at least in the short term.

For all of these reasons therefore, and more, the parties are now even better placed to adapt and to control. It is in this sense that their general capacity to constrain choice and change has been enhanced, and it is in this way that the 'old' parties manage to survive. They simply keep themselves going. Still dominated by the much adapted successors of the parties which first settled into place in the wake of full electoral mobilization,[11] western democracies remain essentially party democracies, their governments remaining party governments. Going further afield, it is also striking to observe how, at a time when democratic theory appears more and more convinced of the relevance of new social movements, citizen empowerment, and a vital civil society, it is political parties in particular which have come to play such an important, and even essential role in the most recent waves of democratization, with the newly emergent democracies themselves being defined, as noted in Chapter 6 below, not just in terms of the rights of citizens, but also, and more appropriately, in terms of the existence of a plurality of parties which compete against one another in free elections.

Adaptation and control are not simply matters of party capacity. They also derive from the structure of the party system itself, and from the stabilization of a given pattern of interactions between the parties, a theme which is more fully developed in the final section of this volume, and especially in Chapter 9. In brief, and echoing Schattschneider's (1960: 60–75) notion of the development and eventual displacement of conflicts, it can be argued that a given party system, and a given structure of competition, act to 'freeze' into place a specific language of politics. Party competition, and politics more generally, then becomes dominated by a particular overriding choice, to which other considerations are subordinated.

and parties are discussed. For a more recent and more extensive discussion, see Poguntke (1995).

[11] As Rose and Mackie (1988) have observed, it is also striking to note how few major parties ever really become extinct. Indeed, when we look at the increase of new party formations in the last decade or so, what is really striking is not the sheer numbers and variety that are involved, but rather their relative lack of success (see Shaddick, 1990, and Mair, 1991; see also Chapter 4 below).

This is not just a matter of what one party does or what another party does. Rather, it is something around which the party system as a whole, or at least the core of that system, revolves. Much as rival cigarette manufacturers have a mutual interest in the promotion of smoking, however competitive they may be *vis-à-vis* one another as far as the marketing of their own particular brands may be concerned, the established parties in a party system may be seen to have a mutual interest in the survival of their particular conflict and their particular form of competition. As Schattschneider (1960: 63) underlines, 'the development of one conflict may inhibit the development of another because a radical shift of alignment becomes possible only at the cost of a change in the relations and priorities of *all* the contestants' (emphasis added).

In this sense, and again echoing Schattschneider, the real essence of a party system may be seen not in the competition between the principal protagonists, be they Labour and Conservative, Christian Democrat and Social Democrat, or whatever, but rather in the competition between those who wish to maintain that principal dimension of competition, on one hand, and on the other hand, those who—'the invisible people' (ibid.)—are trying to establish a wholly different dimension. This is what the freezing of party *systems* entails. Party systems become 'about' something; they centre around a particular structure of competition. In Britain, it is the conflict between Labour and Conservative; in the US, it is that between Democrats and Republicans; in France, it is 'left' and 'right', often without a particular party specification; in Sweden, it is the Social Democrats and the bourgeois bloc; in Northern Ireland it is Unionism and Nationalism; and in the Irish Republic it is, or was until recently, Fianna Fáil and 'the Rest'.

It is especially the latter case which helps to alert us to the importance of this particular dimension of the freezing process (Mair, 1987*a*). By all normal standards, the party system of the Irish Republic should have proved highly unstable. To begin with, it is a system which is relatively young in west European terms, and which, moreover, was born in civil war. It is a system which apparently lacks the sort of deep-rooted cleavages which might have helped to hold parties in place—in the late John Whyte's (1974) terms, it reflects a 'politics without social bases'—and in which seats are allocated under an electoral system which gives precedence to the selection of individual candidates rather than parties as such, which is said to breed a strong sense of localism and clientelism. Finally, with the exception of the record maintained by Fianna Fáil, and despite some recent revitalization, it is a system which has long been characterized by quite loosely and poorly organized parties, with an apparently limited capacity to intervene on the ground. If electoral markets are closed only by strong cleavage structures and/or major party organizational effort, then in Ireland we should expect to have seen little other than a history of wholesale volatility and instability: a most 'unfrozen' party system, as it were. But this has not in fact been the case. Instead, what we have actually witnessed, and it is for this reason that the Irish case is often cited as an example in the subsequent chapters, is a history of remarkable electoral and partisan stability, with more or less the same parties competing and with more or less the same degree of success, through election after election, through decade after decade, and through generation after generation. This is in fact, or at least was until very recently, a 'frozen' party system *par excellence*.

But how then can we account for this freezing? If not through the cleavage structure, and if not through the organizational efforts of the parties themselves, then it can only be by reference to the structure of competition (see Chapter 9 below)—by reference, that is, to the establishment of a language of politics in which one particular conflict is prioritized, and in which any potentially alternative alignment of forces is either absorbed or marginalized. Politics in Ireland has been 'about' Fianna Fáil versus the Rest. This has been the core dimension of competition around which the party system has revolved and the means by which it became frozen. But this was not, it must be emphasized, a result of some *deus ex machina*. Rather, this dimension became established and consolidated as a result of the strategies of the parties themselves—the issues on which they competed, the ways in which they appealed to voters, the approaches they adopted to the process of government formation, and the various alliances and divisions which they fomented. The party system is thus the creature of the parties, but at the same time they also become its prisoners. Stasis is the norm, and for party systems, as for institutional structures more generally (Krasner, 1984: 235), there is a 'capital stock' embodied which cannot easily be dispensed with.

This is what is meant by the notion that party *systems* also enjoy a capacity to adapt and to control. Moreover, this is also precisely what is involved in the establishment of an equilibrium and in 'the mobilization of bias' (see above). And it follows from this that when that equilibrium is disturbed, whether exogenously (for example, the influence of the end of the Cold War on the Italian case) or endogenously (for example, the fundamental shift in Fianna Fáil strategy in the Irish case), and when that potentially vulnerable structure of competition collapses, the party system can be subject to quite a dramatic transformation. In the Irish case, at any rate, there is, or was, little else to anchor it into place.

Party change and party system change are multi-faceted. Especially at the level of the individual parties, it is a constant phenomenon, an ongoing process of continuous adaptation to changing social, political, and policy circumstances. Adaptation here is the key to survival, for without it the party risks decline and decay. To speak of parties being frozen into place is in this sense misleading, for it misses the sort of plasticity or flexibility which is required in order to endure.[12] This is especially so today, in that parties are now much less rooted in society than before, and seem less and less capable of— or even interested in—closing off sections of the electorate within more or less self-contained political communities. Party systems, on the other hand, as was suggested above, are much more prone to stasis. To be sure, adaptation is also crucial here, with the interactions between the established parties being constantly adjusted and trimmed in order to forestall new challengers and take advantage of new opportunities. In this case, however, a core often does remain frozen into place, in that a structure of competition can persist even when the protagonists who are involved in its promotion may have changed beyond almost all recognition. Going further, and this is perhaps the most consistent argument which echoes through the subsequent chapters of this book, it might even be suggested that party systems freeze into place precisely because the parties themselves refuse to be so pinned down.

---

[12] Addressing a similar point, Rose and Mackie (1988: 533) lead off their discussion with a very pertinent quote from Lampedusa's *The Leopard*: 'If things are going to stay the same, there will have to be some changes made.' The Red Queen's remark to Alice in *Through the Looking Glass* (in Carroll, 1982: 152) is equally apposite: 'Now, *here*, you see, it takes all the running *you* can do, to keep in the same place.'

PART II

Persistence and Change

2
Continuities, Changes, and the Vulnerability of Party

Let us start with the apparent certainties: we are living in an era of political change; the contemporary west European political parties now exist in an environment of quite pervasive electoral instability; over the past fifteen years this electoral flux, which is evident at both the aggregate and individual level, has been more pronounced than at any other comparable period since the end of World War II; finally, as we move towards the end of the twentieth century, there is little evidence to suggest that this flux is likely to abate.[1]

It goes without saying that the interpretations, explanations, and implications of this pervasive instability vary quite considerably. For some, it is a flux which signals the end of conventional political patterns, which challenges traditional modes of political representation and reflects the emergence of new issue-concerns and a new system of political values. For others, it is largely ephemeral, representing change at the margins of a structure which, to say the least of it, has remained consolidated since the 1920s. But this is by the way; for now, and at least for the purposes of this present argument, the problem of explaining change seems substantially less important than that of specifying the level at which it is occurring. Before we can begin to explain, we must first identify what it is that needs to be explained.

What needs to be underlined here is that, concurrent with the evident instability of contemporary European electorates, there also exist two other phenomena which, in themselves, represent fundamental forces for continuity, and which therefore suggest the

---

[1] For an overview of the relevant arguments and the evidence which is cited, see Pedersen (1979, 1983); Maguire (1983); Shamir (1984); and Crewe and Denver (1985).

presence of a substantially more complex situation than is often taken to be the case. Each of these phenomena pertains to a set of predispositions which is at once part of the logic of party choice while also being of a wider and more inchoate character than simple party choice itself. I refer here to generalized *ideological* predispositions on the one hand, and to generalized *political* alignments on the other. One is expressed in the somewhat more abstract identification with 'left' or 'right', while the other relates to the sense of belonging, at least in behavioural terms, to an often fragmented political family.

To be sure, the existence of these phenomena and the extent to which they represent forces of continuity cannot be asserted with equal conviction in each case. The evidence for stability at the level of ideological predispositions is at once more fragmentary and more questionable than is the case for the evidence which can be drawn at the level of political alignments. None the less, at the general European level, the presence of both phenomena can be confirmed to a greater or lesser extent, and the continuities which they reflect, when contrasted with the instability of party choice in contemporary Europe, suggest that we can begin to identify more precisely what is changing and therefore where the explanations for such change might be sought.

WHAT PARTIES ARE AND WHAT PARTIES DO

It is becoming increasingly necessary for comparative studies of political parties and party systems to distinguish between two key characteristics of their object of study: the historic political identity of parties, on the one hand, and the contemporary appeals of parties, on the other. Or, to put it another way, they need to distinguish between *what parties are* and *what parties do*.

It is the variation in the traditional identities of parties—what parties are—which largely accounts for the diversity of the contemporary west European mosaic, reflecting a legacy which can be traced back to the prevalence of certain cleavages at the time of mass electoral mobilization, to the inculcation of particular political loyalties during the formative years of mass democracy, and to the persistent relevance of key issues and unresolved conflicts during the period of party system structuration (Lipset and Rokkan,

1967). The result is a widespread contrast in the configuration of contemporary party systems, indicated most clearly in the uneven distribution of special interest parties such as Christian parties or agrarian parties, and reflected also in the contrasting degrees of fragmentation of the traditional class left. Thus explanations for the presence or absence of a Christian Democratic party towards the right of the party system, or for the presence or absence of a Communist party on the left, or for the various balance between liberals, radicals, and/or centre parties in between, are largely historically oriented, focusing more on the genesis and early consolidation of the party system rather than on present conflicts and dilemmas. It is to these necessarily diverse national histories that we owe the present heterogeneity among the party systems of western Europe.

What the contemporary parties now do, on the other hand, often seems to bear little relation to these historically derived identities. Moreover, it is at this level that the ostensible diversity of the west European systems gives way to a certain uniformity. This level of analysis deals with the policies of parties and the programmes and commitments which they enunciate in the everyday process of party competition, as well as with their priorities in government and their attitudes to contemporary social and economic problems.

To be sure, some linkage does exist between these policies and the party identities. However modern and secular it may have become, for example, no Catholic party is likely to promulgate a pro-abortion policy, and no agrarian party, nor even a formerly agrarian party, is likely to propose an end to subsidies for agricultural production. In this sense, past identities continue to have persistent policy implications and, as Budge and Farlie (1983) have argued in another context, certain issues can be identified as clearly 'belonging' to certain parties. In addition, the policies which parties pursue will also inevitably be constrained by the strategic imperatives imposed by the system of competition in which they operate; this, in turn, is at least partially determined by the configuration of the system and by the numbers of competing parties and their ideological profiles (Sartori, 1976: especially 131–216); and this is finally at least partially determined by the genesis of the system, and the cleavages which prevailed at the time of party system structuration.

But while various links can be established between what parties are and what they do, there is no inevitable correspondence between the two. Catholic parties may not be likely to promulgate pro-abortion policies; at the same time, however, their present policy appeals tend to make little reference to religious questions. Agrarian parties may not wish to remove subsidies to agriculture, but there are now few if any such parties which seek to represent only the special interest of farmers. More specifically, as can be seen in the party systems which exist on either side of the Irish border, even the most idiosyncratically derived identities tend to coexist with quite conventional and mundane policy appeals. Thus, in the Irish Republic, where the cleavage giving birth to the party system was quite *sui generis*, and where the party identities are such that even the most conscientious comparativists find difficulty in locating the parties within the terms of reference of the broader European political families, most of the policy debate has centred around questions of the welfare state, economic growth, and employment policy (Mair, 1987*a*: 138–206; 1987*b*). North of the Irish border, in the even more unconventional confines of Ulster politics, one finds a similar pattern, in that the bulk of unionist and nationalist party policies in the Stormont period (i.e. when Northern Ireland elected its own parliament and executive) were devoted to 'normal' socio-economic rather than sectarian or religious concerns (Laver and Elliott, 1987).

It also seems clear that the linkage between historically derived identity and contemporary political appeal is more likely to be attenuated in the case of those parties which emerged from the pre-industrial cleavages, such as those which grew from religious, territorial, or cultural divides. These parties have persisted for a long time, and in many cases they have achieved as much as they could have expected. The issues on which they mobilized have been more or less settled, one way or the other, and in some cases a recognition of this has even led to a recasting of the role of the party (as, for instance, when agrarian parties have redefined themselves as centre parties) or has led to a new strategic orientation (as, for instance, in the Netherlands, when the Calvinist Anti-Revolutionary Party joined forces with the Dutch Reformed Christian Historical Union and the Roman Catholic People's Party to form the multi-denominational Christian Democratic Appeal). In general, however, even though the impulse underlying the mobilization of a distinct political identity may have faded, and even though the original identity itself may have little relevance in terms of contemporary issues and conflicts, these older parties have rarely actually disappeared (Rose and Mackie, 1988), and therefore one must assume that they have discovered a new rationale on which to base their appeal. Hence, as far as these older parties are concerned, it can be argued that the old identities will come back into play only in exceptional circumstances. Certainly, the relevant examples are few: the question of the growing demand for abortion in relation to Catholic parties (Lovenduski and Outshoorn, 1986); the re-awakening of centre–periphery tensions in Norway at the time of the EEC referendum (Valen, 1976); the stimulation of hardline nationalism in the Irish Republic in the wake of the recrudescence of violence in Northern Ireland in the late 1960s (Mair, 1987c). Of course, this is not to deny that these older identities are no longer relevant as far as *voting behaviour* is concerned. On the contrary, there is sufficient evidence to suggest that, despite the imputed decline of traditional cleavages, electorates remain heavily structured by their social and organizational circumstances, and that the role of language, religion, race, and class continue to play a crucial role in determining partisan preferences. What I am suggesting, however, is that these older concerns no longer structure the *policy alternatives* of the parties, and that they therefore no longer form the basis of policy competition.

This is more or less the same contention as that advanced by Sani and Sartori (1983) with their emphasis on the crucial distinction between 'domains of identification' on the one hand and 'dimensions of competition' on the other. The former simply refers to the various dimensions of partisan identification in a given electorate; that is, to the various identities which tie particular voters to particular parties, and which may encompass religion, language, region, or whatever. The latter, however, refers to the space of competition; that is, to the issues on which parties find it useful or rewarding to compete. As Sani and Sartori (1983: 330) note, 'the finding that the electorates are distributed into multiple dimensions of competition does not attest in the least that parties also compete along the same dimensions. Conversely stated, the space of competition may well be a single space, regardless of how many cleavage and/or identification dimensions exist.' Or, to put it another way, despite their importance as far as partisan predispositions are concerned, traditional party identities may bear little relation to contemporary competitive appeals. The point is also sustained by more recent evidence derived from a survey of the contents of post-war party election programmes in a wide range of western democracies, which shows, for example, that despite the importance of the religious cleavage, 'a religious dimension [of competition] is strikingly absent from the majority of countries' (Budge and Robertson, 1987: 396).

LEFT, RIGHT, AND POLICY COMPETITION

But if policy competition does not normally involve issues related to these core identities, what then is involved? According to the survey of manifestos, the answer is clear, as is the evidence of uniformity: in almost all countries, 'some form of Left–Right dimension dominates competition at the level of the parties . . . where there is no overriding preoccupation with national identity or security'. Moreover, this dominant dimension also has a clear policy connotation, and principally 'refers to economic policy-conflicts—government regulation of the economy through direct controls or takeover . . . as opposed to free enterprise, individual freedom, incentives and economic orthodoxy' (Budge and Robertson, 1987: 394–5). Hence, almost regardless of the diversity of traditional identities, and despite the many differences which exist in terms of what parties are, there appears to be a substantial degree of uniformity regarding what these parties actually do.

This is not surprising. All governments and all parties, of whatever party system type and of whatever genesis, are obliged to formulate policies—whether more to the left or more to the right—on the welfare state, on taxation, on employment policy, on industry, on farming, on the environment, and so on. And while the various parties may differ substantially on what they consider to be the best approach to be adopted *vis-à-vis* these concerns; and while these differences may be associated with particular trans-national party families on one hand, or even with particular types of party systems on the other;[2] there nevertheless exists a sufficiently common core of concerns, as well as a sufficiently limited range of options relat-

[2] See, for example, Seiler (1980), who focuses on the cross-national similarities between particular party families in western Europe, and Katzenstein (1985), who focuses on the shared policy concerns of the smaller, more consensual democracies in western Europe.

ing to these concerns, to allow one to speak legitimately of uniformity rather than diversity in western Europe. In this sense, for example, although the contrast between the Social Democratic versus Christian Democratic opposition in Germany and the Labour versus Conservative opposition in Britain can be considered as relevant to an understanding of differences in the genesis of each of the two party systems, it can be argued that there exists a functional equivalence in terms of the policy alternatives now offered to both national sets of voters.

The reasons for this uniformity are also quite evident. The western European democracies are all capitalist democracies, with a more or less similar balance of social classes and demographic profile. All share an effectively common notion of citizenship, including social citizenship, and are led by governments which have all taken on a broadly equivalent set of obligations towards the citizenry (Flora, 1986). Within broad limits, these governments, and hence the parties which form them, confront similar problems and, with varying degrees of success, attempt to reconcile similar conflicts. The result is, inevitably, that the major dimensions of competition in the countries of western Europe revolve around a limited range of themes and emerge as being broadly comparable, particularly in left–right terms.

This pervasive importance of left and right as organizing principles of politics is also apparent at the mass electoral level. This is emphasized in a paper by van der Eijk, Niemoeller, and Oppenhuis (1988), who set out to use 1984 cross-national survey data in order to measure the relationship between party labels, ideologies, and left–right self-placement. As their country-specific analyses show, this latter category remains strongly related to identification with the different ideological groupings even to the extent that 'the ordering in terms of average left–right position of those who associate with the principal ideologies is by and large the same in all countries'; moreover, 'in terms of the left–right location of their would-be voters the parties are ordered as one would expect on the basis of related information'. Finally, when taking all the countries together, the authors find that 'the 10 categories of the left–right scale emerge as a perfectly ordered, curved dimension. The various ideologies are arranged perfectly along this dimension, hardly employing the rest of the space, which attests to the common foundation of substantive political ideas from which left–right positions and ideological labels derive their meaning' (van der Eijk *et al.*, 1988: 17, 18, 29).

That left–right differences should be so pervasive and at the same time so closely associated with a wide range of other ideological and partisan cues is itself not unexpected. As Gordon Smith (1990) notes, the left–right division is remarkable for its sheer plasticity and its capacity to be moulded to a variety of different concerns. A similar sense of the catch-all character of left–right divisions is also apparent in Sani and Sartori's assessment of survey attitudes reported from a variety of different European countries, and their finding that left–right locations were strongly related not only to issues concerning social equality and social change, as might be expected; and not only to attitudes towards the Great Powers, which is also perhaps unsurprising; but also to attitudes towards the religious dimension and towards politically significant groups including, among others, the police, the women's movement, and the student movement. As in the more recent analysis of manifestos, therefore, they find that the dominant dimension of competition in the modern west European democracies is constituted by left–right divisions, and that these divisions appear to encompass a variety of different concerns. Their conclusion is quite unambiguous (Sani and Sartori, 1988: 314):

We are not claiming that the variety of conflict dimensions relevant in the various countries can be squeezed into a single [i.e. left–right] dimension without loss. Clearly, if we are interested in a particular domain we are likely to be better off by using more specific and direct indicators. What we are asserting is that the left–right yardstick mirrors fairly well the voters' stands on some of the major conflict domains and echoes much of the voters' feelings towards significant political objects.

The final point to note here is that the absorption capacity of left and right now also appears to have accommodated many of the 'new politics' concerns. Many of these concerns, such as issues relating to gender rights, ecology, and quality of life, might have been considered as likely to cut across traditional left–right divisions, particularly in so far as they were likely to provoke a conservative response within the traditional working class. Moreover, the early evidence on mass attitudes towards these questions did indeed suggest that they constituted quite a new dimension in politics, highlighting, for example, the opposition of blue-collar working class and new middle class (e.g. Hildebrandt and Dalton, 1978). More recently, however, despite potential incongruence in class alignments, the prevailing language of left and right appears to have embraced many of these new concerns, such that both sets of attitudes now seem quite closely aligned. This is shown quite clearly by Inglehart's (1987: 1299) more recent evidence on the shifts in the partisan predispositions of 'materialists' and 'postmaterialists' over the period from 1970 to 1985:

In 1970, 61 percent of the Materialists intended to vote for parties of the Right and Centre, as compared with 40 percent of the Postmaterialists. Materialists were likelier than Postmaterialists to vote for the Right by a ratio of almost exactly 1.5 to one. This already was a sizeable difference— but it has grown steadily larger since 1970. In 1973, the ratio had increased to 1.8 to 1. In 1976–1978 it grew to 1.9 to 1. By 1979–1981 it was slightly more than 2 to one. And in 1982–1985, the ratio had risen to 2.3 to one. This changing ratio was mainly due to a loss of Postmaterialist votes by parties of the Right. In 1970, 40 percent of the Postmaterialists supported parties of the Right and Centre; in 1982–1985, only 25 percent did so; 75 percent were voting for the Left.

In short, left–right divisions, which predated but at the same time were cemented by the political mobilization of the working class in early twentieth-century Europe, and which came to focus principally on the question of the degree of government intervention, have proved sufficiently flexible to endure as well as to absorb, and have thus acted as a fundamental force for continuity. For all the changes experienced in recent years, it is clear that left and right not only remain the major organizing principles in modern west European politics, but also help to create a uniform foundation for contemporary patterns of policy competition.

LEFT, RIGHT, AND VOTER ALIGNMENTS

The evidence for continuity in terms of broad political *alignments* can be cited with even more assurance. The relevant data here concern aggregate electoral patterns in western Europe as a whole, and derive from a crucial distinction between the degree of electoral interchange between individual parties on the one hand, and that between blocs or families of parties on the other. Details of the different patterns need not be presented here; suffice it rather to summarize the findings of a larger and more detailed recent study of levels of electoral volatility across the class cleavage line (Bartolini and Mair, 1990; see also Chapters 3 and 4 below).

The first point which needs to be underlined here is that, when discussing the political alternatives deriving from cleavages in modern mass politics, and particularly when discussing the political alternatives deriving from the class cleavage, we cannot simply speak of individual parties. Rather, we must be concerned with *blocs* or families of parties, and with the notion of parties which are cleavage allies as against those which are cleavage opponents. In other words, individual parties do not exist in isolation, but rather form parts of broader political pluri-party political alignments. Given this, then should party A lose votes while party B gains votes, and should party A and party B represent opposing sides in terms of, say, the traditional class cleavage (e.g. in the case of a socialist party and a Christian democratic party), then we are dealing with a very different situation from one where party A loses and party B gains while *both* parties organize on the same side of that cleavage line (e.g. in the case of a socialist party and a communist party).

In short, the electoral instability which results from individual party volatilities reflects two distinct processes with quite different systemic implications. At the extreme, these processes can be characterized as follows. In one case, the individual party volatilities result exclusively from an exchange of votes between the parties of a given political family while, at the same time, leaving the overall alignment wholly unscathed. In the other case, the individual party volatilities are the exclusive result of an exchange of votes across the broader blocs and thus involve a major shift in the balance of the overall alignment. In practice, of course, any level of electoral interchange is bound to involve both processes, combining some intra-bloc and some inter-bloc reshuffling.

This in itself can be seen to be quite self-evident; what has been less commonly noted, however, is that when we look at the recent increase in levels of electoral instability in contemporary Europe, and when we control for levels of electoral interchange across the class-cleavage boundary, we can see that the greater part of this increase has in fact been contained *within* each class-cleavage bloc, and that the degree of electoral volatility *between* the major blocs has actually tended to decline over time. In other words, while the contemporary west European democracies are characterized by a relatively pronounced degree of electoral instability, this instability is regularly contained within broader and more stable political alignments. In effect, therefore, and certainly as far as the class blocs are concerned, partisan flux has coexisted with a more generalized aggregate electoral persistence. The families have remained stable while their individual members have proved volatile (Bartolini and Mair, 1990: 96–124).

This contrasting pattern can be illustrated quite easily by taking the examples of two party systems which have experienced considerable flux during the postwar period: the Netherlands, where partisan alignments began to become adrift in the late 1960s (Andeweg, 1982; van der Eijk and Niemoeller, 1983); and Denmark, which was riven by an earthquake election in 1973 and which has remained relatively unstable thereafter (Pedersen, 1987; Bille, 1990). Both countries therefore offer clear examples of the new wave of instability which has characterized much of recent electoral history in western Europe. In both cases, however, the broad political alignments of the traditional left and the traditional right have remained relatively stable.

This can be seen in Figure 2.1 (a and b), which charts the aggregate electoral performance of the class left during the postwar period in each country. In the Danish case, for example, the overall vote for the left (constituted by the Social Democrats, the Communist Party, the Socialist People's Party, and the Left Socialists) has generally remained between 45 and 50 per cent, falling substantially outside this narrow range on only two occasions, in 1973 and 1975. In the Dutch case, the stability is even more pronounced, with the class left bloc (constituted by the Labour Party, the Pacifist Socialist Party, the Communist Party, and DS 70) falling noticeably outside quite a minimal range only in 1967. Thus, despite overall levels of quite pronounced electoral volatility, aggregate support for the left bloc as a whole—and therefore also the bloc of the non-left—has proved remarkably persistent over time.

Yet this is clearly not the whole story, for there has also been considerable fluctuation *within* the left in each of these countries. This is also evident in Figure 2.1, which reports values for an index of left fractionalization at each of the postwar elections, and which summarizes the extent to which support for the left is monopolized

by one party (when the index is low) as against a situation in which it is fragmented among a number of different and sizeable parties (when the index is high).[3] In both countries this index proves remarkably unstable. In the Danish case the index falls to a post-war low in 1957, then increases steadily through to 1973, falls again in 1977 and 1979, and finally increases steadily through to 1987. In the Dutch case the erraticism is even more evident: falling in the late 1950s, rising sharply in the early 1970s, and then falling again to a postwar low with the consolidation of PvdA support in 1986.

These two countries are not exceptional; rather, they simply represent quite telling instances of a more widespread phenomenon in postwar European politics: despite overall bloc stability, there has been a considerable degree of intra-bloc reshuffling; party-specific instability has been accompanied by bloc-specific persistence.

A CRISIS OF PARTY?

This, then, is the core of the problem. Generally increasing levels of electoral volatility have occurred despite ideological continuity and increasing uniformity (at least at the level of left–right differences), and despite the general evidence of persistence at the level of broad political alignments (at least at the level of broad class alignments). Instability has been accompanied by persistence.

So what is the nature of this instability and where might we search for its explanation? The first point to emphasize is that the instability does not appear to reflect a 'crisis of ideology'; while values might be changing, the new emphases nevertheless do seem to have the potential to be absorbed into the more traditional organizing principles of left and right, and such principles do still appear to have a large degree of popular resonance. Second, it does not reflect a 'crisis of class', at least in electoral terms, since the class left bloc has remained remarkably stable over time. If only by default, therefore, it appears that we may be confronting a 'crisis of party', that is, a pattern of change which is *party-specific*. Hence,

---

[3] This index is calculated according to the formula of Rae (1971), the difference being that it applies *only* to the parties of the left block. That is, the votes of all constituent parties within the block are summed and treated as being equal to 100 per cent, and the shares of each of the parties are then treated as the relevant units for the calculation of the Rae index. For purposes of comparison with the overall vote of the left, the index as reported in Figure 2.1 has been multiplied by 100.

if we are to understand the reasons for this change, the best place to begin is with those explanatory factors which can be considered to be party-specific and which, at the same time, could not be expected to impinge greatly upon either more generalized ideological predispositions or on the broad electoral alignments.

Three factors in particular can be specified as having a special impact on the individual party organization rather than on general ideological predispositions or broad political alignments. These are: first, the particular party leadership; second, the specific policy appeals (as opposed to the general orientation) on which the party mobilizes; and third, the party's organizational strategy and style. At least in principle, all three factors may be considered as having a capacity to impact upon the fortunes of the individual party while at the same time leaving the overall parameters of the system unchanged. In other words, all three factors may encourage voters to shift from one party to another while remaining within the same general tendency.

It is not my intention to explore each of these three factors, at least as far as this present chapter is concerned. The leadership factor, for example, which might be extended to include the impact of a party's specific contribution when in government or opposition, is notoriously difficult to measure at a cross-national level (but see Graetz and McAllister, 1987) and merits the type of in-depth inquiry which is quite beyond the scope of this study. I am also going to avoid any discussion of the impact of specific policies and programmes, although here Inglehart's evidence of the differential preferences—within the left—of postmaterialists (see above) is clearly relevant. Rather, at least for now, I wish to concentrate on the *organizational* factor as a cause of party instability, and this will be the subject of the remainder of this chapter.

What I am basically proposing here, and this comes to the core of the argument, is that, while remaining tied to the broader family, bloc, or tendency, the voter may no longer feel any special ties to any particular *party* within that bloc. Wider and possibly more abstract or diffuse loyalties may persist—hence the continuity in ideological predispositions and broader alignments—but the sense of belonging to a specific party may decline.

Why should this be the case? One reason may simply be that the *organizational* link between the party and the voter has been eroded. The party, qua organization, has become remote and distant, and as organizational ties have loosened so an electoral market has been created. But it must be emphasized that this putative electoral market is not a completely open market. Those voters who see themselves on the left do not readily vote for those parties which they see as being on the right, or vice versa; and those who traditionally supported the parties of the class left, the workers' parties, do not easily switch to support the more bourgeois parties. The market has limits. The space is not continuous.[4] Choice is largely constrained. Thus, those who have voted communist might now vote socialist, or vice versa, and those who voted socialist might now vote left socialist. On the right, former liberals may vote Christian democratic, or vice versa, while former conservatives may now vote liberal. When there is a multiplicity of parties, even a constrained choice offers substantial room for manoeuvre, and it is my contention that room for manoeuvre may at least partially be derived from change at the level of the party organizations and from a loosening of the organizational ties which link parties and voters.

To the extent that this is correct, three lines of enquiry can be suggested, which can be ordered according to their relative lack of immediacy. First, and perhaps most important of all, there is a need to explain how broader familial or bloc loyalties can persist *despite* the evident vulnerability of individual party organizations. But this is necessarily a more long-term and theoretically wide-ranging line of enquiry, and cannot be adequately treated here. Second, there is a need to gather systematic, cross-national, time-series data on party organization in order to measure to what extent, if any, there has been a genuine loosening of organizational ties, and the extent to which this varies across parties and across countries (see also below). Third, and most immediately, there is a need to develop a set of hypotheses which might indicate how and why the organizational hold of parties may have loosened. This is what I will turn to now.

CATCH-ALL POLITICS AND PARTY VULNERABILITY

In 1918, in a lecture at the University of Munich, Max Weber addressed himself to the question of 'politics as a vocation'. His

[4] For a similar suggestion in a quite different context, see Laver (1976).

theme was the new professionalism of politics, and within that theme he laid particular emphasis on the emergence of the modern mass party. For Weber (1946: 102), the contrast with past political organization was profound:

> The most modern forms of party organization stand in sharp contrast to [the] idyllic state in which circles of notables and, above all, members of parliament rule. These modern forms are the children of democracy, of mass franchise, of the necessity to woo and organize the masses, and develop the utmost unity of direction and the strictest discipline.

Subsequent scholarship was to confirm the pervasiveness of this transformation and its inevitable association with the extension of democratic rights. Mass participation came to mean mass parties, and for many observers, including Schattschneider (1942: 1), it appeared that modern democracy itself was 'unthinkable save in terms of parties'. A brief checklist of the functions normally associated with parties (e.g. King, 1969) underlines their essential role: parties structure the popular vote, integrate and mobilize the mass of the citizenry; aggregate diverse interests; recruit leaders for public office; and formulate public policy. Most important of all, within the liberal democracies it is primarily parties which organize modern government, such that, as Wildenmann (1986: 6) notes, 'party government is the crucial agency of institutional legitimisation'.

At the same time, however, it is impossible to separate the question of the role of parties from that of their legitimacy. The leaders whom parties recruit, the policies which they formulate, and the governments that they seek to control can be legitimized only to the extent that the parties themselves are legitimized; hence the relevance of the mass party. For whatever one can say about the professionalization of politics which came in the wake of mass democracy, it was the popular base of parties which, in the end, was to ensure their legitimacy. Parties reflected the public will and provided the crucial linkage between the citizenry and the state. They did so as mass organizations, for it was as mass organizations that they belonged to the society from which they emanated. In effect, and above all else, the twentieth century has been the century of the mass party.

There are two respects in which this development has been important: first, because of the sheer pervasiveness of the mass party organization in modern democratic politics; second, because of the process of stabilization which resulted from the organizational capacities of the mass party.

The pervasiveness of mass party organization, already noted by Weber, was forcefully underlined in Duverger's (1954) pioneering comparative study of parties and party systems (see also Neumann, 1956). Like Weber, Duverger linked the development of the mass party to the extension of democratic rights, arguing that mass enfranchisement had led to the replacement of caucus-based organizations by branch-based organizations, and of cadre parties by mass parties. Duverger associated this transformation primarily with the left, arguing that the need to secure financial resources made it particularly imperative for socialist parties to develop a mass organization. Parties of the right, on the other hand, which enjoyed the support of wealthy backers and clients, could still afford a more cadre-type organization. Nevertheless, this was not a hard and fast distinction, and Duverger also emphasized the notion of a 'contagion' from the left which could induce the spread of mass party organization right across the political spectrum.

What was even more important, however, was the impact which this had on the stabilization of mass electorates: as Sartori (1968: 292) has argued, 'the critical factor in altering the nature of a party system and in bringing about its structural consolidation is the appearance of the mass party.' Through the encapsulation of sections of the mass electorate, and through the inculcation of political identities which proved both solid and enduring, the mass party became the agency by which political behaviour was structured and by which partisan stability was ensured. Political choice developed into political identity as a result of political organization; in this fashion, the party systems themselves were consolidated.

The critical step was therefore the transition from cadre party to mass party, from loosely-based *networks* of like-minded notables to tightly organized, popularly financed mass *organizations*. These latter organizations, through their mass following, closed off the electoral market and stabilized the modern party systems. As Lipset and Rokkan (1967: 51) have argued:

the narrowing of the 'support market' brought about through the growth of mass parties . . . left very few openings for new movements. Where the challenge of the emerging working-class parties had been met by concerted efforts of countermobilization through nationwide mass organizations on the liberal and conservative fronts, the leeway for new party formations

was particularly small; this was the case whether the threshold of representation was low, as in Scandinavia, or quite high, as in Britain.

The sequence of the process is clear and the logic compelling. The
extension of the suffrage incorporates the mass of the citizenry into
the political system; mass parties mobilize and integrate these new
citizens and inculcate a set of enduring political identities; these
political identities, in turn, act as a force for the stabilization of
alignments and, in Lipset and Rokkan's familiar terms, for the
freezing of party systems. Organization is therefore clearly crucial,
for it was only through the independent organizational intervention
of the mass party, a party which, in many cases, 'permeated and
enveloped other political elites' (Daalder 1966: 58; see also Rokkan
1977) that these identities could be forged and these voters could
be bonded. It is in this sense, as Sartori (1969: 90) has underlined,
that 'a freezed party system is simply a party system that intervenes
in the political process as an independent *system of channelment*,
propelled and maintained by its own laws of inertia'. In sum, the
mass party, which has been the creature of mass democracy, acted
at the same time to ensure the stabilization of mass democracy.

But while the logic is compelling, it is also contingent. The stability which resulted from the capacity of parties to draw voters
firmly into their organizational nets largely depended upon the
immediacy of their links with the wider society. To the extent that
these links were loosened, and to the extent that the party became
more remote from the everyday lives of the citizenry, the organizational preconditions of such stability would be eroded. To be sure,
policy appeals, government performance, and the attraction of particular leaders might help to ensure the maintenance of voter loyalty, but, at the very least, the loosening of organizational ties
implied a certain vulnerability.

Just such a sense of vulnerability was to follow from the emergence of what Kirchheimer (1966) identified as the 'catch-all party'.
While Kirchheimer has proved among the most widely cited of the
modern writers on parties and party systems, he has also been subject to a curiously partial reading; for, in taking on board
Kirchheimer's prognostications concerning the rise of the catch-all
party, most scholars have tended to emphasize the strictly ideological implications of his argument, and have thereby neglected the
arguably more crucial organizational developments which were at

the heart of the original thesis (see, e.g., Wolinetz, 1979; Dittrich, 1983).

Like Duverger, Kirchheimer was concerned with a contrast between two types of party—what he referred to as the 'mass integration' party on the one hand, and the new catch-all party on the other. Moreover, and again like Duverger, he imputed a sequential pattern to the distinction, arguing that the age of the former had passed, and that the west European systems were now faced with the more or less irresistible rise of the catch-all party (Kirchheimer, 1966: 184):

the mass integration party, product of an age with harder class lines and more sharply protruding denominational structures, is transforming itself into a catch-all 'people's' party. Abandoning attempts at the intellectual and moral encadrement of the masses, it is turning more fully to the electoral scene, trying to exchange effectiveness in depth for a wider audience and more immediate electoral success.

Kirchheimer then goes on to list five characteristics of the emerging catch-all party. These are a 'drastic reduction of the party's ideological baggage'; a 'further strengthening of the top leadership groups'; a 'downgrading of the role of the individual party member'; a 'de-emphasis of the *classe gardée*, specific social-class, or denominational clientele, in favour of recruiting voters from the population at large'; and a process of 'securing access to a variety of interest groups' (1966: 190). Crucially, it is only the first of these five characteristics which is explicitly concerned with ideological change. In sum, and above all else, the catch-all party is also an *organizational* phenomenon.

Moreover, the nature of the organizational transformation involved in the emergence of the catch-all party is also clearly specified. Kirchheimer depicts a party which has sundered its close links with the mass electorate and has become essentially remote from the everyday life of the citizen. This remoteness is reflected in a shift of internal party power towards the leadership; a loosening of socially specific bonds with sections of the electorate—be they defined in class terms, denominational terms, or whatever; and a reduction in the role of ordinary members.

Thus the catch-all party severs its specific organizational links with the society of which it is part and begins to operate at one remove from its constituency. It shifts from being a 'bottom-up' party to being a 'top-down' party, and chooses to compete on the market rather than attempting to narrow that market. It builds on conditional support rather than on a sense of identification. It seeks the endorsement of voters rather than their encapsulation.

The result is a greater potential for contingent or even virtually random voting. Thus, it is no accident that the changes in party organization and style which were noted by Kirchheimer in the early 1960s were soon succeeded by the destabilization of the individual party electorates in the late 1960s and 1970s. For, as parties increasingly tended to operate at one remove from the society of which they were once a part, voters themselves tended to shed their sense of partisan belonging and, as Rose and McAllister (1986) put it in a different context, they slowly began to choose. These free-range voters were no longer mobilized by the parties and had ceased to be integrated into the parties. Their horizons widened, their options increased, and, in general, they became more volatile. In effect, as the parties became more remote, the electorate itself became more available. The basis for persistence, which rested on organizational intervention and control, and which thrived on the encapsulation of the mass public, was thereby undermined.

ORGANIZATIONAL CHANGE AND ELECTORAL CHANGE

The shifting electoral alignments which have characterized Western Europe since the late 1960s cannot simply be explained by reference to the changing organizational style of the traditional parties, of course. There is clearly much more to it than this. Over the past few years, a number of crucial factors have been identified as leading to electoral instability, and a particular emphasis has been laid on the impact of changes in the social structure and the blurring of traditional class boundaries (Dalton *et al.*, 1984b; Flanagan and Dalton, 1984) and on the impact of new value systems and the mobilization of a new postmaterialist cleavage (Inglehart 1977; 1984; 1987). In addition, however unwilling one might be to endorse the sweeping assertions of an 'end of ideology' which characterized much of the writing on political attitudes in the 1960s (see the survey in Waxman, 1968), it cannot be denied that many of the great issues which once sustained traditional loyalties have now more or less been solved. The struggles of the working class for political rights have been won; the legitimacy of defending the rights of organized religion has also been accepted, as has the legitimacy of the rights of those who reject religious beliefs; a comprehensive welfare state has become the norm in most of the contemporary west European democracies, and such conflicts over welfare rights as do persist tend to be at the margins of the system. The great struggles are over, and as Pizzorno (1981: 272), echoing Kirchheimer, has noted, the situation in most of the western democracies has become one 'in which no irreducible political identity is at stake and political demands all become negotiable. Interest groups asking for specific policies are the main actors on the political scene whereas the political parties . . . tend to lose their programmatic and organizational identity.' That electoral destabilization should then ensue is hardly surprising.

The changes which have been identified in the previous paragraph do, of course, lie largely outside the control of the parties themselves. Hence the fact that they have been conducive to greater party vulnerability is something which the parties cannot challenge but to which they must adapt. The type of organizational change which was noted earlier, however, is quite another matter, for this does appear to have lain within the control of party. But this surely begs the question: for, to the extent that such organizational change has also acted to encourage electoral destabilization, why then should parties have loosened their societal ties? If electoral vulnerability has been at least the partial consequence of the adoption of a catch-all organizational style, why should the parties have followed this path to begin with?

There are three factors which are important here. First, there are those organizational and institutional developments which, in and of themselves, have facilitated a more catch-all or 'top-down' approach. These include changes in the modes of financing the parties, which have led to a greater reliance on state subventions as against membership subscriptions or other popular forms of finance; the impact of new technologies and of changes in the mass media which have enabled party leaders to appeal directly to voters and thereby undermined the need for organizational networks; the increased availability of new marketing techniques, which help to obviate the need for grass-roots liaison as a means of gaining feedback; and so on.

Second, there is the impact of social change on organization itself (as opposed to its impact on issue-concerns, values, etc.—see above), in that the development of a more knowledgeable, well-informed, and competent electorate, together with the undeniable increase in the individualization and atomization of modern society, have together undermined the sense of collective solidarity which once served as the prerequisite for the traditional mass party. Perhaps ironically, it has sometimes been the very success of the parties which has acted to promote this erosion of collective solidarity. As Einhorn and Logue (1988: 180) note in the case of the Social Democrats in Scandinavia, for example:

the principal cause of demobilization was success . . . Social Democratic housing policy moved a good portion of the blue-collar working class out of the densely populated urban neighborhoods where the party and its organizations had been a way of life; those customs did not move easily to suburbia. Moreover, the centralised mechanisms of the welfare state eliminated the need for solidarity, which had been a crucial characteristic of the labour movement. Previously, solidarity had provided the welfare infrastructure for the working class—trade union benefit societies covering sickness, unemployment, old age and death; housing cooperatives, and the like—but now the need for solidarity and schooling in it were attenuated.

Third, it is also possible that the difficulties which we perceive in attempting to puzzle out the reasons for a shift towards attenuated organizational links are not really difficulties at all, but may simply derive from approaching the problem from the wrong end. In this sense, the catch-all or top-down style of party may actually be the norm, while the more encapsulating or solidaristic party may well be the transitory exception. Thus, for example, Pizzorno (1981: 272) has hypothesized that:

'integration' parties, stable electoral cleavages, and clear alternatives in party programme are more likely to be found in periods of intense social (mainly occupational and geographic) change and of consequent strong pressures by new categories of interests to enter into the political system. If this hypothesis is true, strong parties, with clearly delineated programs and integrated membership, are a temporary phenomenon. They emerge both to strengthen and to control the access of the new masses into the political system and become redundant once both entry and control are achieved. If they are typical of pluralism, then, they are typical only of its first 'generative' phase, when the big collective actors are admitted to share power into a system of representation.

This argument is also reinforced by a second contention of Pizzorno (1981: 253), that 'in principle, there should be no need for organization . . . to unite the followers of a governmental party.' According to this view, governmental resources, or the promise of such resources, offer incentives to the parties to shed those often unwelcome policy and ideological constraints which are an inevitable side-effect of the maintenance of an active organizational network. To the extent that parties gain greater access to government, we might expect them to lay a diminishing emphasis on the need for organization. The importance of this hypothesis is easily indicated by even the most cursory survey of the recent west European experience, for this shows that most of the relevant parties are now governing or potentially governing parties. In the fifteen-year period from 1970 to 1985, for example, only two west European parties of any notable size remained persistently excluded from government: the British Liberal party on the one hand, which despite its increasing electoral support remains a very minor party at the parliamentary level; and the Italian Communist Party on the other, whose exclusion from government has been tempered by sustained periods in office at the regional level, as well as by a semi-governmental role at national level during the period of the *compromesso storico* in the 1970s. With these qualified exceptions, all other European parties of any reasonable electoral size have enjoyed at least one period of incumbency during this fifteen-year span.

ORGANIZATIONAL CHANGE: A RESEARCH AGENDA

This paper has sought to emphasize the link between party organization or styles of organizational intervention and electoral (de)stabilization. While the existence of such a linkage in itself seems hardly contentious, the implicit logic which underlies it has become of crucial importance by virtue of the wave of electoral volatility which began to break over most of western Europe since the late 1960s.

As noted above, there are many potential explanations for this recent electoral volatility. Change in predispositions may reflect the interests of new generations and hence may constitute a crisis of ideology; or it may reflect changes in the social structure and the blurring of traditional social boundaries, and hence may constitute a crisis of class; or, as I have tried to suggest in this essay, it may reflect changes in modes of representation and, as such, may constitute a crisis of party. Indeed, it may well reflect a conjuncture of all three elements, and more.

To the extent that there is a specific crisis of party, however, then this is likely to result in, and possibly also emerge from, changes in party organization and in the forms of linkage which tie parties to the mass electorate. An understanding of these changes must therefore be considered to be a major research priority.

This will need four distinct lines of enquiry. First, we need to go beyond those necessarily simple but now rather crude classifications of party organization which are to be found in the traditional literature. In particular, Duverger's distinction between cadre parties and mass parties offers little help towards understanding contemporary diversity, nor does it contribute to an explanation of contemporary change. The same may be said of Kirchheimer's approach which, while emphasizing the increasing remoteness of party and hence the preconditions for instability, nevertheless fails to take account of those parties which do not develop in a catch-all direction, and also fails to offer any real explanation as to why some parties become catch-all and why others do not. Given the rise of the apparently solidaristic and distinctly purposive 'new politics' parties; and given the political mobilization of new interests reflected in the emergence, however minimally, of new women's parties, pensioners' parties, and so on, this latter aspect is of crucial importance. Hence the need to develop a more exhaustive typology of contemporary party organization—a task in which this essay may be considered as a first and preliminary step.

Second, we need to develop a series of hard, fast, and empirically valid indicators concerning the internal life of modern parties. We need to assess the extent of change in the role of the ordinary party member; the extent to which party organizations have become more centralized; the extent of changes in the locus of internal party power; the extent of change in the relationship between party leaderships and other organizations, be they ancillary agencies, affiliates, or simply related interest groups; the extent of the professionalization of party bureaucracies and leaderships; the extent of the local integration of the party, and so on. In short, we need indicators of the real degree of organizational remoteness, and we need to be able to compare such indicators across the different types of party, across different party systems, and across time.

Third, on the basis of such evidence, and particularly through comparisons across space and time, we need to specify with some precision the relationship between organizational change or adaptation and electoral volatility. Does greater remoteness imply more instability? If so, is the process of party adaptation actually leading to a crisis of party? Does the challenge to traditional politics involve the emergence of new types of party organization which, in turn, can provide the basis for a renewed process of electoral stabilization? On the face of it, and as Kirchheimer emphasized, the trend in modern politics appears to be moving away from solidaristic ties and towards more contingent linkages, and this in itself would imply greater potential for volatility. At the same time, however, new modes of solidaristic organization, together with the mobilization of new interests in politics, suggest the potential for a possible brake on this process.

Finally, and most crucially, we need to develop and test a series of hypotheses which might account both for the diversity of party organizations and for change within party organizations. There are at least two elements involved here. First, we need to analyse those organizational/institutional conditions which might *facilitate* diversity and change. These include changes in the financing of parties; the impact of new technologies and of changes in the mass media which enable party leaders to appeal directly to voters and which may undermine the need for organizational networks; the availability of new marketing techniques, and so on. Second, we need to look at the social/political conditions which may act to *encourage* organizational change. These include the growth of new issues and concerns which, together with the emergence of a more knowledgeable and critical electorate, force parties to become more adaptable and responsive; an increasing individualization and atomization of society which may undermine the basis for solidaristic organizations; the incorporation of more and more parties into the governmental process (if only for short periods in certain cases) which may encourage increasing remoteness; the development of new modes of representation and the increasing attractiveness or effectiveness of unconventional political behaviour, and so on.

In sum, we need to understand the nature of and the basis for party organizational diversity and change in contemporary western

3
The Problem of Party System Change

The catalogue of change grows ever more extensive. The evidence begins in the outlying periphery of western Europe, with the gradual decay of Fianna Fáil predominance in Ireland, and with the sudden emergence of a new party, the Progressive Democrats which, in its first electoral outing in 1987, became the third largest party in the system. There is evidence from Britain, with the long-term erosion of Labour and the concomitant growth of third-party support in the form of, however temporarily, the Liberal/SDP Alliance. In France, the first left-wing government in the history of the Fifth Republic was elected in 1981 and later returned to office in 1988; the 1980s in France have also been characterized by the continued marginalization of the Communists and by the re-emergence of an extreme right party. Italy in the 1980s witnessed the appointment of the first non-Christian Democratic premiers since World War II and, more recently, recorded a relatively major shift in support from the Communist Party to the Socialists and the Ecologists. Ecologists also managed to win parliamentary representation in Austria, with further change being evident in a doubling of the right-wing Liberal Party vote in the more recent election of 1986. In west Germany, the Social Democrats continue to poll less than 40 per cent of the vote, and find themselves facing the increasingly vibrant challenge of the Greens, who now command almost 10 per cent of the seats in the Bundestag. In Belgium the linguistic divisions in all three major parties have now solidified, the ruptures in the Christian Social Party and in the Liberals being paralleled by the division in the Socialist Party in 1978. The late 1970s in the Netherlands also witnessed a major change, with the merger of the three traditional denominational parties into the more broadly-based Christian Democratic Appeal. In Denmark, despite the relative peace which has followed the 'earthquake'

election of 1973, the last decade has seen substantial growth in support for both the Conservatives and the Socialist People's Party. Conservative growth has also been evident in Norway and Finland with, in the latter case, the return of the KOK to government in 1987 for the first time in more than twenty years. In Sweden, the past decade has witnessed the continued challenge to the long-term dominance of the Social Democrats, which first lost office in 1976, and which now must face a new challenge from the Green Party, which first entered parliament in 1988.

Patterns are also evident; there seems little that is random. One thread which can be identified in recent years involves the growth of ecology parties, which have now gained representation in the parliaments of Austria, Belgium, Finland, Germany, Italy, Switzerland, and, more recently, Sweden. A second thread is the apparent decline of the traditional class left, or at least, its re-equilibrium, following the erosion of support for significant components of the left. The growth of the non-social democratic left in Denmark and Norway offers a clear example of this trend. In France, on the other hand, the re-equilibrium has favoured more moderate forces on the left, in that the Communist Party has lost substantial ground in favour of the Socialists, and it is also possible that a similar centripetal realignment may be beginning in Italy. A third thread, discerned with perhaps more difficulty and dispersed less evenly, is the challenge to the Christian parties. The pan-Christian merger in the Netherlands, for example, represented an unabashed attempt to restore some electoral credibility to the fading fortunes of the three constituent denominational parties. In France, no confessional alternative has emerged since the demise of the MRP in the early 1960s. In Italy, despite a revival in 1987, the Christian Democrats continue to command a smaller proportion of the vote than at any postwar election prior to 1983, while in Austria, the 1986 election left the People's Party with a smaller proportion of the vote than at any election since 1953. Even in Switzerland, where symptoms of change are rare in postwar politics, the 1980s have seen the Christian Democratic People's Party commanding a smaller share of the vote than at any election since 1939.

Neither the changes nor their patterning are wholly unexpected. A lot has been happening on the ground, as it were, and the very evident social and economic flux in recent years in postwar western Europe cannot but be anticipated to have had an impact on mass politics. Since at least the early 1960s, both sociologists and political scientists have emphasized the importance of changes in the class structure and conventional value systems of advanced industrial Europe, and have offered clear indications of how such changes may impact upon prevailing political styles. The decline in the traditional working class, growing white-collar employment, and the increasing economic and social importance of service industry all combine to create a potential challenge to the traditional shibboleths of social-democratic politics. Increasing secularization and a more widespread politicization of gender offer a threat to traditional confessional alignments. Finally, a growing concern with environmental issues, an increasing distrust of authority, and the prioritization of quality-of-life issues offer the basis for a new alignment in politics which, when socially differentiated, appears to draw lines between age-groups or generations, rather than between classes or religions.

If conventional patterns of mass politics are challenged by the changing *substantive* concerns of voters, then so also do they appear vulnerable to a changed perspective of the *relationship* between the individual and the wider society. More widespread educational qualifications, a greater sense of individual competence, and a reluctance to tolerate simple elite direction all combine to suggest an increasing distaste for the conventions of mass party organizations. Political mobilization, if and when it occurs, now appears more easily reflected in the ebbs and flows of single-issue interest organizations, which seem to offer a more meaningful and flexible outlet for the demands of younger generations than can be afforded by the relatively moribund parties of the past. Thus, the traditional political alternatives qua organizations are more vulnerable; affective attachments have declined, and patterns of political representation are in flux.

There is little need to cite the literature which catalogues such change; the images are pervasive, their import underlined by a diverse range of scholars, all seeking to identify the kernel of these transformative processes and to predict their future direction. One important study, however, does capture the ethos of this literature quite succinctly; in a concluding chapter to a major collection of essays published in 1984, Russell Dalton and his colleagues (1984*b*: 451) note that:

Electoral alignments are weakening, and party systems are experiencing increased fragmentation and electoral volatility. Moreover, the evidence suggests that the changes in all of these nations reflect more than short-term oscillations in party fortunes. This decomposition of electoral alignments often can be traced to shifts in the long-term bases of partisan support—party identification and social cleavages. Virtually everywhere among the industrialised democracies, the old order is changing.

Drawing on the extensive country studies in their volume, Dalton and his colleagues find evidence of change in the weakening of alignments, increased fragmentation, and increased volatility. This change is seen as long-term rather than short-term, involving shifts in both the pattern of social cleavages and the orientation to mass party organizations. This strong but considered conclusion also contains little of the ephemeral. The changes which have been observed are substantial, undermining and potentially transforming a pattern of political alignments which has more or less persisted since the beginning of mass democratic politics in western Europe. We are not just talking about marginal change, therefore; something much more fundamental is at stake. The problem is understanding what it actually means.

In general, many of the shifts in the west European political environment are conventionally grouped as symptoms of an all-embracing phenomenon called *party system change*, a phenomenon about which much evidence is adduced, but which is itself rarely defined in any rigorous sense. Indeed, it can even be argued that it is this very definitional fuzziness which allows the multiplicity of symptoms to be cited with such equanimity. Aggregate electoral shifts are therefore seen as indicative of party system change, as are shifts in the balance of partisan support among the different strata of the population. Further symptoms include changes in coalitional alignments, as well as changes in the balance of representative power between parties on the one hand and interest groups on the other. Finally, changes in the cleavage system, whether resulting from the emergence of new cleavages or from the decline in old cleavages, are also seen to indicate change in party systems, with the 'hold' of a given cleavage system often being taken as a surrogate indicator of the degree of entrenchment of the party system itself.

The range of symptoms is extensive, and those mentioned above constitute a far from exhaustive catalogue. It is therefore tempting to conclude that, lacking a precise definition, the concept of party system change can be (and usually is) taken to mean virtually anything which, for those who work in the area, represents something of a problem. Hence this particular chapter, the purpose of which is not to propose some rigorous definition of party system change which may enable us to circumvent the quagmire, but rather is simply to identify some of the problems involved in the understanding of party system change, and, through this approach, to place some key questions on the agenda for future debate and future research.

PARTY CHANGE VERSUS PARTY SYSTEM CHANGE

The first problem which needs to be indicated is the distinction between *party change* on the one hand, and *party system change*, on the other, and, with this, the allied problem of when precisely the former also implies the latter (see also Chapter 1 above).

In many ways, it is party change which is the more difficult to specify. When can we speak of party change as such? Must we restrict the definition only to those cases when we can clearly identify the emergence of a new party—as perhaps in the case of the CDA in the Netherlands or of the linguistic fractures in the three traditional parties in Belgium? Or can we speak of party change when only some of the characteristics of the party have been transformed?

The key problem here is perhaps insurmountable, in that it involves the specification of the 'essence' or 'identity' of a given political party. Strictly speaking, we can speak of change only when we first can define what it is that has changed. Unfortunately, if inevitably, parties are rarely discussed in such terms. Rather, we tend to frame our discussion of a party *tout court* in terms of certain aspects or characteristics of that party—whether it is the electoral base, the policy profile, the governing role, or whatever. It is also inevitable that many of these aspects are in a state of almost permanent flux. Thus the electoral base of a party will change as the society itself changes, either as a result of socio-economic change or demographic change. The policies of party will also be subject to modification with time, in response to changing needs, changing demands, and changing constraints. It is also very likely that the governing role of parties will change, as the parties themselves respond to shifts in the electoral balance or to new strategic opportunities. As Carl Friedrich (1968: 452) has observed: 'Party development is more highly dynamic than any other sphere of political life; there is no final rest, no ultimate pattern . . . Rather, there is constant change in one direction or another, with never a return to the starting point.'

Since changes in specific aspects of parties are a permanent feature of the political landscape, and since the process of party adaptation is also continous, it may be tempting to conclude that party change is so pervasive as to be almost irrelevant. To be sure, the extent and pace of the change will vary, and the implications of change in different times and in different circumstances may be very different. But this is not to talk about change as such; rather it is to specify different levels and types of change, which necessitates an alternative but equally rigorous set of criteria. In short, it necessitates a leap from talking about change as such, which is pervasive, to talking about when change matters, which may be quite rare.

Moreover, we remain with the problem of change in the different aspects of the party rather than change in the party *tout court*, and with the difficulty of moving from one level to the other. Let us try to pin this down to a specific example, of which perhaps the best is the British Labour party. Between 1945 and 1987, for example, a number of aspects of the British Labour party have been substantially transformed. In terms of electoral strength, the party's share of the vote declined by more than one-third, from 48 per cent to just 31 per cent. The party 'within the electorate' has also changed, a crude indicator of which is that its support among manual workers declined from some 60 per cent in the immediate postwar years to some 42 per cent in 1987.[1] In ideological terms, despite the revitalization of the left in the late 1970s, it is also now a markedly more moderate party, with a parliamentary leadership which, in terms of social profile, is increasingly indistinguishable from that of its Conservative opponents. For now, at least, one can also speak of a change in the party's governing role since, having been out of office since 1979, and having being challenged in its role of major opposition by the Liberal/SDP Alliance in the 1983 and 1987 elections, it is not just the case that Labour is no longer a 'natural' party of government—if this ever was the case—but also that it is no longer even the 'natural' alternative government.

---

[1] The figures are derived from data reported in Alford (1963) and the *Sunday Times*, 14 June 1987.

One can argue at length about the extent and importance of changes in these and other aspects of the party, as well as about their possible future pattern. For our purposes, however, the problem is more basic: how are these changes to be interpreted? Do they matter, and do they mean that the party as such has changed? Is Labour now a different party than it was in 1945? In short, what are the criteria which can be adopted in order to determine whether this particular party has changed? The problem is acute, for if such criteria are absent, then we are really no nearer to differentiating Labour *party* change from Labour *party* continuity. That is to say, until we can distil the essence of what constitutes the British Labour party—the core of the party, as it were—we must inevitably restrict ourselves to a discussion of change in certain aspects of the party rather than of change in the party *tout court*.

PARTY SYSTEM CHANGE

In this sense, we may be on surer ground in talking about party *system* change, for here it does seem possible to identify an essence of what constitutes any given party system and thereby to determine whether that system has changed. A party system clearly involves something more than the sum of its component (party) parts, and incorporates some element of understanding of the mode of interaction between these parties. Sartori (1976: 43–4) offers the clearest definition:

The concept of system is meaningless—for purposes of scientific inquiry—unless (i) the system displays properties that do not belong to a separate consideration of its component elements and (ii) the system results from, and consists of, the patterned interactions of its component parts, thereby implying that such interactions provide the boundaries, or at least the boundedness, of the system . . . Parties make for a 'system,' then, only when they are parts (in the plural); and a party system is precisely the *system of interactions* resulting from inter-party competition.

Once the nature of what constitutes a party system has been established, then it becomes possible to identify different types of party systems, and hence to specify criteria which will enable one to determine whether any given system has changed from one type to another. In some ways this can lead us to the simplest and clearest definition: *party system change occurs when a party system is transformed from one class or type of party system into another.* To be sure, the mode of classifying party systems is itself quite hotly disputed, and change defined in this fashion is likely to be a relatively infrequent phenomenon. Nevertheless, such an approach enjoys the advantages of strict criteria and quite unambiguous conclusions. In short, it offers one way in which to circumvent the quagmire.

Such an approach also enjoys the advantage of enabling us to relate party change to party system change; that is, it allows us to assess whether the appearance or disappearance of a party— which is the most unambiguous case of party change—results in party system change. When is this the case? At what point can one say that a new party system has emerged?

At one level, the answer appears straightforward: change at the core of a party system is relevant; change at the margins is not. For example, the replacement of a left socialist party by a new ecology party in Norway might not be considered to involve a change in the party system. On the other hand, were the Greens in Germany to retain their Bundestag representation at a time when the Free Democrats fell below the 5 per cent threshold, such a change might be considered momentous. Clearly then, the importance of the appearance or disappearance of a party is not simply a function of its size, or even of its ideological appeal; rather, the question relates to the *systemic role* of the particular party, and the extent to which its presence or absence might alter either the direction of competition in the system or the process of government formation.

Party system change might therefore occur when, as a result of ideological, strategic, or electoral shifts, there is a transformation of the direction of competition or the governing formula. If, on the other hand, the change involves simply the realignment of the social bases of party support, or the emergence of a new set of issue concerns, while leaving the pattern of competition essentially untouched, this might not be considered of major significance—at least in terms of the party *system*.

Let us therefore return to the question of the classification of party systems. Turning to Sartori's (1976) own approach, for example, it can be suggested that the appearance/disappearance of a party leads to party system change when the number of relevant parties is altered to an extent which shifts the party system in question from, say, the limited pluralism class to, say, the extreme pluralism class. On the other hand, it can be argued that even this level of change is insufficient to constitute a change of the system unless it also involves either an extension or abbreviation of the breadth of ideological polarization. Thus the disappearance of one of the relevant anti-system parties from a system of polarized pluralism might be considered sufficient to eradicate the existence of bilateral oppositions, reduce the level of polarization, encourage the emergence of centripetal competition, and thereby transform the system into one of moderate pluralism. Conversely, the appearance of a new anti-system party, such as the French National Front, might be considered sufficient evidence of the existence of bilateral oppositions and of maximum ideological polarization, thus possibly shifting the direction of competition and thereby transforming the French party system from one of moderate pluralism to one of polarized pluralism. In neither instance, however, might we attribute much significance to the appearance or disappearance of a small centre party.

These are indisputably relevant changes, and they are also easily noted and categorized. Other cases are more problematic, however. For example, Sartori (1976: 192–201) defines a predominant party system as one in which the major party is constantly supported by a winning majority of voters. As such, as he himself admits (Sartori, 1976: 196), it is a type of party system which may cease to exist at any moment—the loss of a certain proportion of votes or seats being sufficient to transform the party system into one of moderate pluralism or whatever. Here the change may not seem momentous, and may indeed result from a very minimal level of electoral volatility. Yet, following Sartori, even such a small shift may indicate a change of the party system as such. The same is obviously true if the criteria for change are linked to Blondel's (1968) classification of party systems, which hinges almost exclusively on the aggregate distribution of electoral support.

In sum, despite the multiplicity of symptoms cited in the literature, it does seem possible to specify at least minimal criteria for a definition of party system change in a way which is not readily apparent in the case of party change.[2] To the extent that discussions of the former are linked to accepted classifications, then the essence of a particular party system can be distilled, and the

[2] For a useful discussion of the difficulties in establishing criteria for systemic change in general, see Dowding and Kimber (1987).

question of change versus continuity can be answered quite unambiguously. In the case of party change, on the other hand, the essence is elusive, and whether a party actually has changed, or become a new party, or whatever, is difficult to ascertain. To be sure, in this case also one can relate the question of change to accepted classifications. Thus, following Kirchheimer (1966), for example, one can speak of a party *tout court* changing from a mass integration party to a catch-all party; or, following Duverger (1954), one can speak of a mass party becoming a cadre party; or, following Daalder (1984), one can speak of an agrarian party becoming a centre party. Here, however, the classifications themselves are quite ambiguous, in that typologies of parties have not been subject to the rigour associated with the elaboration of typologies of party systems, with the result that strict criteria concerning what constitutes a 'catch-all' party, or a 'mass' party, or a 'centre' party are not easily conceived. The difficulties persist and hence, inevitably, discussions of party change will continue to avoid the question of actual party change as such and will focus instead on those ongoing processes of change which characterize particular aspects of parties.

ELECTORAL VOLATILITY AND CLEAVAGE CHANGE

As noted above, the contemporary literature is awash with references to the transformation of west European politics, references which frequently confuse the notions of party change on the one hand and party system change on the other. More specifically, an emphasis on *electoral* change, which has occupied the lion's share of recent scholarly attention, and which in most cases refers to just one particular aspect of party change, has usually been extended to imply change in party systems in general, and change in the cleavage structure in particular.

The reasoning here is both direct and indirect. First, taking the direct arguments, it is suggested that electoral change—whether at the aggregate or individual level—leads to party system change. The problems involved in such reasoning have already been discussed above, and do not need to be rehearsed again. In brief, I have argued that, strictly speaking, electoral change should be seen to lead to party system change only when it brings about a shift from one type of party system to another. In some cases, as in the predominant party system, even a very small electoral change may necessitate such a reclassification. In other cases, however, the matter is more complex, and it may only be through effecting the appearance or disappearance of a party which, in turn, will alter the direction of competition that electoral change may also involve party system change. In other words, the *location* of the electoral change is crucial, as is the systemic role of the party or parties affected (Mair, 1983).

Second, there is the indirect argument. Here, electoral change is seen as symptomatic of change in the cleavage system and this, in turn, is seen to imply a transformation of the party system: *electoral change = cleavage change = party system change*. The difficulties with this line of reasoning are manifest. The first and most evident difficulty has been highlighted by Gordon Smith (1988: 3), who addresses the second link in this equation, and who questions whether cleavages should actually be considered of systemic relevance. As he suggests, from what he admits to being a 'heretical' position:

The cleavage structure relates to the social make-up of support accruing to individual parties—not to the 'system', not that is if we follow a definition based on interaction. Social cleavages, and changes in them, naturally do have important consequences for the system as a whole, but those effects are registered through the other dimensions: affecting the number and relative size of the parties, the extent/intensity of polarisation, the volatility of the party system. This view is contentious, since it implies that a clearer line should be drawn between the study of parties and their electorates on the one hand and party systems on the other. But if no line at all is established it becomes difficult to find any acceptable limits as to what should be brought into discussion.

Smith's argument—that cleavage change may not in itself imply party system change—is both interesting and provocative; that said, however, it also inevitably involves opening up another Pandora's box which, for now, might best remain closed. For the purposes of this chapter, therefore, it seems more fruitful to challenge this indirect line of reasoning from another perspective, and that is by looking at the first link in the equation, which relates electoral change to cleavage change.

In other words, if, in common with most interpretations, and *pace* Smith, we do accept that cleavage change implies party system change, is it also reasonable to assume that electoral change implies cleavage change? This is certainly the assumption which underlies much of the contemporary emphasis on change in West European party systems, in that the recent waves of electoral volatility which have been experienced by many of the West European countries have been explicitly interpreted as an indication of cleavage decline. The question remains, however, as to whether this interpretation is valid.

Testing Lipset and Rokkan

Recognition of the importance of the cleavage structure underlying west European politics derives mainly from Stein Rokkan's pioneering efforts to chart the broad macro-historical parameters of European political development (Lipset and Rokkan, 1967; Rokkan, 1970). According to Rokkan, mass politics in modern Europe has been structured by four major cleavages. Two of these cleavages, which were the earliest in chronological terms, derived from the national revolutions in modern Europe, when the central nation-building cultures came into conflict with peripheral subject cultures on the one hand, and with the corporate privileges of the Church on the other hand. The two cleavages which emerged from this process—centre versus periphery/subject versus dominant culture, and Church versus state—were to have a profound effect on the pattern of mass politics as it emerged following democratization, although clearly they varied significantly in their impact in different nation states.

The other two cleavages derived from the Industrial Revolution in modern Europe, and crystallized oppositions between the old landed interests and the new industrialists on the one hand, and the owners of capital and the new working class on the other. These cleavages were also to have a profound effect on the pattern of mass politics following democratization, but whereas the conflicts involving the primary versus the secondary economy, like those of centre versus periphery and Church versus state, varied significantly between the different nation states, the conflict of owners versus workers was to prove 'more uniformly divisive' (Lipset and Rokkan, 1967: 21), with workers' movements mobilizing in each of the modern European democracies.

This complex of cleavages, emerging in different forms as it did across Europe, largely accounted for the variation among the party systems which developed in the wake of universal suffrage, and, more significantly, established a set of parameters which proved remarkably enduring. The introduction of universal manhood suffrage at the beginning of the twentieth century proved the crucial catalyst which, as it were, 'froze' these cleavage structures into place, institutionalizing a language of politics which was to prove more or less immutable. Thus, even in the 1960s, when Lipset and Rokkan were writing, the cleavage structures were still all too apparent. Their analysis may have stopped with the 1920s, but, as they argued, there was little reason to continue beyond that point, for 'the party systems of the 1960s reflect, with few but significant exceptions, the cleavage structures of the 1920s . . . [T]he party alternatives, and in remarkably many cases, the party organizations, are older than the majorities of the national electorates' (Lipset and Rokkan, 1967: 50).

The reasons for such persistence or 'freezing' are complex, and neither the Lipset–Rokkan essay nor Rokkan's subsequent work found the necessary scope to explore this aspect more fully (although see Sartori, 1969; Alford and Friedland, 1974; Rokkan, 1977; see also Chapter 1 above). One crucial element of the process, however, was the notion of what Lipset and Rokkan (1967: 51) defined as 'the narrowing of the "support market" ', whereby the party organizations which developed around these crucial cleavages entrenched themselves through mass mobilization in the wake of the extension of the franchise, and, through the incorporation of virtually the entire 'mobilizable' electorate, pre-empted the emergence of alternative alignments.

Thus the closure of the electoral market and the enduring capacity of cleavages to structure political behaviour left little room for the emergence of new cleavages or new politics. To be sure, no wholesale immutability was implied. The 'support market' may not have narrowed completely; certain electoral concerns would always remain on the margins, and the issues which were derived from the major cleavages would undoubtedly wax and wane through time. In general, however, and especially in the longer term, the cleavage structure retained a profound impact on partisan predispositions, and there remained a powerful bias in favour of those party alternatives which mobilized along the cleavage divides. More significantly, universal suffrage and the final incorporation of all adults into the democratic process left little or no scope for the mobilization of *new* cleavages, and hence, in this crucial sense, the parameters remained as they had been in the 1920s.

The emphasis on electoral change in the contemporary literature is now read as portending a substantial revision of this view, in that it seems difficult to square more recent evidence of electoral volatility with a theory which emphasizes the persistence of cleavages and the 'freezing' of party systems. Survey evidence, which points both to a loosening of electoral bonds and a widespread decline in affective attachments towards parties, also appears to run counter to the emphasis on persistence.

Hence, for example, the pervasive references to cleavage decline and the possible emergence of new cleavages in the work of Dalton and his colleagues (1984a). In a separate article derived from the project, for example, Flanagan and Dalton (1984: 8) explicitly link their work to a testing of the Lipset–Rokkan thesis, linking electoral change to cleavage decline and thence to party system change in that, as they note, 'within a single decade the major research question has changed from explaining the persistence of party systems to explaining their instability and volatility'. The utility of survey data in the analysis of cleavage persistence is also emphasized, since such data can tap into the crucial 'cyclical pattern' inherent in the development of any cleavage, whereby the divide is sharply polarized when first mobilized, is then characterized by convergence, and finally, as it becomes institutionalized, generates less commitment within the mass public, resulting in an ageing of the party alignment pattern and a decline in popular attachment (Flanagan and Dalton, 1984: 8–10). The authors then contend (p. 10) that just such a pattern is evident in the case of the class cleavage:

Throughout the postwar period the dominant partisan cleavage in most Western democracies distinguished between the working-class and bourgeois parties. Recently, however, there have been increasing signs that this dominant class cleavage may also be moving into eclipse . . . [T]he contributors to *Electoral Change* assembled convincing [survey] evidence that the traditional middle-class/working-class cleavage is weakening.

Dalton and his colleagues also see signs of the emergence of new cleavages being derived from a new revolution—the postindustrial revolution. These new cleavages, observable through survey data,

pit proponents of the established industrial order against supporters of the goals of the new politics; manual workers against knowledge workers; the public sector against the private sector, and so on
(Dalton *et al.*, 1984*b*: 455–7). Although admitting that 'any of the
new social cleavages . . . must cross many hurdles before becoming
integrated into the political process,' they also see clear signs that
'the structure of democratic party systems, frozen for so much of
our lifetimes, is beginning to thaw' (Dalton *et al.*, 1984*b*: 457, 460).
Their views are echoed by Inglehart (1984: 26):

To a considerable degree, Lipset and Rokkan were correct in speaking of
a 'freezing of party alignments' dating back to an era when modern, mass-
party systems were established. Although deep-rooted political party alignments continue to shape voting behaviour in many countries, they no
longer reflect the forces most likely to mobilise people to become politically
active.

These various data therefore suggest that while class and other
traditional cleavages retain a profound impact on electoral behaviour, their impact has been withered by both age and changed
social conditions. A new society—a postindustrial society—is
emerging in advanced capitalism which, in turn, will act as the har-
binger of new cleavage patterns that will eventually displace traditional alignments.

The arguments also seem quite convincing. They build on data
which offer a level of detail which is not available from aggregate
electoral analysis, they depict trends common to a wide variety of
countries, and, in general, they are developed with immense rigour.
That said, they also suffer from one immense drawback, and that
is the inevitable constraint of time. Survey analysis is the child of
the late 1960s and 1970s and, in the end, the information which it
affords on the social basis of partisan support, the pattern of affective attitudes, and the links between citizens and political organizations, remains contemporary information. Trends may be
apparent, but they can be traced back only through a limited period
of time, and the situation which now pertains can be contrasted
only with that which prevailed at most fifteen or twenty years ago.
To be sure, trends over the longer term can be imputed through
contrasts between different age cohorts; but, at best, these remain
estimates, and we lack genuinely equivalent data from earlier
generations. In short, there is a severe problem of perspective.

The evidence of aggregate data

Hence the need to turn to aggregate electoral data which, while less informative, offer a necessary longer-term perspective. Hence also the need to return to the seminal analysis of Rose and Urwin (1970), which was the first study to use aggregate electoral data to test the Lipset–Rokkan theory.

Rose and Urwin (1970: 287–8) posit their analysis within the context of four distinct theories of the dynamic properties of parties and party systems: those emphasizing evolutionary trends; those emphasizing secular trends; those emphasizing a static equilibrium; and those emphasizing the constancy of party strength—'the null hypothesis'—which they associate with Lipset and Rokkan. They then go on to elaborate three testable hypotheses concerning this 'null hypothesis': 'old parties (i.e. pre-1914) are least likely to have their vote trend down'; 'old parties are least likely to have their vote show a significant trend'; and 'the older the party, the steadier its vote should be'; all derived on the basis that 'Lipset and Rokkan have argued that the party systems of Western nations tended to be "frozen" by cleavages established at the time of the enactment of universal suffrage, since parties then had already organized large blocs of the electorate' (Rose and Urwin, 1970: 296).[3]

Rose and Urwin's empirical findings—which supported the null hypothesis—are not of immediate interest here. What is relevant, however, is the explicit link which they drew between the Lipset–Rokkan theory on the one hand and the electoral fortunes of individual parties on the other. If party support remained reasonably stable, the argument went, then Lipset and Rokkan's theory was sustained; if party support proved volatile, however, the theory could no longer be considered valid. This crucial linkage has been maintained in the subsequent literature analyzing aggregate electoral patterns, although, in this more recent literature, the emphasis is on change rather than persistence.

Thus Wolinetz, for example, who was primarily concerned to test Kirchheimer's thesis on the development of catch-all parties, also reiterated the Rose–Urwin linkage between the aggregate electoral

---

[3] Later in their essay, Rose and Urwin (1970: 306) derive a fourth hypothesis, viz. 'the greater the age of a party system, the more likely it is to be static. This hypothesis reflects the Lipset–Rokkan emphasis upon the importance of the early institutionalisation of party support.'

fortunes of individual parties and the Lipset–Rokkan theory. For Wolinetz (1979: 7–8; see also Kirchheimer, 1966), Rose and Urwin had come to the 'same conclusion' as Lipset and Rokkan, although, as he pointed out, subsequent electoral volatility had meant that, by the mid-1970s, the picture had become different. A more recent study by Pedersen (1983) has also underlined an explicit linkage between aggregate electoral change and the Lipset–Rokkan theory. Commenting on the evidence of increased electoral volatility, and taking the Lipset–Rokkan theory as his starting-point, he notes (34–5):

> During the 1960s it was widely held among political scientists that European party systems were inherently stable structures which—with a few exceptions—reflected the societal cleavage structures of the past . . . Recent political history, however, has produced some rather unexpected events which make it somewhat difficult to reconcile the theoretical view and the empirical realities . . . [and which] seem to indicate that, even if party systems may still reflect the traditional cleavage structures in the society, the significant exceptions that Rokkan and Lipset were talking about are no longer few, but constitute a larger and growing part of all European party systems.

Pedersen then goes on to substantiate this position, reporting trends in a summary index of party system volatility to demonstrate a pervasive pattern of change. These patterns are also confirmed by Maguire (1983), who replicates and updates the Rose–Urwin study, again couching the evidence in the context of the freezing hypothesis, and concludes from the more recent data that 'it is clear that European party systems cannot now be regarded as inherently stable structures' (Maguire, 1983: 92).

Each of these cited studies confined the analysis to postwar electoral trends, and there was little ambiguity in their respective findings: party support had remained more or less steady from the late 1940s through to the late 1960s, thus confirming the freezing hypothesis, whereas the 1970s had witnessed quite a considerable increase in electoral fluctuations, thus challenging the hypothesis.

Yet, even here, it is evident that there remains a problem of perspective. The 1970s and the 1980s are clearly different, and in this sense the aggregate data are compatible with the conclusions which are drawn from the survey analyses; but the contemporary period is different only with respect to the 1950s and 1960s, and it is difficult to know which pattern constitutes the norm. If volatility is the exception, then we can perhaps conclude that the freezing hypothesis no longer holds true (but even this is arguable, as we shall show below). If, on the other hand, the 'steady state' period of the 1950s and 1960s is the exception, and volatility is the norm, are we then to conclude that the freezing hypothesis *never* held true?

What was needed, therefore, was evidence which dated back to the beginnings of mass politics and which, at the very least, incorporates data from the 1920s, when the freezing process allegedly ocurred. This is the more meaningful approach adopted by two studies of aggregate electoral patterns. In the first of these, Ersson and Lane (1982; see also Lane and Ersson, 1987: 94–132) assess the broad sweep of electoral trends since the beginning of the 1920s, again situating their analysis in the context of the Lipset–Rokkan argument and the findings of Rose and Urwin, and again, as with the more recent literature, finding that 'the widely accepted hypothesis that West-European party systems are characterised by no change or stability is not in accordance with the data' (Ersson and Lane, 1982: 93). In this case, however, the longer time-span accords the findings significantly more weight, for the evidence of instability is apparent throughout the period since the 1920s, with, if anything, even more pronounced instability during the interwar years. Thus not only does the recent volatility of the 1970s challenge the continued validity of the Lipset–Rokkan hypothesis, but the longer-term analysis also suggests that the hypothesis never really carried much validity in the first place. Party systems have never been particularly stable, and hence the freeze has been exaggerated.

Much the same conclusion is reached by Shamir's (1984) extensive analysis of patterns of change and stability, which is the second major study to go beyond the relatively short-term postwar perspective. In this case, the perspective is even longer than that adopted by Ersson and Lane and, in many cases, trends are traced back to the nineteenth century. As the title of the study indicates, Shamir's explicit intention is to test the Lipset–Rokkan hypothesis, and, as with Rose and Urwin, Wolinetz, Pedersen, Maguire, and Ersson and Lane, the evidence adduced relates primarily to the aggregate electoral performance of parties over time. Although, like Ersson and Lane, data on ideological polarization are also incorporated, Shamir (1984: 39) nevertheless emphasizes that 'the freezing notion of party systems has been taken most often to refer to the party units comprising the system, the stability of support for those parties, and the cleavage dimensions delineating the system.' According to Shamir, two alternative models can be derived from the Lipset–Rokkan theory. The first of these implies the complete absence of change in party systems, which, Shamir states, is an unreal expectation. The second model, which is more realistic, implies the existence of a stable equilibrium, where short-term changes coexist with long-term stability, and where no significant change occurs which is not predictable on the basis of past observations. In the event, however, the data fail to support either model: most party systems evidence no increased stability following the period in which they were allegedly institutionalized, and hence they 'cannot be regarded as stable and surely not as frozen. The freeze hypothesis . . . has to be rejected' (Shamir, 1984: 70).

On the face of it, therefore, this cumulated empirical evidence offers little to sustain the Lipset–Rokkan theory. Postwar trends in aggregate party support suggest that, even if the thesis was valid through to the end of the 1960s (Rose and Urwin, 1970), the volatility of the 1970s and 1980s has undermined its continued relevance (Wolinetz, 1979; Pedersen, 1983; Maguire, 1983). The longer-term aggregate trends are even more damaging, for they indicate a prolonged pattern of instability which can be traced back to the 1920s (Ersson and Lane, 1982) and beyond (Shamir, 1984).

In short, observed trends in the aggregate electoral support for political parties in western Europe are incompatible with the Lipset–Rokkan thesis. There are two possible implications which can be drawn from this statement. First, the Lipset–Rokkan thesis is wrong; however useful it may be in terms of its contribution to our understanding of the processes by which party systems were structured, its emphasis on persistence or freezing was essentially misconceived. Or second, the measures of aggregate electoral trends which have been adopted in the literature are inadequate indicators of the original thesis and therefore fail to indicate party system change—at least in the intended sense.

Parties and cleavages

Let us stay with the second alternative for the moment—not least because the implications of the first seem quite drastic—and look at the measures which have been adopted by the authors cited above. All share one common feature: while a variety of different indices is used by these authors, in the end each is based on measures of persistence/change in the aggregate support for *individual parties*. Whether it is the Rae (1971) fractionalization index (Wolinetz, Ersson and Lane, Shamir) or simple trends in party support; that is, the regression of a party's vote against time (Rose and Urwin, Maguire); or measures of volatility or fluctuation (Pedersen, Ersson and Lane, Shamir), the unit of analysis is the individual party organization.[4] It is here that the essential problem may lie, for there is little to suggest that the Lipset–Rokkan theory can be tied so explicitly to the fortunes of individual parties. Indeed, as Lybeck (1985: 109) clearly emphasizes, 'there is really nothing in the original Lipset–Rokkan formulation to indicate that they believed the fraction of voting support going to a party should be constant.'

It is necessary to recall that the main question addressed by Lipset and Rokkan (1967: 1) did not concern parties as such, but rather 'the conditions for the development of a stable system of cleavage and oppositions in national political life'—of which parties were the organized expression. At one stage in their analysis, for example, there is a telling reference to 'the three cases of France, Germany, and Italy [where] the continuities in the alternatives are as striking as the disruptions in their organizational expressions' (Lipset and Rokkan, 1967: 52–3). The substance of this distinction between 'the alternatives' and 'their organizational expressions' is not of immediate importance here; what is relevant is that a distinction is made in the first place. Second, and more crucially, Lipset and Rokkan nowhere imply an inevitable correspondence between inter-party conflict on the one hand and the representation of a cleavage dividing line on the other. For while a cleavage will give rise to competing party organizations, the presence of particular patterns of competition does not in itself represent a cleavage.

---

[4] Ersson and Lane (1982) and Shamir (1984) also measure ideological polarization, which Shamir (1984: 40) links explicitly to the Lipset–Rokkan thesis: 'probably the most important part of the freezing theory refers to party systems cleavage structure. Lipset and Rokkan maintain that the cleavage dimensions delineating the party systems they studied have frozen . . . I will not study the party systems cleavage dimensions, that is, their substance, directly. Instead I will examine the closely related structural dimension of ideological polarisation . . . Clearly a freezing in the cleavage structure translates structurally into little variability in a party system's ideological polarisation.' However, little theoretical evidence is offered for this linkage between cleavage dimensions and ideological polarization, and certainly no necessary link is apparent in the Lipset–Rokkan theory.

This point can be clarified when one takes the example of competition between socialist parties and communist parties, a conflict which has been present in varying degrees throughout twentieth-century Europe. It goes almost without saying that although this inter-party conflict is significant, it certainly does not represent a distinct *cleavage*. While the socialist and communist parties *together* represent one side of a cleavage dividing line—that between workers and employers—their internal dispute is clearly of a different order. Thus, as Lipset and Rokkan (1967: 48) note:

The conditions for the development of distinctive working-class parties varied markedly from country to country within Europe. These differences emerged well before World War I. The Russian Revolution did not generate new cleavages but simply accentuated long-established lines of division within the working-class elite.

Putting these points together suggests an important distinction between the individual party organization, on the one hand, and the organized expression of the cleavage, on the other, in that the latter is capable of incorporating more than one party. In other words, there is no simple one-to-one correspondence between an individual party organization and the presence of a cleavage, for while the political relevance of the latter requires expression in some form of political organization, such a political organization may nevertheless include two or more parties competing for more or less the same constituency. Thus while individual parties may rise and fall, the major 'alternatives' may therefore persist. In France, for example, despite 'marked organizational fragmentation both at the level of interest articulation and at the level of the parties . . . no analyst of French politics is in much doubt about the underlying continuities of sentiment and identification on the right no less than on the left of the political spectrum' (Lipset and Rokkan, 1967: 53).

In sum, the evidence of persistence in the first postwar decades, and of instability since the late 1960s, as well as in the interwar years, points to little more than electoral persistence or change at the level of the individual party. Thus, if party A gains, party B loses, and party C remains the same, the index of instability is the same as if party B had gained, party C had lost, and party A had remained the same, even though party A may organize on the same 'side' of a cleavage as party B, and on the opposite 'side' to party

C (see also Chapter 2 above). More specifically, none of the indices of electoral change used in the above literature can distinguish between shifts between cleavage allies on the one hand and between cleavage opponents on the other. Should a Communist party cede votes to a Socialist party, for instance, while the overall left vote remains stable—and contemporary western Europe is now replete with such examples—the change would be seen to carry equivalent weight to a situation in which both Communist and Socialist parties had ceded votes to the right. Both situations would reflect electoral instability, yet it is clear that only the latter reflects 'cleavage' instability. Hence the difficulty involved in translating evidence of electoral change into evidence of cleavage change; the two need not coincide. That there are also difficulties in translating evidence of cleavage change into evidence of party system change is, of course, as noted above, also apparent.

In sum, the general assumption which links electoral volatility to systemic instability must be subject to serious qualification. In its direct form, that is *electoral change = party system change*, the qualifications derive from the type of party system in question and from the location of the electoral change itself. In its indirect form, that is *electoral change = cleavage change = party system change*, the qualifications are derived from both sets of linkages: those between cleavage change and party system change, already noted by Smith (1988); and those between electoral change and cleavage change, which have now been discussed at some length. For while the various indices of aggregate electoral change may tell us a great deal about electoral stability/instability in general, they appear to tell us little about the persistence/decay of cleavages. And this, surely, is the real brunt of the freezing hypothesis.

HOW MUCH ELECTORAL CHANGE?

This is not to deny the relevance of electoral volatility as such. Notwithstanding the difficulties involved in treating volatility as an indicator of cleavage decline, aggregate electoral change, if only in certain circumstances, is likely to have at least some bearing on the extent of party system change. But even if we loosen the criteria, and forget for the moment about the possible need to restrict discussions of party system change to those cases where there is a clear shift from one class or type of party system to another (see above), there remain problems concerning the level at which electoral volatility matters.

Once again, given the emphasis on electoral change in the contemporary literature, we are left with a number of key unanswered questions. At what point does volatility become important? Do we rate as significant levels of volatility above 5 per cent, above 10 per cent, or only above 15 per cent? Given Shamir's point that total electoral stability is an unreal expectation, what then are the cut-off points beyond which volatility can be seen to reflect meaningful party (if not party system) change? Should such cut-off points be established in absolute terms, or should they be relative to the individual country or period? Finally, is it necessary to distinguish between one-off volatile elections and a sequence of volatile elections?

The problem of cut-off points becomes particularly acute once it is recognized that there exists a clear bias towards aggregate electoral stability in the history of mass politics in western Europe. In theory, the Pedersen index can range from 0 (where there is no aggregate change) to 100 (where all existing parties lose all their votes and are replaced by wholly new parties). In practice, however, a survey of volatility levels in 303 elections in thirteen European countries between 1885 and 1985[5] shows that the actual range runs from 0 to 32 (Germany in 1920), with an overall mean of just 8.6. In fact, as can be seen from Table 3.1, volatility levels tend to cluster at quite low values, with more than two-thirds of the cases registering a level below 10, and with just 11 per cent registering a level above 15.

As against this, however, it can be argued that even low levels of volatility acquire a degree of significance if they reflect a cumulating trend, in that a sequence of even low volatile elections may create a substantial change in the overall electoral balance of the system. A highly volatile election, on the other hand, may prove relatively insignificant if followed by a second highly volatile election which acts to restore the prior partisan electoral balance.

In an effort to test this latter proposition, Table 3.2 reports a detailed breakdown of the 24 elections characterized by a level of volatility in excess of 17.2 (that is, in excess of twice the overall

[5] The full presentation and analysis of these data were subsequently reported in Bartolini and Mair (1990).

TABLE 3.1. *European elections by levels of volatility, 1885–1985*

Volatility levels	0–5	5–10	10–15	15+
N elections	79	134	56	34
% elections	26.1	44.2	18.5	11.2

Source: Bartolini and Mair (1990).

TABLE 3.2. *High-volatility* elections, 1885–1985*

Country	One-off elections (TV)	Consecutive elections (TV)
Belgium	1936 (17.7)	—
Denmark	1945 (18.4)	1973 (21.2)
	—	1975 (17.8)
	—	1977 (18.3)
France	—	1906 (31.1)
	—	1910 (30.5)
	1924 (18.7)	
	—	1951 (20.0)
	—	1956 (20.2)
	—	1958 (26.7)
	—	1962 (19.2)
Germany	1953 (21.2)	1920 (32.1)
	—	1924 (27.1)
		1930 (22.0)
	—	1932 (21.2)
Ireland	1927 (20.8)	—
	1943 (20.6)	—
Italy	1948 (23.0)	—
Netherlands	1897 (19.4)	
Switzerland	—	1917 (22.8)
	—	1919 (23.4)
United Kingdom	1931 (19.2)	

Note: * Total Volatility > 17.2 (i.e. twice overall mean).
Source: As Table 3.1.

mean). The most striking point to note about these elections is that the majority (15 or 62.5 per cent) occur in sequence, with a minority (9 or 37.5 per cent) being one-off elections. How do we interpret these sequential patterns?

There are two possible explanations for such a clustering. First, as suggested above, it may be that we are actually witnessing a process of *restoration*, within which the sudden transformation reflected in the high level of volatility in the first of the sequential elections is redressed in the subsequent volatile election(s), with the once losing parties regaining their electoral strength. In these circumstances, the party system could be considered to have received a sudden shock, but without any lasting effects.[6] Were this to be the case, then we should expect a relatively low level of net volatility across the elections which bracket the sequence of highly volatile elections. In the Danish case, for example, we would anticipate that volatility between the last election prior to 1973 and the first election after 1977 should be substantially lower than that at any of the intervening elections.

The second and alternative explanation, however, is that we are witnessing a more *enduring* shift in the partisan balance, in which the parties which experience major losses (or major gains) in the first of the sequence of elections find that their erosion (or growth) continues thereafter. In this case, net volatility calculated between the pair of bracketing elections should be at least as high as that which characterizes the intervening elections.

These alternative explanations are tested through the data in Table 3.3, which reports levels of volatility across the bracketing elections (treating these as if they were consecutive elections). The evidence is quite unequivocal: in all cases (with the possible exception of Denmark), volatility across the bracketing elections remains relatively high, and in most case exceeds that of even the most volatile election in the intervening sequence. It is clear from these data that these sequences of highly volatile elections therefore reflect enduring shifts in the partisan balance, and that they offer no real evidence for any restorative effect. Moreover, as can be seen

---

[6] If, on the contrary, rather than a clustering of highly volatile elections, there is simply a one-off highly volatile election, then it seems plausible to assume that this has involved a reasonably enduring (and radical) redistribution of votes; restoration of the partisan status quo, to the extent that it will have occured, will have taken place gradually, in that it is not reflected in an immediately subsequent high-volatility election.

TABLE 3.3. *Net volatility between those elections bracketing sequences of high-volatility*

Country	Bracketing elections	Net volatility	Number of parties gaining/losing > 5%
Denmark	1971 and 1979	19.7	2
France	1902 and 1914	37.4	5
	1946 and 1967	37.8	5
Germany	1919 and 1924(ii)	36.9	7
	1928 and 1932(ii)	38.0	5
Switzerland	1914 and 1922	33.6	3

Source: As Table 3.1.

in the last column in the Table, these periods are also characterized by the erosion or growth of support of relatively large numbers of parties (again, the very fragmented Danish system may be considered a possible exception).

In sum, it is clear that these clusters of highly volatile elections indicate periods of a fundamental electoral realignment of party systems. Not one of these sequences offers any real evidence of a restoration of the status quo. The nearest approximation to such a situation is that of Denmark in the 1970s, but even here net volatility across the bracketing elections is almost 20 per cent. To the extent that aggregate electoral volatility does have some bearing on the extent of party system change, and to the extent that the criteria for specifying instances of the latter may be loosened, then it is therefore around these exceptional cases of sustained electoral flux that we might best begin to explore the dimensions of party system change. To be sure, instances of such change will inevitably prove less frequent than those indicated in Tables 3.2 and 3.3; at the electoral level, however, these appear as the paradigmatic cases and, as such, deserve closer attention.

THE ELECTORAL BIAS

Voter fluctuation—be it at the aggregate or individual level, and be it between blocs of parties or single parties—is but one of the potentially relevant dimensions along which party system change can begin to be understood. Perhaps inevitably, however, particularly when applied at the level of the individual party, it is also the aspect which has received most attention in the recent literature, to the neglect of assessments of change with regard to other aspects, such as, for example, party ideology, organization, or strategy.

This electoral bias is certainly understandable. Electoral results are easily tabulated, change at the electoral level is easily compared across time and space, and, in the end, electoral performance is perhaps the key indicator of party strength. At the same time, however, this bias inevitably carries its own problems. In particular, an emphasis on the electoral dimension suggests that one can only speak of party or party system change if and when electoral change is seen to occur. And to the extent that this is the case, then the absence of electoral change becomes interpretable only in terms of party or party system stability. The possibility of change occurring despite electoral stability is therefore largely discounted, as is, perforce, the whole notion of party or party system adaptation.

This problem becomes acute when attempting to categorize party systems as stable or changing. Restricting the focus to the electoral dimension affords one particular categorization; enlarging that focus to take account of the ideological, competitive, or organizational dimensions may afford quite different results. In other words, before we can determine when a party system is changing, it is necessary to define the parameters along which change is to be measured.

For Kirchheimer, for example, party system change clearly involved something other than simple aggregate electoral change. In his classic essay, appropriately entitled 'The Transformation of the Western European Party Systems', Kirchheimer (1966) developed a major thesis on party system change which, to all intents and purposes, effectively ignored the electoral dimension. In this case, the transformation of party systems involved change at the level of ideology, organization, and competition, and while such change would inevitably provoke an electoral response (see the interpretation of the Kirchheimer argument in Wolinetz, 1979), such a response would not necessarily be visible at the electoral level—or at least at the aggregate electoral level, where adaptation could ensure maintenance of the given aggregate electoral equilibrium (Dittrich, 1983).

Indeed, one might go so far as to suggest that aggregate electoral stability could be due in large part to processes of change along other dimensions, and that the capacity of parties to maintain their electoral support derives from an ability to transform their appeals, their organizational style, and/or their mode of competition, while aggregate electoral change may result from an incapacity or an unwillingness to adapt along other dimensions. In such paradoxical circumstances, the apparently stable party systems would prove to be those characterized by parties which were more adaptable, whereas the apparently changing party systems would be those characterized by more obdurate political actors.

The Irish case offers a particularly useful example of the process by which adaptation—and change—at a variety of levels has coexisted with a striking degree of electoral continuity (Mair, 1987a; see also Chapter 1 above). Notwithstanding the sudden disruption caused by the emergence of a new party, the Progressive Democrats, in the 1987 election, for example, the overall shifts in the long-term electoral balance in the Irish Republic have appeared quite minimal. Over the two elections of 1982, for example, the leading Fianna Fáil party averaged some 46 per cent of the popular vote; half a century previously, in 1932, it had won 45 per cent. Fine Gael, the second party, averaged 37 per cent in 1982; in 1932 its predecessor, Cumann na nGaedheal, had won 35 per cent. Labour, the third party, averaged 10 per cent in 1982; in 1932 it won 8 per cent. In summary figures, and taking account of other minor parties and independents, net aggregate volatility across this fifty-year span was just 8.9, only marginally higher than the mean figure of 8.6 which emerges from the analysis of 303 consecutive elections in thirteen European countries between 1885 and 1985 (see above).

To be sure, this overall measure of electoral stability in the Irish case ignores quite a substantial degree of intermediate fluctuation in the intervening years. None the less, at least at the aggregate level, the impression of continuity—or at least of restoration—is striking, and the inevitable temptation in the Irish case is therefore to speak of party system stability. Yet, as a closer assessment reveals, such a conclusion is in many ways misleading. At the level of organization, for example, party–voter linkages have been transformed beyond recognition. A similar wholesale transformation has occurred at the level of ideology, with the substantive concerns of the parties and the nature of their appeals undergoing a total sea-change across this fifty-year span. Finally, in terms of party system dynamics, the situation now is wholly incomparable with that which pertained previously: the parties themselves are more competitive in terms of their electoral strategies; the electorate is increasingly dominated by voters who are in competition between the parties, and whose declining affective attachments render them available to virtually each of the competing alternatives; and, since at least the early 1970s, there is now a real possibility of alternation in government. In short, the system itself has become immensely more competitive (Mair, 1987*a*: especially 221–8).

In the Irish case, then, it can be concluded that there has been a transformation in the strategies of the parties as well as in the strategic constraints of the system itself. The pattern of competition has also changed, as has the means by which voters are mobilized. Ideologically transformed parties now compete for radically different voters. This surely is substantial change. Yet, in the end, these parties win more or less the same level of aggregate support as they did half a century before (or at least did so prior to 1987). In effect, the parties in Ireland have been constrained to work very hard in order to remain in the same place and preserve the same equilibrium. And given such a sustained process of adaptation, is it not then possible to speak of party system change in Ireland, *despite* long-term electoral continuity?

More generally, the Irish example suggests that an undue emphasis on the electoral dimension blocks out consideration of patterns of change which may offer a much more complete understanding of when and how party systems change, and when and how they persist. In sum, it cautions against a simple categorization of party system change/persistence which derives largely, if not solely, from aggregate electoral trends.

KEY PROBLEMS

This chapter has sought to identify some of the key problems in the understanding of party system change, and has judiciously avoided the prescription of strict criteria as to how such change might be measured. In other words, and following the path of least resistance, the intention has been to raise questions rather than to provide answers.

Four key problems have been identified. First, I have emphasized the need to distinguish party change on the one hand and party system change on the other, two notions which are often confused in the context of much of the contemporary literature. In emphasizing this distinction I have also suggested that it may prove more feasible to establish criteria for party system change than for party change since, at least by means of the accepted classifications of party systems, it seems more feasible to distil the essence or core of a particular party system than is the case for a particular party. Once such a core has been identified, then it is possible to say when a given system has changed. Finally, I have also suggested that, strictly speaking, it may be inappropriate to speak of party system change in cases other than the transformation of a party system from one class or type to another.

Second, I have discussed some of the problems involved in assuming a linkage between electoral change and cleavage change on the one hand, and between cleavage change and party system change on the other. Focusing particularly on the former linkage, I have suggested that while much of the evidence of aggregate electoral change which has been adduced in order to challenge the Lipset–Rokkan freezing proposition tells us a great deal about electoral stability/instability in general, in and of itself it tells us little about the persistence or decline of cleavages. To the extent that the hypothesis about party system change rests on the assumption of cleavage decline, therefore, in these terms at least the case is, as yet, unproven.

Third, I have discussed some of the problems associated with the interpretation of electoral volatility itself, particularly those relating to the question of when volatility matters. The most important point to note here is that the evidence of a century of mass politics points to quite extensive electoral stability, and that the instances of 'substantial' volatility, and particularly the instances of sustained high volatility, are relatively infrequent. None the less, the identification of such instances does help to specify those cases and periods where party system change may be most radical, and where a more complete understanding of the dimensions of change may be sought.

Finally, and with particular reference to the Irish case, I have discussed some of the problems associated with the electoral bias, and the concomitant neglect of other and potentially more fundamental dimensions of change. As the study of the Irish case indicates, it is perhaps paradoxical that the most far-reaching processes of party system change may occur in those cases which are characterized by relative electoral stability, whereas the more volatile systems may well be symptomatic of party rigidity and party obduracy, characteristics which, in a certain light, can be read as evidence of stability.

In general, however, it is clear that an understanding of party system change must focus on that which defines the system in the first place: the pattern of interactions among the parties. Electoral developments, ideological change, organizational revitalization, and so on, are all important aspects of party change, but they are appropriate indicators of party system change only when they also begin to have a bearing on the pattern of interactions which characterize the system itself; or, in other words, when they have systemic relevance.

4

Myths of Electoral Change and the Survival of the 'Old' Parties[1]

Stein Rokkan's contribution to the contemporary understanding of European politics and political development remains unparalleled. In many ways, and particularly for my generation, which first learned political science in the late 1960s and early 1970s, it has been Rokkan's interpretation which has done most to frame our long-term understanding of how our political environment has been shaped. Moreover, despite the burgeoning of the literature on comparative European politics in recent years, his is an interpretation which has also remained largely unchallenged. Few, if any, would seek to redraw the contours which he established in his geopolitical map of Europe, for example, and few, if any, would seek to question the importance of the cleavage structures which he identified as crucial to the development and consolidation of mass politics and party systems.

But while very little may have been proposed in order to qualify Rokkan's understanding of the origin and early development of mass politics in western Europe, there is nevertheless a large and growing body of opinion which seeks to suggest that this essentially genetic approach is no longer suited to an understanding of contemporary patterns of politics. There is, in particular, a large volume of literature which seeks to assert that Rokkan's specific emphasis on the freezing of party systems was largely misconceived. For while party systems, and the traditional parties which make up these systems, may well have been frozen up to the time in which Rokkan, together with Lipset, advanced his famous freezing proposition (Lipset and Rokkan, 1967), what we have subsequently wit-

[1] First presented as the Stein Rokkan Lecture, Joint Sessions of the European Consortium for Political Research, University of Limerick, 1992.

nessed has been evidence of pervasive instability and change. In other words, while it is widely accepted that Rokkan's work can help us to understand the past, it is less and less often accepted that his work, at least in this particular regard, can help us understand the present.

Let us recall the freezing proposition: writing of the political patterns which were prevalent more than a generation ago, Lipset and Rokkan stated that 'the party systems of the 1960s reflect, with few but significant exceptions, the cleavage structures of the 1920s'. Moreover, they added that the party alternatives which were then contesting elections, and in many cases the party organizations themselves, were 'older than the majorities of the national electorates' (Lipset and Rokkan, 1967: 50). There was, in short, little that was then new under the sun of European politics.

Well and good, say many of the more recent observers. The party systems, as well as the party alternatives of the 1960s, did indeed seem frozen into place. But this can no longer be seen to be the case. Looking at west European politics today, it is argued that party systems are no longer frozen, and that many of the party alternatives are no longer older than the majorities of the national electorates. *Pace* Rokkan's proposition, it is contended, the old order *has* changed since the late 1960s, and there is *now* a new politics abroad. It is not so much that Rokkan was wrong; rather, what has happened is simply that his analysis has been overtaken by events.

There are three main sources of evidence which are usually cited to justify this contemporary revision, or even rejection, of the freezing hypothesis. First, there is the evidence of trends in aggregate electoral volatility—the net shifts in votes from one election to the next. Since the late 1960s, it is argued, votes have begun to shift their preferences in ever greater numbers. Electorates and their party systems have become much more volatile, and hence they have also become less frozen. This was first emphasized by Pedersen (1979), who was one of the earliest in the new wave of writing to chart patterns of electoral volatility in postwar Europe.

Second, there is the evidence of the mobilization and success of new parties, which suggests that mass politics is no longer simply dominated by 'old' parties, or by parties older than their national electorates. Rather, a whole host of new parties have been seen to emerge, which seek to challenge and displace their older and more traditional rivals. These new parties are, moreover, radically different from the old, both in terms of issues (new politics parties) and organizational style. Kitschelt (1988) and Poguntke (1987) are among the most recent of those highlighting the importance of this particular change, but the point is also emphasized throughout the contemporary literature (see, for example, Dalton and Kuechler, 1990).

Third, and more generally, there is the (often imputed) evidence of the decline of party in organizational and representational terms, and as a device for linking citizens to decision-making, as well as the evidence of new and emerging forms of interest intermediation. It used to be said that this particular challenge to party was due to the development and strengthening of neo-corporatist style structures and interest groups, but of late this particular argument has tended to dissipate, and more recent emphasis has been placed upon the 'new social movements', and so on. Whatever the character of the particular challenge, however, be it based on neo-corporatism or new social movements (and the shared emphasis on 'newness' should be noted), it is none the less damaging to party. Thus, for example, Lawson and Merkl (1988*b*) can discuss *when* parties fail, rather than *if* parties fail or *whether* parties fail. There is little room for doubt here.

Each of these three patterns of change is more or less rooted in varieties of electoral change—whether these result from dealignment (the decline of party), realignment (the emergence of new parties), or both (aggregate electoral instability). It is my contention in this chapter, however, that this image of electoral change is largely mythical. It is a popular image, and even an exciting image; above all, it is a new image, and newness is always very appealing to our fashionable profession; but like many new, exciting, and fashionable images, it is also lacking in foundation, bearing little or no relation to the actual patterns of electoral alignments in contemporary Europe. In reality, as I will argue, the empirical evidence suggests that European electorates continue to be stable; that alignments continue to be relatively frozen; and that the old parties continue to survive. I will argue, in other words, that much of what Lipset and Rokkan contended in the late 1960s concerning freezing, ageing, and stability, still continues to be valid today.[2]

[2] In this, as throughout this paper, I am drawing heavily on the evidence presented in and updated from Bartolini and Mair (1990).

This is not, of course, to imply that one can speak of wholesale stagnancy in the electoral markets of western Europe, and in some cases, even at the aggregate level, change has been both radical and abrupt. In general, however, and when looking at the west European experience as a whole, large-scale flux is exceptional. Moreover, even in countries such as Denmark, the Netherlands, Norway, and Germany, whose national experiences have loomed so large in those various books of evidence which emphasize widespread change, the impression of persistence often remains much more striking than does that of discontinuity.

LEVELS OF ELECTORAL VOLATILITY

Let me begin with aggregate levels of electoral volatility, the increase in which, as noted, is often cited as evidence that European party systems are no longer frozen. The question here is the precise extent of the supposed increase in volatility which has taken place since the late 1960s; that is, since the period in which Lipset and Rokkan spoke of frozen party systems.

According to the index devised by Pedersen (1979), who was among the first scholars to drew our attention to the increasing electoral instability, levels of electoral volatility can range from 0, indicating no change, with all parties receiving the same proportion of votes in one election as they had received in the previous election, to 100, indicating a complete and total change, when all existing parties are replaced by wholly new parties.[3]

These are of course, the theoretical limits of the index. In practice, however, while levels never do reach 100, they can reach quite substantial heights. Among the 303 elections analyzed in the period 1885–1985 in Bartolini and Mair (1990), for example, the highest level reached was 32.1 (Germany in 1920), while the level reached in the Danish 'earthquake' election of 1973 was 21.2. Indeed, the *average* level of volatility in France in the 1950s was 22.3. Thus, even though the theoretically maximum level has never been recorded, the range of actual values recorded in west European elections has sometimes proved substantial.

---

[3] The value of the index is equivalent to the sum of the aggregate electoral gains of all winning parties or (which is the same) the sum of the aggregate electoral losses of all losing parties (Pedersen, 1979).

But, it must be emphasized, these are the exceptions. For if we take western Europe as a whole, in a period which includes very quiescent as well as quite volatile contests, the average level of aggregate volatility in the period from 1945 to 1989 is just 8.7; which means that there has been an average net shift of less than 9 per cent of the votes from one election to the next in postwar Europe. And this, in turn, means that there has been a net aggregate stability of 91 per cent.

What is even more striking, however, is that this average level of volatility is actually *lower* than that reached in the interwar period, when everybody agrees that the party systems became frozen, and when average volatility was 9.9 (Bartolini and Mair, 1990: 100). Moreover, not only has there been a decline in volatility from the prewar to the postwar period, but there has also been a decline during the postwar period itself. Thus the average in the period of 'steady-state' politics, from 1945 to 1965, when most commentators agree that Rokkan's view made sense, was actually 9.0. Between 1966 and 1989, on the other hand, in a period when all the talk has been of instability, change, and a defreezing of systems, the average volatility has been 8.5—a level which is *below* that of the steady-state period, and even further below the mean level recorded in the interwar period. In fact, if one looks at the three broad electoral epochs which have occurred since universal suffrage and the age of mass politics—the interwar period, the first postwar decades, and then the most recent postwar decades—aggregate electoral volatility, aggregate electoral instability, has shown a consistent decline. This hardly signifies transformation or crisis; it hardly even signifies a defreezing.

It also must be emphasized that even when aggregate change is occurring in this limited way, it is not very significant as far as the cleavage boundaries are concerned. Rather, looking at the aggregate evidence, it is readily apparent that when voters switch, they are more likely to switch between friends rather than between enemies. This is certainly true in terms of the traditional socialist–bourgeois cleavage line, which is the alignment with which the evidence in Bartolini and Mair (1990) was most concerned. Thus, when parties of the right lose votes, they then to do so to the benefit of other parties of the right; and when parties of the left lose votes they tend to do so to the benefit of other parties of the left—there is little shifting across cleavage boundaries.

The result is that the actual levels of aggregate volatility between the socialist bloc and the bourgeois bloc are even more muted than those across the party system as a whole. In the 1945–89 period, for example, and again taking an index which runs from 0 to 100, mean cross-cleavage volatility has been 2.9, as against 3.2 in the interwar years. These levels are astonishingly low, averaging less than a 3 per cent shift from election to election, and once again reflecting a decline in the mean level since the period in which the freezing process occurred.

In this case, however, it must be admitted that when we again break the postwar period into two, and contrast the steady-state period (1945–65) with that of the period of supposed turbulence and collapse (1966–89), we do see signs of increasing instability. In fact, class bloc volatility has increased from an average level of 2.85 in the early postwar decades, the frozen decades, to 2.95 in the later postwar decades, that is, in the age of the new politics. This is an increase of 0.1, which, indeed, is truly striking. We live in interesting times.

The third observation which must be underlined is that this absence of substantial electoral change is not, of course, true for all countries; but then neither is the evidence of even marginal change true for all countries. In recent decades, some countries have become more volatile, notably Denmark, Iceland, the Netherlands, and Norway, while others, at least for now, have become less volatile, notably France, Germany, Ireland, and Italy. It is also clear that the locus of electoral change has tended to shift from the larger countries to the smaller ones. The main point that must be made, however, is that there has been no *Europe-wide* trend towards electoral instability.[4] Rather, across Europe as a whole, the picture is one of maintaining the status quo in electoral terms. Moreover, during what might be called the 'post-Rokkan' period, or the alleged defreezing period, even the most 'volatile' countries, such as Denmark, Iceland, Luxembourg, the Netherlands, and Norway, record mean levels of aggregate change of just 10, 11 or 12 per cent—and this, it will be recalled, is on a scale of 0 to 100.

---

[4] That Pedersen (1979), in his own original analysis, also pointed to the absence of a Europe-wide trend, has tended to be overlooked by those who tend to cite his article as evidence of pervasive change.

THE SURVIVAL OF THE 'OLD' PARTIES

All this, one might say, or at least the proponents of the myth of electoral change might say, is beside the point. Aggregate changes from election to election tell us little—what matters is the cumulation of such changes and the direction in which they are going. Thus even if aggregates of only 5 or 10 per cent of votes change between elections, this misses the point, for these election-to-election changes may all build in the same long-term direction, spelling the gradual erosion of the old parties and the gradual rise of new alternatives. So is this the case?

The best way in which to test for this is to look precisely at the electoral strength of parties which had already been contesting elections in the early 1960s and which are still contesting elections now; that is, to look at those parties which had already entered politics at the time when Lipset and Rokkan concluded that the party systems were frozen, and which are still around today. These are the 'old parties' and include many of the parties which Lipset and Rokkan described as being then, in the early 1960s, older than the majority of the national electorates.[5] So how have these old parties been doing in recent elections? Have they experienced substantial decline? Have they lost out to new parties which are now clearly younger than the majority of the national electorates?

The evidence certainly does not suggest this; or rather, the evidence certainly does not suggest that these parties have experienced substantial losses. To be sure, these old parties do not now gain as high a share of the vote as they did in the early 1960s. Given that thirty years have elapsed since the early 1960s, this is hardly surprising. On the other hand, they have not lost that great a share.

In the early 1960s, for example, these old parties gained an average of just less than 95 per cent of the vote in the fourteen

[5] For the purposes of this analysis, simple splits and mergers are not regarded as having necessarily led to the disappearance of old parties and to the creation of new parties. The formerly united but now linguistically divided Christian, Socialist, and Liberal parties in Belgium, for example, are still regarded as 'old' parties, as is the CDA in the Netherlands, which involved a merger of three long-established denominational parties, and the Left Wing Alliance (the successor of the old People's Democratic League) in Finland. The French UDF, on the other hand, which brought together both old and new centre-right tendencies in French politics, is regarded as a 'new' party, as are the Social Democratic party in the UK, and both the Progressive Democrats and the Workers' party in Ireland.

European countries I have looked at,[6] ranging from about 75 per cent in France (where I have treated the UDF as a wholly 'new' party) to almost 100 per cent in Sweden. In the more recent elections, by contrast, in the late 1980s and in 1990 and 1991, these 'old parties' have averaged 84 per cent of the vote, ranging from 66 per cent in France to 92 per cent in Austria (see Table 4.2). This spells a long-term average net loss of less than 11 per cent in thirty years, a loss which, by definition, will have been ceded to parties which first entered politics in the period following the mid-1960s. Given the vast political transformations which have been said to have beset politics in this period, an overall loss of this small size can hardly be considered as earth-shattering. Indeed, in some countries, as is evidenced in the more recent elections in Austria, Finland, and in the west German part of the all-German elections, these old, *passé* parties together polled more than 90 per cent of the vote.

But even this surprisingly high level of resilience is not the most striking feature of the survival of the old, pre-late-1960s parties. For there is also one other trend which is worth emphasizing and which has been far too neglected in the recent writing on European politics: that is, in terms of sheer numbers, there has actually been an *enormous expansion of the European electorates* in the past thirty years—an expansion which derives partly from the lowering of the voting age, and partly from the coming to political age of the baby-boom generations. On average, and excluding Switzerland, where the electorate has more than doubled since 1960 as a result of the enfranchisement of women, the size of the average European electorate has increased by more than one-third since the early 1960s. In some cases, such as the Netherlands, the increase has been in the order of 65 per cent, and in Ireland more than 45 per cent. In other cases, such as Austria or Belgium, it has increased by a more muted 17 or 18 per cent (see Table 4.1). In all cases, however, the increase has been quite substantial (see also Katz, Mair *et al.*, 1992). There are, in short, a whole host of new voters out there, and, as we have

[6] The remaining 5 per cent of the vote in the early 1960s therefore belonged to old parties which have not survived through to the beginning of the 1990s, and therefore can be cited as offering some minimal support for the proponents of the 'de-freezing' argument. My point here would simply be that this 5 per cent for 'disappeared' parties pales into insignificance by comparison to the 95 per cent won by those parties which were to persist.

TABLE 4.1. *The growth of electorates in western Europe*

Country	Electorate in 1960–64 ('000)		Electorate in 1987–91 ('000)		Growth percentage
Austria	1962:	4,805.4	1990:	5,628.9	+ 17.1
Belgium	1961:	6,036.2	1991:	7,144.9	+ 18.4
Denmark	1960:	2,842.3	1990:	3,941.5	+ 38.7
Finland	1962:	2,714.8	1991:	4,060.8	+ 49.6
France	1962:	27,540.4	1988:	36,977.3	+ 34.3
(W) Germany	1961:	37,440.7	1990:	48,099.3	+ 28.5
Iceland	1963:	99.8	1991:	182.8	+ 83.1
Ireland	1961:	1,670.9	1989:	2,448.8	+ 46.6
Italy	1963:	34,201.7	1987:	45,583.5	+ 33.3
Netherlands	1963:	6,748.6	1989:	11,112.2	+ 64.7
Norway	1961:	2,340.5	1989:	3,190.3	+ 36.3
Sweden	1960:	4,972.2	1991:	6,413.2	+ 29.0
Switzerland	1963:	1,531.2	1991:	4,510.8	+194.6
UK	1964:	35,894.1	1987:	43,180.6	+ 20.3

Source: Mackie and Rose (1982/1991); Mackie (1991; 1992); Koole and Mair (1992 *et seq.*).

seen, the old, 'pre-defreezing' parties are also managing to hold a reasonably strong share of this new electorate.

What is also striking is that these old parties are not only holding a reasonably strong *share* of the expanded electorate, but, given this expansion, they are also polling substantially more votes in absolute terms. Thus in twelve of the fourteen countries I have looked at, and even in those countries where the share of the vote won by the old parties has fallen, the actual number of votes won by the old parties has increased. More precisely, despite losing an average of some 11 per cent share of the vote, the actual number of votes going to the old parties has increased by almost 17 per cent, and by almost 21 per cent if the Swiss case is included (see Table 4.2). Indeed, across Europe as a whole, the *number* of votes won by old parties has declined only in Austria and in Belgium.

This general increase in the number of votes won by old parties is also true in precisely those countries which have been cited most often as the inspiration for the myth of electoral change, and for the belief that events have now overtaken the freezing hypothesis. In the 1990 election in Denmark, for example, the 'old' parties

TABLE 4.2. *The survival of traditional parties**

Country (years of first and most recent elections)	% Vote for 'old' parties in first election	% Vote for 'old' parties in late 1980s/ early 1990s	Change in % vote for 'old' parties	% Change** in *number* of votes won by 'old' parties
Austria				
(1962, 1990)	99.5	92.0	−7.5	−2.4
Belgium				
(1961, 1991)	97.1	76.1	−21.0	−8.2
Denmark				
(1960, 1990)	94.8	81.5	−13.3	+14.1
Finland				
(1962, 1991)	94.5	90.8	−3.7	+13.9
France				
(1962, 1988)	75.4	66.8	−8.6	+15.9
(West) Germany				
(1961, 1990)	94.3	90.6	−3.7	+13.9
Iceland				
(1963, 1991)	99.8	87.4	−12.4	+54.5
Ireland				
(1961, 1989)	90.9	84.2	−6.7	+31.2
Italy				
(1963, 1987)	97.4	90.9	−6.5	+17.1
Netherlands				
(1963, 1989)	90.5	84.9	−5.6	+33.2
Norway				
(1961, 1989)	96.9	84.7	−12.2	+25.8
Sweden				
(1960, 1991)	99.9	80.4	−19.5	+5.2
Switzerland				
(1963, 1991)	96.3	78.1	−18.2	+72.1
United Kingdom				
(1964, 1987)	99.4	87.6	−11.8	+3.7
Mean by country	94.8	84.0	−10.8	+20.7 (+16.8)***

Notes:

* Traditional, or 'old' parties, are those parties which contested both the first and recent elections.

** Expressed as a percentage of the number of votes won by these parties at the first election.

*** The figure in brackets is the mean excluding Switzerland.

Source: As Table 4.1.

polled 14 per cent more votes than they did in 1960; in Germany, the 1990 election in the western part of the country also gave the old parties 14 per cent more votes than they had won in 1961; while in the Netherlands, where talk of the crisis of the traditional parties is extraordinarily pervasive, the elections in 1989 gave the old parties a full 33 per cent more votes than they had polled in 1963.

In short, electorates in Europe in the 1980s have in general proved more stable and more predictable than they were even in the period in which Rokkan referred to the freezing hypothesis. At least up to now, the general pattern shows more rather than less stability. Moreover, even though their share of the vote has fallen by an average of 11 per cent in thirty years, the old parties, that is, those which were already around in the early 1960s, at the time when Rokkan was developing his analysis, continue to win the lion's share of popular support; now, in fact, they poll a substantially greater number of votes from their newly enlarged electorates than was the case thirty years ago. Despite the widespread myths of electoral change, it is therefore electoral continuity and persistence which now emerge as far more striking phenomena.

WHAT SUSTAINS THE MYTHS OF ELECTORAL CHANGE?

Given such evidence of continuity, how is it that there exists such a widespread conviction that party alignments have changed, and that party systems are no longer frozen? What, in other words, sustains these myths of electoral change?

There are three factors which are relevant here. First, and most simply, there is the shock of the new and the appeal of the new. Since newness is exciting, we also assume it to be very important, and thus focus on the fact that 5 per cent of voters support the Greens, while forgetting the more obvious fact that 95 per cent do not. I find it somewhat ironic that we now know much more about Green parties, for example, and have access to many more books and articles written about these Green parties, then we do about, say, Social Democratic parties—even though the latter still poll about seven or eight times as many votes as the former. Comparative politics may not be a very precise profession, but it is certainly a fashionable one.

Second, and more important, we still tend to think of the political as a more or less automatic reflection of the social. Thus, when society changes, we assume that politics also automatically changes, and thus, when class or other social boundaries become blurred, we assume that electoral change must inevitably follow. New class structures, new social and demographic patterns, therefore inevitably imply new politics.

But while this may well be true as far as the issues which divide parties are concerned, in that, almost of necessity, substantive policy differences can and always do change in line with new social problems and new government concerns (see Chapter 2 above), such social changes do not necessarily imply the emergence of new political parties. Indeed, perhaps the most striking feature of the survival of the old parties of western Europe is that this survival has occurred within a context of massive social change.

The Irish experience, which is most appropriate to the setting of this chapter, offers a case in point. Between 1961 and 1989, for example, the percentage of the Irish labour force engaged in services rose from 39 per cent to 57 per cent, while the percentage engaged in agriculture fell from around 37 per cent to just 15 per cent.[7] In that same period, aggregate electoral support for Labour (the long-term Cinderella party) has gone from 12 per cent to 10 per cent; aggregate electoral support for Fine Gael (traditionally the second-biggest party) has gone from 32 per cent to 29 per cent; and aggregate support for Fianna Fáil (the traditionally dominant party) has remained unchanged at 44 per cent. Massive social change has therefore been accompanied by pronounced levels of aggregate electoral stability.

One possible, and to my mind largely plausible, and indeed, generalizable explanation of this is that, despite the massive social change, and despite the enormous structural mobility, which has seen large sections of the population move from rural areas to urban areas, and from agriculture to services and industry, large numbers of voters have nevertheless maintained their traditional voting preferences. The class structure may have changed, but the political boundaries have survived. Yet when we read much of the literature

---

[7] Incidentally, the image of Ireland as a traditional farming and rural community is far from the contemporary reality—the unemployment level is currently some 33 per cent higher than the percentage of the labour force which is engaged in agriculture.

on the supposed realignment and dealignment of European electorates, and on the supposed decay of traditional cleavages—in
other words, when we read much of the literature which remains
caught up with the myths of electoral change—the potential for such
continuity is largely ignored. As class and other social boundaries
change, then it is argued, or often simply assumed, that political
boundaries *must* also change; and the possibility that individual or
structural mobility may *not* actually impact on broad political iden-
tifications thus remains largely neglected.

The problem here is that many analysts have far too easily
assumed that the Lipset and Rokkan freezing proposition implied
that more or less the same social forces must always remain sup-
portive of more or less the same parties. Thus a party which traditionally won the majority of its support from the working class
must, if the freezing proposition is correct, also continue to win the
majority of its support from the working class; and similarly for
parties which traditionally won the majority of their support from
Catholics, or from farmers, or whoever. But this, as has been
argued at length elsewhere (Bartolini and Mair, 1990: 212–25), is
actually a very *narrow* view of cleavages and of their capacity to
structure political alignments. It is also a largely misconceived view,
since it sees cleavages simply as indicators of social stratification,
and thus as phenomena which must change as these social strata
themselves change. It is a view of cleavages which ignores the
importance of the values, collective identities, and organizational
components of the cleavage structure, and which thus severely
impoverishes the concept of cleavage which Rokkan sought to
apply in his analysis of the growth and structuring of mass politics
in western Europe. Indeed, to regard the cleavage structure as simply another term for the system of social stratification is to imply
that one can only have frozen party systems, and frozen cleavage
structures, in what is essentially a *frozen society*. And this is clearly
untenable. More than twenty years ago, in an early laudatory
assessment of the importance of Lipset and Rokkan's analysis,
Giovanni Sartori (1969) warned against what he called the sociology of politics, and against an approach which sees the political
as simply a dependent of the social. It is this continued emphasis
on the sociology of politics, and the concomitant neglect of a genuine, Rokkanian, political sociology, which now helps to sustain
the myths of electoral change.

Third, and following on from this, the insistence, despite the evidence to the contrary, that electoral change is the inevitable consequence of social change, neglects the capacity of parties to adapt to their changed circumstances, and hence neglects their own capacity to maintain the support of their electorates (see also Chapter 1 above). Parties, as Rokkan as well as Sartori constantly reminded us, are also independent actors, capable, at least in part, of moulding the environments in which they compete. Thus, while the social bases of party support change—inevitably so—in line with changes in the social structure; and while the policies and priorities of parties and governments change—also inevitably so—in line with new social problems, conflicts, and commitments; so, in turn, do parties adapt and modify their appeals and their methods of mobilizing support. That they do so successfully is more than clear from their proven capacity to survive.

The past is indeed, as L. P. Hartley observed, a foreign country; they do things differently there. For parties too, the past is another country, and they too did things differently there than they do now. But this does not necessarily make them less powerful parties; nor does it make them 'unfrozen' parties; it simply means that they are different parties, which adapt their policies, strategies, and styles of competition to a different set of circumstances, and which do so in order to survive. They have been doing this for a long time now, and they have usually been successful. Even now, in the 1990s, and despite all the myths of electoral change, they continue to be successful, and hence they continue to survive.

THE NEGLECT OF PARTY

By way of a conclusion, it is my belief that all of this emphasis on electoral change, most of which I regard as misconceived, has led us down a path where we find ourselves devoting almost all our attention to questions of how parties fail, or how they are in crisis, or how they are *passé*. The result is that we forget to ask how it is that parties can and do survive. Yet this surely remains one of the most pressing questions for comparative research on mass politics.

At the same time, it must be added that it is no accident that we neglect to ask how parties survive, for we also have neglected the analysis of party *per se*, and of party as organization (see Katz and

Mair, 1992*b*). Much of the best of the early postwar work on mass politics—by Duverger, Kirchheimer, Neumann, and others—focused on parties as organizations, and as the essential political linkage between citizens and the state. Since the end of the 1960s, however, attention has focused more on citizens themselves and their responses to parties, in the form of the vast literature on individual electoral behaviour; and on the parties as teams of leaders or as governors, in the form of the vast literature on coalitions and policy formation. And thus what came in between these two, the party *as organization*, was effectively displaced.

One result of this displacement was the obliteration of much of what was distinctive about party as a mode of interest representation, and thus also the obliteration of the distinction between party on the one hand, and other forms of interest representation on the other. Hence, with time, our profession also witnessed a renewed interest in alternative channels of intermediation, ranging from neo-corporatism to new social movements. The other result of this displacement, however, as I have sought to emphasize here, was the decreasing ability to perceive parties as independent actors in their own right, actors which were not simply forced to come to terms with environmental changes lying wholly outside their control, but which were also capable of structuring that environment in a way which could help to ensure their own persistence.

Parties continue to matter. Parties continue to survive. The old parties which were around well before Rokkan elaborated his freezing proposition are still around today, and, despite the challenges from new parties and new social movements, most of them still remain in powerful, dominant positions. They have not suffered substantial electoral erosion. The electoral balance now is not substantially different from that of thirty years ago, and, in general, electorates are not now substantially more volatile than once they were.

Following Rokkan, the party alternatives of the 1960s were older than the majority of their national electorates. Thirty years on, these self-same parties still continue to dominate mass politics in western Europe. Nowadays, in short, they are even older still.

PART III

Party Organizations and Party Systems

5

Party Organization, Party Democracy, and the Emergence of the Cartel Party (with Richard S. Katz)

One common thread which has run through the literature on political parties, essentially since the time of Ostrogorski (1902), and which has also run through the vast variety of typologies and analyses (both normative and empirical) that have been presented in that literature, has been the view that parties are to be classified and understood on the basis of their relationship with civil society (see, for example, Duverger, 1954; Neumann, 1956; Panebianco, 1988). This has had two implications. The first has been a tendency to set up the mass party model as the standard against which everything should be judged (Lawson, 1980, 1988; Sainsbury, 1990). The other has been to undervalue the extent to which differences between parties may also be understood by reference to their relations with the state.

It is the contention of this chapter that both of these implications are ill-founded. As will be argued, the mass party model is tied to a conception of democracy (see also Pomper, 1992) and to a particular, and now dated, ideal of social structure, neither of which is characteristic of postindustrial societies. Moreover, the mass party model implies a linear process of party development that, even when elaborated to take account of more recent developments (e.g. Kirchheimer's catch-all party or Panebianco's electoral-professional party), suggests an end-point from which the only options are stability or decay, and which, like all hypotheses of the end of evolution, is inherently suspect. In contrast, it can be argued that the development of parties in western democracies has been reflective of a dialectical process in which each new party type generates a reaction which stimulates further development, thus leading to yet another new party type, and to another set of reactions, and so on. From this perspective, the mass party is simply one stage in a continuing process.

It is also important to recognize that the factors which facilitate this dialectic are not derived solely from changes in civil society, but also from changes in the relations between parties and the state. In particular, it can be argued that there has been a tendency in recent years towards an ever closer symbiosis between parties and the state, and that this then sets the stage for the emergence of a new party type, 'the cartel party'. Like previous party types, the cartel party implies a particular conception of democracy; moreover, also like previous party types, it stimulates further reactions and sows the seeds for yet further evolution.

THE MASS PARTY AND THE CATCH-ALL PARTY

Emphasis on the mass party as model entails two assumptions, one concerning the essential meaning of and institutional prerequisites for democracy, and the other concerning the organizational prerequisites for electoral success. Both of these have been developed most prominently by Duverger (1954), but are also evident in the model of British democracy described by Beer (1969: chapter 3) under the sobriquet 'Socialist Democracy', as well as in a variety of prescriptions for American democracy generically identified as 'Responsible Party Government' (Ranney, 1962).

In the archetypical mass party model, the fundamental units of political life are pre-defined and well-defined social groups, membership in which is bound up in all aspects of the individual's life (Neumann, 1956: especially 403). Politics is primarily about the competition, conflict, and cooperation of these groups, and political parties are the agencies through which these groups, and thus their members, participate in politics, make demands on the state, and ultimately attempt to capture control of the state by placing their own representatives in key offices. Each of these groups has an interest, which is articulated in the programme of 'its' party. This programme is not just a bundle of policies, however, but a coherent and logically connected whole. Hence, party unity and discipline are not only practically advantageous, but are also normatively legitimate. This legitimacy depends, in turn, on direct popular involvement in the formulation of the party programme, and, from an organizational perspective, this implies the need for an extensive membership organization of branches or cells in order to provide avenues for mass input into the party's policy-making process, as well as for the supremacy of the extra-parliamentary party, particularly as embodied in the party congress.

Individual electoral choice is constrained by the encapsulation of the mass of the electorate into one of the subcultural groups that the parties represent, so that electoral politics is less about differential rates of conversion than it is about differential rates of mobilization. None the less, at the system level, the socialist/mass party model provides for prospective popular control over policy, in that the voters are supporting one or other party and its well-defined programme, and the party (or coalition of parties) with a majority of the votes gets to rule. Parties, in this view, provide the (not an) essential linkage between citizens and the state (Lawson, 1988: 36). This also involves a particular conception of organizational expediency. Since electoral competition is primarily about mobilization rather than conversion, the key requirement for a successful party is to increase the level of commitment of those who are already predisposed to offer it support—that is, the members of its 'natural' social constituency. For reasons of both legitimacy and expediency, therefore, the expectation was that there would be a 'contagion from the left', whereby parties representing other interests/segments in society would be obliged to adopt the basic features and strategy of the socialist/mass party model, or they would otherwise perish (Duverger, 1954: xxvii). From this perspective, the mass party was seen as the party of the future.

The emergence of what Kirchheimer (1966) called the 'catch-all party' severely challenged this notion of the party as representative of pre-defined sectors of society. In the first place, the beginnings of an erosion of traditional social boundaries in the late 1950s and 1960s implied a weakening of formerly highly distinctive collective identities, making it less easy to identify separate sectors of the electorate and to assume shared long-term interests. Second, economic growth and the increased importance of the welfare state facilitated the elaboration of programmes which were no longer necessarily divisive or partisan, but which could be claimed to serve the interests of all, or almost all. Third, with the development of the mass media, party leaders began to enjoy a capacity to appeal to the electorate at large, an electorate made up of voters who were learning to behave more like consumers than active participants.

The result was the formulation of both a new model of party and, linked to this, a new conception of democracy, which observers sometimes, albeit unsystematically, identified as an 'Americanization' of European politics. Elections were now seen to revolve around the choice of leaders rather than the choice of policies or programmes, while the formation of those policies or programmes became the prerogative of the party leadership rather than of the party membership. Popular control and accountability were no longer to be ensured prospectively, on the basis of clearly defined alternatives, but rather retrospectively, on the basis of experience and record (e.g. Fiorina, 1981). Electoral behaviour was no longer believed to be moulded by predispositions, but was now based on choice (Rose and McAllister, 1986). The mobilization of voters was no longer emphasized, and nor, indeed, was their conversion, in that both processes assumed a capacity to engender affective loyalty; rather, voters were believed to have become free-floating and uncommitted, available to, and also susceptible to, any and all of the competing parties.

The problem with this new model was that, whereas the earlier conception of parties had seen their role as essential to the functioning of democracy, and had thus taken their organizational survival as given, the new conception of parties and of democracy viewed their role as much more contingent. Thus, although the modality may have changed, party continued to be evaluated primarily in terms of the linkage between party and civil society, and it was precisely this linkage which was being undermined; hence, the voluminous literature on 'the decline of party'; and hence also the variety of different efforts to explain why parties might be able to survive such a change (e.g. Pizzorno, 1981; see also Finer, 1984). If, instead, attention is paid to the linkages between party and the state, then both the survival and the evolution of party organizations become more readily understandable.

STAGES OF PARTY DEVELOPMENT

The models of party which have been discussed assume a sharp distinction between parties and the state. The classic mass party is a party of civil society, emanating from sectors of the electorate, with the intention of breaking into the state and modifying public policy in the long-term interests of the constituency to which it is accountable. The catch-all party, while not emerging as a party of civil society, but as one which stands between civil society and the state, also seeks to influence the state from outside, seeking temporary custody of public policy in order to satisfy the short-term demands of its pragmatic consumers.[1] In short, despite their obviously contrasting relations with civil society, both parties lie outside the state, which remains, in principle, a neutral, party-free arena.

While the assumption that political parties are neatly separated from the state is quite conventional and commonplace, nevertheless it has been characteristic only of particular periods of history. Just as the clarity of the boundary between party and civil society varies over time (a sharp distinction in the period of the catch-all party and a fusion in the case of the mass party), so the clarity of the boundary between party and the state may also vary. Rather than a simple and static trichotomy (party, state, civil society), we see instead an evolutionary process, running roughly from the mid-nineteenth century to the present day, which is driven by a series of stimuli and responses, and which has moved both the relationships among and the clarity of the boundaries between parties, the state, and civil society. This process may be simplified as involving four separate stages.

The first of these four stages is that of the liberal *régime censitaire* of the late nineteenth and early twentieth centuries, with its restrictive suffrage requirements and other limitations on the political activity of the property-less. While the conceptual distinction between civil society and the state was valid, this was much less so in practical terms. Barring movements that would mobilize the (socially as well as politically) disenfranchised, the people who made up the politically relevant elements of civil society and the people who occupied the positions of power in the state were so closely connected by ties of family and interest that even when the two groups were not simply coterminous, they were heavily interpenetrating. This era was characterized by a conception of politics

---

[1] The same can be said of Panebianco's (1988) electoral-professional party, which differs from the catch-all party primarily in the sense that its organization is staffed by professionals and consultants rather than by party bureaucrats.

that assumed there to be a single national interest which it was the role of government to find and implement, and, in this context, the political parties that arose naturally claimed to be as Burke described: groups of 'men' in pursuit of the public interest—or perhaps in pursuit of their private interest, as a less charitable reading of history might suggest. There would be little need for formal or highly structured organization in such a context. The resources required for election, which often involved local status or connections as much as anything tangible, would be raised at the local level, and those who were in a position to make demands on the state would not need intermediaries.

Of course, the harmony of interest was more obvious in theory than in practice, and more obvious from the perspective of those in the ruling class than that of those excluded. Similarly, the advantages of organizing in areas with relatively large bourgeois and petty-bourgeois electorates (e.g. the Birmingham caucus of Joseph Chamberlain) and of taking concerted action within the parliament soon became clear, and vitiated the anti-party spirit that generally characterized the age. Still, in this conception, parties remained primarily of the cadre or caucus type, and schematically would have to be portrayed as in Figure 5.1, in the intersection of the state and civil society. That is, parties were basically committees of those people who jointly constituted both the state and civil society.

As industrialization and its attendant urbanization proceeded, the number of people able to meet the suffrage requirements of the *régime censitaire* increased, even while those requirements themselves were being relaxed. Additionally, restrictions on working-

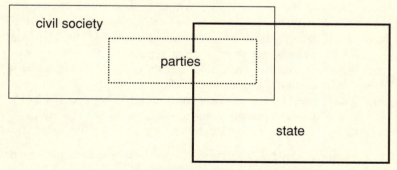

Fig. 5.1 Parties of the cadre or caucus type

class organization were increasingly seen to be incompatible with the liberal rationale of the bourgeois state, and, in any event, were unable to prevent the working class from organizing and taking action in the political as well as in the industrial spheres. Together, these processes created a far clearer separation between the state and the now vastly larger politically relevant portion of civil society, with the latter now growing to include large numbers of people who were not personally connected to those managing the state, and who perceived the state in terms of 'them' rather than 'us'.

The mass party, with its organized membership, formal structures and meetings, and so on, is the characteristic form of this second stage in the relationships among parties, state, and civil society. The mass party arose primarily among the newly activated, and often disenfranchised, elements of civil society as part of their (ultimately successful) struggle to gain a voice in, and eventually control over, the ruling structures of the state. Where the old cadre party had relied on quality of supporters, this new party relied on quantity of supporters, attempting to make up in many small membership subscriptions for what it lacked in large individual patronage; to make up in organized numbers and collective action for what it lacked in individual influence; and to make up through a party press and other party-related channels of communication for what it lacked in access to the commercial press.

As the instruments of the political 'outs', these new parties were naturally dominated by those whose principal base was in the party rather than in government. Because their strength lay in formal organization, this dominance by what would later come to be called the extra-parliamentary party tended to become formalized, and thus survived as a matter of principle even after the new parties succeeded in winning first the vote for their supporters and ultimately power in government as well. Reflecting their far more activist political agenda, the life experiences of their supporters, and an ethos of struggle, these parties naturally were more amenable to the idea of enforced party cohesion and discipline than were the bourgeois caucus parties. Most significantly in this regard, these were the first parties that explicitly claimed to represent the interests of only one segment of society. As a result, the representative's job was less to search for the national interest than it was to act as the agent of 'his' segment of society in pursuit of its own interest. The political party was the forum in which the political interest of the social group it represented was articulated. Thus, it was not only practically and experientially appropriate that the party be disciplined, but it was also normatively desirable.

In these terms, the rise of the mass party, and ultimately of universal suffrage, was associated with a redefinition of the politically appropriate. Not only was an oligarchic system made democratic by the extension of the suffrage to nearly all adult citizens, but there was also a changed conception of the proper relationship between citizens/voters, whether numerous or not, and the state. Elections became choices of delegates rather than trustees, and thus rather than vehicles by which the voters gave consent to be governed by those elected, they became instead devices by which the government was held accountable to the people. The political party was to be the mechanism that made all this possible. Schematically, the relationships among parties, civil society, and the state in this conception of politics would be as shown in Figure 5.2, with the state and civil society clearly separated, and parties serving as a bridge or linkage between the two. The parties nevertheless remained clearly anchored within civil society, even though penetrating the state through patronage appointments to the state service as well as through the occupation of ministerial office.

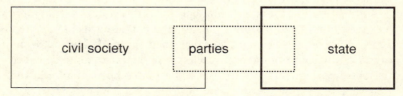

Fig. 5.2 Mass parties linking state and civil society

Both the mass party model of democracy and the mass party as an organizational form presented a challenge to the established parties, to which their organizations, such as they were, had to respond. On one hand, with electorates numbering in the millions rather than in the thousands, the informal networks of the caucus party were inadequate to canvass, mobilize, and organize supporters. On the other hand, growing acceptance of the mass party model of democracy (popular control of government through choice among unified parties) undermined support, even among

their own natural electoral base, for the more traditional organizational and governmental styles practised by the established parties.

This said, one response that clearly was not available to the leaders of the traditional parties was to adopt the mass party ethos root
and branch. In particular, they could not accept the idea that parties exist to represent well-defined segments of society, because the
segments which would have been left to them (farmers, industrialists, etc.) were obviously and increasingly permanent minorities.
Similarly, the idea that the extra-parliamentary organization ought
to be dominant was unappealing to those already established in
government. Further, while they needed to organize and mobilize
electoral supporters, they were not so dependent on them for material resources; as the parties of the upper and middle classes, they
could still draw on large individual contributions; as the parties in
government, they could deploy many of the resources of the state
for their own advantage; as the parties of the establishment, they
had privileged and sympathetic access to the 'non-partisan' channels of communication.

As a result, the leaders of the traditional parties tended to establish organizations that looked like mass parties in form (regular
members, branches, a party congress, a party press), but which in
practice often continued to emphasize the independence of the parliamentary party. Rather than emphasizing the role of the parliamentary party as the agent of the mass organization, they
emphasized the role of the mass organization as supporters of the
parliamentary party. Equally as significant, while these parties
recruited members, they did not, and in practical terms could
not, restrict their appeal to particular classes, but rather had to
make broader appeals, trying to catch support from all classes, albeit
with rates of success that varied markedly across class lines. In
ideological terms, then, they could maintain the earlier commitment
to an idea of a single national interest that cut across sectional
boundaries.

At the same time as these older parties of the right were adopt-
ing this new 'catch-all' model, there were also a number of factors
emerging which served to undermine the mass party model, both as
a normative ideal and as a practical imperative. In many respects,
the mass party model became a victim of its own success. The 'big
battles' for political and social rights had united the emerging
constituencies of the mass parties in a way which could not be

maintained once these rights were won. The need for solidarity was further reduced when the state began to provide on a universal basis the welfare and educational services that before had been the responsibility of the party and its *parentela*. Moreover, the amelioration of social conditions, increased mobility, and the development of mass media all served to reduce the distinctiveness of experience of once well-defined social constituencies (e.g. Einhorn and Logue, 1988). Not only had the social and political prerequisites for the mass party therefore begun to erode, but, once they had gained a taste of office, and especially once they had achieved power on their own, the parliamentary leaders of the original mass parties had also begun to find the catch-all model more attractive. Having enjoyed the fruits of electoral victory—which included the ability to alter policy in ways they thought desirable or beneficial for their electoral supporters—these politicians naturally wanted to continue winning, and so became more interested in broadening their electoral appeal beyond their original *classe gardée*. Moreover, once in office, they found that further compromises were being forced by the constraints and demands of practical government, and by the need to work with groups that were among their erstwhile electoral opponents.

All of this gave rise to a third stage of evolution, with the old mass parties beginning to emulate the response of the old parties to their own rise, and thus with parties from both the traditional left and the traditional right beginning to converge on the catch-all party model. While such parties may (continue to) have members, they no longer seriously attempt to encapsulate them; rather party membership becomes just one of many independent memberships that an individual may or may not maintain. Instead of emphasizing social homogeneity, the party accepts members wherever it finds them, and moreover recruits members on the basis of policy agreement rather than social identity. In place of the defensive electoral strategy of the mass party, which laid most stress on the mobilization and retention of a limited constituency, the party adopts an offensive strategy, exchanging 'effectiveness in depth for a wider audience and more immediate electoral success' (Kirchheimer, 1966: 184). In making this transition, there is a waning of the ideological and/or policy distinctiveness of the parties, and, with the emergence of a growing policy consensus, the need for and capacity to maintain a distinctive electorate becomes further undermined. Moreover, changes in systems of mass communications, most particularly the rise of television as the most widely used source of political information, enhance the conditions which allow, or indeed compel, parties to make universal appeals directly to voters, rather than communicating principally to and through their core supporters.

Contemporaneously, the relationship between parties and the state also changes, suggesting a new model which is illustrated in Figure 5.3. In this model, parties are less the agents of civil society acting on and penetrating the state, and are rather more like brokers between civil society and the state, with the party in government (i.e. the political ministry) leading an essentially Janus-like existence. On one hand, parties aggregate and present demands from civil society to the state bureaucracy, while on the other they are the agents of that bureaucracy in defending policies to the public.

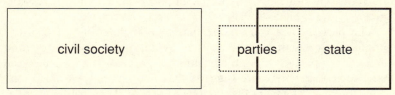

FIG. 5.3 Parties as brokers between state and civil society

Although the mass parties also perform these functions, they are nevertheless fundamentally altered by the loosening of ties between particular parties and particular segments of society as implied by the catch-all model. While there remain differences among parties with regard to their receptiveness to inputs from differing groups, and with regard to the policies they are prepared to defend—that is, while it still makes some difference which party is in office (e.g. Castles, 1982)—most groups expect and are expected to be able to work cooperatively with any party that is in power. Thus, for example, while there may remain some formal links between trade unions and social democratic parties, not only do the unions deal directly with the bourgeois parties when they are in power, but they also deal with the social democratic parties when in power in much the same way. Conversely, social democratic parties may find themselves defending anti-union policies apparently made necessary by circumstances beyond their control.

The idea that parties act as brokers is particularly appropriate to the pluralist conception of democracy that, not coincidentally, developed along with it (Truman, 1951; Dahl, 1956). In this view, democracy lies primarily in the bargaining and accommodation of independently organized interests. Parties build constantly shifting coalitions among these interests, and it is vital to their function as facilitators of compromise and guarantors against unreasonable exploitation of one group by another that each party be open to every interest. Elections are properly choices between teams of leaders rather than contests among closed social groupings or fixed ideologies. The old mass party, as Michels (1962) suggested, may well have been dominated by its leadership rather than embodying the true democracy which its ideology implied, but, in this new conception of democracy, party oligarchy actually becomes a virtue rather than a vice. Thus, the catch-all model is not only attractive from the self-interested perspective of party leaders, but proves normatively desirable as well.

The parties-as-brokers model has several potentially important implications regarding the further evolution of the nature and activities of parties. First, the position of parties as brokers between civil society and the state suggests that the parties themselves may have interests which are distinct from those of their clients on either side of the relationship. Moreover, they are in effect able to extract a commission for their services. Although not usually cast in precisely these terms, the role assigned to the personal rewards of office in, for example, the Downsian model of rational politics (Downs, 1957), corresponds to this commission for services rendered.[2] This commission need not be limited to material rewards to individuals (e.g. office and its perquisites), but can also include payments to the party as an organization, as well as deference to policy preferences, whether those of the party or of particular individuals. Second, the capacity of a party to perform the brokerage function depends not only on its ability to appeal to the electorate, but also on its ability to manipulate the state. But if a party can manipulate the state in the interests of its clients in civil society, it should also be able to manipulate the state in its own interests. Thus, as Epstein (1986:

---

[2] It is just these terms that David Mayhew (1974) employs to describe the personal rewards of leadership positions in the American Congress.

171) noted with regard to his 'parties as public utilities' model of American parties, it is possible to imagine 'that parties, like many regulated business enterprises, [succeed] in using the power of the state to protect their own interests'.

Most important, looking at Figures 5.1 to 5.3 as a dynamic rather than as three isolated snap-shots suggests the possibility that the movement of parties from civil society towards the state could continue to such an extent that parties effectively become part of the state apparatus itself. Indeed, it can be contended that this is precisely the direction in which the political parties in the modern democracies have been heading over the past two decades.

PARTIES AND THE STATE

A variety of social, cultural, and especially political developments may be cited as facilitating or even encouraging this movement towards an anchoring of parties within the state. These include a general decline in the levels of participation and involvement in party activity, with citizens preferring to invest their efforts elsewhere, and particularly in groups where they can play a more active role, where they are more likely to be in full agreement with a narrower range of concerns, and where they feel they can make a difference. The more immediate local arena thus becomes more attractive than the remote and inertial national arena, while open, single-issue groups become more appealing than traditional, hierarchic party organizations (e.g. Lawson and Merkl, 1988*a*; Dalton and Kuechler, 1990). One result of this is that the sheer size and commitment of party memberships have generally failed to keep pace with the growth in electorates on the one hand, and with the rapidly escalating costs of party activity on the other.

Parties have therefore been obliged to look elsewhere for their resources, and in this case their role as governors and law-makers made it easy for them to turn to the state. Principal among the strategies they could pursue was the provision and regulation of state subventions to political parties, which, while varying from country to country, now often constitute one of the major financial and material resources with which the parties can conduct their activities both in parliament and in the wider society (see Katz and Mair, 1992a, and Chapter 6 below).

The growth in state subvention over the past two decades, and the promise of further growth in the coming years, has come to represent one of the most significant changes to the environment within which parties act. At the same time, however, it must be emphasized that this environmental change is far from exogenous to the parties, in that it is the parties, in their role as governors, who are ultimately responsible for both the rules regarding state subventions, as well as for the amounts of money and resources which are made available. Moreover, it is also necessary to underline that precisely because these subventions are often tied to prior party performance or position, whether defined in terms of electoral success or parliamentary representation, they help to ensure the maintenance of existing parties while at the same time posing barriers to the emergence of new groups. In a similar vein, the rules regarding access to the electronic media, which, unlike the earlier printed media, are subject to substantial state control and/or regulation, offer a means by which those in power can acquire privileged access, whereas those on the margins may be neglected. Again, the rules vary from one country to another, and in some cases are clearly less restrictive and less important than others; nevertheless, the combination of the importance of the electronic media as a means of political communication on the one hand, and the fact that these media are regulated by the state, and hence by the parties in the state on the other, offers the parties a resource which was previously inconceivable.

In short, the state, which is invaded by the parties, and the rules of which are determined by the parties, becomes a fount of resources through which these parties not only help to ensure their own survival, but through which they can also enhance their capacity to resist challenges from newly mobilized alternatives. The state, in this sense, becomes an institutionalized structure of support, sustaining insiders while excluding outsiders. No longer simple brokers between civil society and the state, the parties now become absorbed by the state. From having first assumed the role of trustees, and then later of delegates, and then later again, in the heyday of the catch-all party, of entrepreneurs, parties have now become semi-state agencies.

There are risks involved in such a strategy, however, and principal among these is that of the party becoming dependent on continuous access to resources that in principle lie outside its own control. In particular, there is the danger that a party that is excluded from government will also be excluded from access to resources. With the earlier models of party, winning or losing an election might make a great deal of difference to a party's political objectives but mattered little to its survival, since the resources required for organizational sustenance came from within its own reservoir of support. With this new approach, by contrast, winning or losing may make less difference to a party's political objectives because of the absence of great policy battles, but could make a good deal of difference to its sheer survival, since the resources for its sustenance now come increasingly from the state. But it must be emphasized that parties need not be in competition for survival in the same way that they once competed to determine policy; for while there could be only one policy at a time, all of the parties can survive together. It is in this sense that the conditions become ideal for the formation of a cartel, in which all the parties share in resources, and in which all survive.

THE EMERGENCE OF THE CARTEL PARTY

In fact, the differences in the material position of winners and losers have been dramatically reduced. On the one hand, the set of 'governing parties' is no longer as limited as it once was. At the risk of over-generalization, almost all substantial parties may now be regarded as governing parties. All have access to office. There are, to be sure, a variety of extremist minority parties which have always remained on the fringes of power, including the Danish and Norwegian Progress Parties; but a full catalogue of such exceptions would simply serve to emphasize how few significant parties are persistently excluded, particularly if regional and other forms of sub-national government are considered. On the other hand, even when a party is excluded from government, or even when, as in the case of the British Labour party, a party languishes for a long period in opposition, this rarely implies a denial of access to the spoils of the state, nor to at least some share of patronage appointments. More often than not, media access is largely unaffected by absence from government. Access to state subventions is also unaffected; indeed, in some systems, such as Ireland and the United Kingdom, parties currently in opposition are actually accorded a higher level of subvention precisely because they lack the immediate resources of parties currently in government.

Hence we see the emergence of a new type of party, the cartel party, characterized by the interpenetration of party and state, and also by a pattern of inter-party collusion. In this sense, it is perhaps more accurate to speak of the emergence of cartel parties, since this development depends on collusion and cooperation between ostensible competitors, and on agreements which, of necessity, require the consent and cooperation of all, or almost all, relevant participants. Nevertheless, while at one level this development relates to the party system as a whole, it also has important implications for the organizational profile of each individual party within the cartel, and so it is reasonable to speak of a cartel party in the singular.

As yet, however, this process remains at an early stage. Moreover, given the nature of the conditions which facilitate the emergence of cartel parties, it is also uneven, being more evident in those countries in which state aid and support for parties is most pronounced, and in which the opportunities for party patronage, *lottizazione*, and control are most enhanced. Finally, it is also a process which is likely to develop most easily in those political cultures marked by a tradition of inter-party cooperation and accommodation. Pending a closer and more rigorous enquiry, therefore, it can be suggested that the process is likely to be most developed in countries such as Austria, Denmark, Germany, Finland, Norway, and Sweden, where a tradition of inter-party cooperation combines with a contemporary abundance of state support for parties, and with a privileging of party in relation to patronage appointments, offices, and so on. Conversely, the process is likely to be least developed in a country such as the United Kingdom, where a tradition of adversary politics combines with relatively limited state support for party organizations, and where the possibilities for patronage, while growing, also remain relatively limited.[3]

---

[3] The United Kingdom is a curious case in which the behaviour associated with the cartel party model is becoming less prevalent. While the emphasis on the parliamentary party would appear to facilitate the formation of a cartel, this depends on the strong expectation of alternation in office. Labour's apparent inability ever to get back in office, and the Conservative's apparent permanent hold on office, have led both to anti-cartel behaviour. Thus, for example, Labour has become more favourably disposed towards PR which would break the two-party monopoly (now effectively a one-party monopoly) in office, while the Conservatives have become much less willing to share appointments and honours with Labour party members (see Webb, 1994).

THE CHARACTERISTICS OF THE CARTEL PARTY

As noted above, the most obvious distinction between the different models of party—the élite or cadre party, the mass party, the catch-all party, and now the cartel party—concerns the particular social and political context within which each of these parties emerged, and which, for reasons of convenience, may be identified with distinctive time-periods (see Table 5.1, where the various characteristics of the four models of party are juxtaposed to one another). At the same time, however, this was far from the only influence on party development, in that particular types of party often outlived the circumstances which had facilitated their initial emergence. Thus mass parties did not displace élite parties *tout court*; rather, both continued to coexist even after the advent of universal suffrage, in much the same way that mass parties continued even after the development of the catch-all party, and, most recently, catch-all parties continue to exist notwithstanding the emergence of cartel parties. Moreover, contemporary parties are not necessarily wholly cartel parties any more than parties of previous generations were wholly élite parties, or wholly mass parties, or wholly catch-all parties. Rather, all of these models represent heuristically convenient polar types, to which individual parties may approximate more or less closely at any given time.

Among the key characteristics of party which have varied with time have been those involving the goals of politics and the basis of inter-party competition. In the period of dominance of the élite party, political goals and conflicts largely revolved around the distribution of privileges, and the parties competed on the basis of the ascribed status of their adherents. As the mass party developed, the key opposition in politics began to revolve around the question of social reform (or opposition to social reform), and the parties competed in terms of their representative capacity. With the emergence of the catch-all party, the goals of politics remained largely purposive, but came to revolve around questions of social amelioration rather than wholesale reform, with parties competing less on the basis of their representative capacities, and rather more on the basis of their effectiveness in policy-making. Finally, with the emergence of the cartel party, comes a period in which the goals of politics, at least for now, become more self-referential, with politics becoming

TABLE 5.1. *The models of party and their characteristics*

Characteristics	Élite party	Mass party	Catch-all party	Cartel party
Time-period:	19th century	1880–1960	1945–	1970–
Degree of social-political inclusion:	restricted suffrage	enfranchisement and mass suffrage	mass suffrage	mass suffrage
Level of distribution of politically relevant resources:	highly restricted	relatively concentrated	less concentrated	relatively diffused
Principal goals of politics:	distribution of privileges	social reformation (or opposition to it)	social amelioration	politics as profession
Basis of party competition:	ascribed status	representative capacity	policy effectiveness	managerial skills, efficiency
Pattern of electoral competition:	managed	mobilization	competitive	contained
Nature of party work and party campaigning:	irrelevant	labour-intensive	both labour-intensive and capital-intensive	capital-intensive
Principal source of party's resources:	personal contacts	members' fees and contributions	contributions from a wide variety of sources	state subventions
Relations between ordinary members and party élite:	the élite are the 'ordinary' members	bottom up (*pace* Michels); élite accountable to members	top down; members are organized cheerleaders for élite	stratarchy; mutual autonomy

Character of membership:	small and élitist	large and homogeneous; actively recruited and encapsulated; membership a logical consequence of identity; emphasis on rights and obligations	membership open to all (heterogeneous) and encouraged; rights emphasized but not obligations; membership marginal to individual's identity	neither rights nor obligations important (distinction between members and non-members blurred); emphasis on members as individuals rather than as an organized body; members valued for contribution to legitimizing myth
Party channels of communication:	inter-personal networks	party provides its own channels of communication	party competes for access to non-party channels of communication	party gains privileged access to state-regulated channels of communication
Position of party between civil society and state:	unclear boundary between state and politically relevant civil society	party belongs to civil society, initially as representative of the newly relevant segment of civil society	parties as competing brokers between civil society and state	party becomes part of state
Representative style:	trustee	delegate	entrepreneur	agent of state

a profession in itself: a skilled profession, to be sure, and one in which the limited inter-party competition which does ensue takes place on the basis of competing claims to efficient and effective management.

Patterns of electoral competition have also therefore differed. Among the élite parties, competition was effectively managed and controlled. This pattern was radically undermined by the extension of the suffrage, and by the emergence of mass parties which sought to gain victory on the basis of popular mobilization. The new style of electoral competition could best, if not always most typically, be seen in the attempts by the mass parties to segment the electorate into a series of exclusive constituencies, and in what Lipset and Rokkan (1967: 51) refer to as the attempts 'to narrow the support market'. With the catch-all party, electoral strategies became more competitive. Voters could be won, and parties found it worth their while to try to win them, even if the basis for this competition had ceased to involve major issues and come instead to revolve around questions of policy effectiveness. Even this pattern, however, can now be said to have been challenged, for, with the emergence of the cartel party, competition is once again contained and managed. Certainly, the parties still compete, but they do so in the knowledge that they share with their competitors a mutual interest in collective organizational survival, and, in some cases, even the limited incentive to compete has actually been replaced by a positive incentive not to compete. Perhaps nowhere was this better exemplified than by the sharing of patronage between the major Italian parties, including sometimes the Communists, who ostensibly were in opposition. Other very obvious examples include the sharing of seats and rotation of the presidency of the Swiss Federal Council among the four main parties; the sharing of mayoral appointments in the Netherlands; and the 'incumbent protection' gerrymander in many American state reapportionment decisions.

This new style of electoral competition also has implications for, and is partly a consequence of, changes in the resource base of the parties and in the type of party work and campaigning which is required. Élite parties, as has been noted, derived much of their resources, whether financial or otherwise, from among personal contacts, and paid little attention to the need for campaigning. Mass parties, on the other hand, built up highly labour-intensive organizations, financing their activities on the basis of membership

fees and subscriptions, and developing their own independent channels of communication. This was less evidently the case with the
catch-all party, which, while leaning heavily on its membership base
for both finances and campaign work, also began to win contributions from a wider variety of sources, and began to shift towards a
more capital-intensive approach to campaigning. These new parties
also laid less emphasis on their own independent channels of communication, and spent an increasing effort in competing for access
to non-partisan communication networks, devoting more and more
resources to the employment of professional publicists and media
experts (Panebianco, 1988: especially 220–35). This latter pattern
has now been even further pushed forward by the cartel parties,
whose campaigns are now almost exclusively capital-intensive, professional, and centralized, and who rely increasingly for their
resources on the subventions and other benefits and privileges
which are afforded by the state.

All of this also affects the character of party membership and the
relations between the party members and the party leadership. For
the élite party, of course, the party leaders are the only members,
and so these questions do not arise. With the mass party, by contrast, there is a large and homogeneous membership which claims
the right to control the party élite, and in whose name the party
élite acts. However, while members are actively recruited and enjoy
rights and privileges within the party, membership also entails substantial duties and obligations. The catch-all party continues to
emphasize membership and to afford its members rights within the
organization, but opens its ranks to a wider range of supporters
and no longer requires the same level of commitment. Leaders are
no longer primarily accountable to the members, but rather to the
wider electorate. The members in this sense are more like cheer-
leaders, and the pattern of authority is more top-down than bottom-up. Finally, although members of a cartel party may have even
more rights than those of catch-all parties, their position is sometimes less privileged. The distinction between members and non-
members may become blurred, with parties inviting all supporters,
whether formally enrolled or not, to participate in party activities
and decisions. Even more important, when members do exercise
their rights, they are more likely to do so as individuals rather than
through delegates, a practice which is most easily typified in the
selection of candidates and leaders by postal ballot rather than by

selection meetings or party congresses. This atomistic conception of party membership is further facilitated by allowing people to affiliate directly with the central party, obviating the need for local organizations, and hence also for local organizers. Indeed, it becomes possible to imagine a party which manages all of its business from a single central headquarters, and which simply subdivides its mailing list by constituency, region, or town when particular sets of candidates have to be selected or when subnational policies have to be approved.

The result is a leadership that can legitimize its position both inside and outside the party by pointing to a large and formally empowered membership. At the same time, its autonomy is enhanced, since an atomized membership is less likely to provide the basis for the mobilization of challenges, and since the position of local activists as necessary intermediaries is undercut. Parties do of course still need and want local office-holders, and these might be troublesome for the central party were they to advocate policies or strategies which ran counter to those advanced by the national leadership. That said, these local leaders will always be discouraged from intervening in national affairs by the knowledge that the national leadership, if challenged, can appeal directly to the individual members. As far as local matters are concerned, on the other hand, both sides have an interest in encouraging local autonomy. From the local office-holders' point of view, a relatively free hand is always desirable, while from the central party side an autonomous local party is more likely to encourage involvement and participation, and is more likely to make the party attractive to potential members and supporters. Each side is therefore encouraged to allow the other a free hand. The result is stratarchy.

DEMOCRACY AND THE CARTEL PARTY

Just as each of the models of party organization (élite party, mass party, catch-all party) that preceded it had an associated model of democracy, so the rise of the cartel party model as an empirical phenomenon is also associated with a revision of the normative model of democracy. In this revised model, the essence of democracy lies in the ability of voters to chose from a fixed menu of political parties. Parties are groups of leaders who compete for the opportunity to occupy government offices and to take responsibility at the next election for government performance. In one sense, this is simply an exaggeration of the catch-all party, or élitist liberal model of democracy, and the significant element is what is missing from this formulation. Democracy lies in the currying of public favour by élites, rather than public involvement in policy-making. Voters should be concerned with results rather than policy, which is the domain of the professional. Parties are partnerships of professionals, not associations of or for the citizens.

In other senses, however, the cartel party model of democracy is fundamentally different. Central to the earlier models was the idea of alternation in office—not only were there some parties that were clearly 'in' while others were clearly 'out', but the fear of being thrown out of office by the voters was also seen as the major incentive for politicians to be responsive to the citizenry. In the cartel model, on the other hand, none of the major parties is ever definitively 'out'. As a result, there is an increased sense in which electoral democracy may be seen as a means by which the rulers control the ruled, rather than the other way around. As party programmes become more similar, and as campaigns are in any case oriented more towards agreed goals rather than contentious means, there is a shrinkage in the degree to which electoral outcomes can determine government actions. Moreover, as the distinction between parties in office and those out of office becomes more blurred, the degree to which voters can punish parties even on the basis of generalized dissatisfaction is reduced. At the same time, participation in the electoral process implicates the voter, and by casting elections as the legitimate channel for political activity, other, potentially more effective channels are made less legitimate. Democracy becomes a means of achieving social stability rather than social change, and elections become 'dignified' parts of the constitution.

To put it another way, democracy ceases to be seen as a process by which limitations or controls are imposed on the state by civil society, and becomes instead a service provided by the state for civil society. Political leadership needs to be renewed, and elections provide a peaceful ritual by which this may be accomplished. Feedback is necessary if rulers are to provide government that is broadly acceptable, and contested elections, which signal public pleasure (or displeasure) with policy and outcomes, provide that feedback. Thus, the state provides contested elections. And since democratically contested elections, at least as currently understood, require political parties, the state also provides (or guarantees the provision of) political parties. In the end, of course, it is the parties in power that are the state and that provide this service, and it is thus their own existence that they are guaranteeing.

Recognition of party politics as a full-time career entails acceptance, and even encouragement, of a number of tendencies that earlier conceptions of democracy regarded as undesirable. While the relationship of these to the idea of a party cartel, either as preconditions or as likely consequences, is straightforward, they nevertheless imply a fundamental reorientation towards parties and elections. Most important, politicians feel an increasing need to lower the costs of electoral defeat. This is, of course, a universal desire, which has often led to the wholesale suspension of elections in countries without strongly established norms of electoral politics. In the western countries, where this is clearly not a viable option, the alternative is to provide subventions and support for all, allowing different coalitions to be in office at different levels or in different places, and so forth. One result of this is the toning down of competition. Furthermore, as politicians pursue long-term careers, they come to regard their political opponents as fellow professionals, who are driven by the same desire for job security and who confront the same kinds of pressures as themselves, and with whom business will have to be carried on over the long term. Stability becomes more important than triumph, and politics becomes a job rather than a vocation.

CHALLENGES TO THE CARTEL PARTY

But while the cartel parties may be able to limit competition among themselves, they are of course unable to suppress political opposition more generally. This is especially the case as parties, both singly and as a group, become ever more closely connected to the state; and as they cease to be effective channels of communication from civil society to the state. Instead of parties making demands on the state on behalf of particular groups in civil society, these groups find that they themselves need to make demands on the party/state. Increasingly, therefore, demand articulation becomes the province of interest organizations. In some cases, of course, and particularly as far as the interest organizations of the larger and more established groups (e.g. trade unions, employers' associations) are concerned, these have developed relationships with the state which are not unlike those developed by the parties themselves. This is the phenomenon which has been labelled 'neo-corporatism', and, among other things, involves the granting of a privileged and secure position to certain groups in exchange for 'good behaviour'. But precisely because these established groups have been co-opted into the system, they often prove unwilling or unable to express some demands, and this, in turn, can lead to the rise of alternative organizations, which are often short-lived and strident.

As this suggests, the self-protective mechanisms that the cartel parties have created therefore have their own, internal contradictions. To the extent that cartel parties limit the possibility of intraorganizational dissent, minimize the consequences of competition within the cartel, and protect themselves from the consequences of electoral dissatisfaction, they prevent elections from performing even the minimal feedback function that the new model of democracy assigns to them. This is only furthered if the major interest organizations have also been brought within the self-protective umbrella of neo-corporatist arrangements. At the same time, however, this cannot prevent the emergence of challenges from outside the cartel, even though it might be possible to place barriers in the path of new parties seeking to enter the system, such as, for example, the predication of state subventions on prior electoral performance or the restriction of ballot access. More important, attempts at exclusion may also prove counter-productive, offering to the excluded neophytes a weapon with which to mobilize the support of the disaffected. Thus, in much the same way as the élite parties created the social and political conditions for the emergence and success of mass parties, and as the mass parties, in turn, created the conditions for the emergence and success of catch-all parties, and as the catch-all party led to the conditions that generated the cartel party, so the more recent success of the cartel inevitably generates its own opposition.

New parties seeking to break into the system may, of course, campaign for support on the basis of a wide variety of ideological appeals. Increasingly, however, experience suggests that one particular rallying cry which seems common to many new parties, and which seems particularly effective in mobilizing support, is their demand to 'break the mould' of established politics (see, for example, Poguntke, 1994b; Scarrow, 1994b). In many cases, this demand is largely rhetorical, and its protagonists, particularly those seeking support among the new middle classes—parties ranging from Democrats 66 in the Netherlands, to the Social Democrats in Britain, and the Progressive Democrats in Ireland—often prove more than willing to join the establishment which they once initially decried. Even in other cases, as with many of the Green parties, where the opposition is more deep-rooted, these demands also prove capable of accommodation and co-optation.

In some cases, however, the protest taps into a more radical disaffection. This is certainly the case for a variety of new extreme-right parties, such as the Vlaams Blok in Belgium, the National Front in France, National Action in Switzerland, and even possibly New Democracy in Sweden, which seems intent on following the path of the Progress parties in neighbouring Denmark and Norway. This is also increasingly true of the established but now increasingly strident and excluded Freedom Party in Austria. All of these parties appear to espouse a profoundly undemocratic and often xenophobic opposition to the consensus which now prevails in most of the western democracies, and this obviously provides a major basis for their support. But what is perhaps more striking is that many of these parties also appear to be gaining great mileage from their assumed capacity to break up what they often refer to as the 'cosy' arrangements which exist between the established political alternatives. In effect, therefore, by operating as a cartel, by attempting to ensure that there are no clear 'winners' and 'losers' among the established alternatives, and by exploiting their control of the state to generate resources which can be shared out among themselves, the cartel parties are often unwittingly providing precisely the ammunition with which the new protesters of the right can more effectively wage their wars. These new protesters do not represent a challenge to party; their protest is, after all, organized by party. But they do see themselves as representing a challenge to the cartel party, a challenge which may well be fuelled by the actions of the cartel parties themselves, and which, in the longer term, may therefore help to legitimate their protest.

As was noted at the beginning of this chapter, much of the contemporary literature speaks of the decline or failure of parties, an emphasis which, from this perspective, is largely misconceived. In fact there is little real evidence to suggest that the age of party has waned. On the contrary, while in some respects parties are less powerful than before—enjoying, in the main, less intense partisan loyalties, lower proportions of adherents, less distinctive political identities—in other respects their position has strengthened, not least as a result of the increased resources which the state (the parties in the state) places at their disposal (see also Chapter 6 below). To be sure, if one takes as the standard the model of the mass party, as much of this literature appears to do, then the mainstream parties are perhaps less powerful than before; that is, they are less powerful mass parties. But this is an inappropriate standard, which fails to take account of the ways in which parties can adapt to ensure their own survival, and which ignores the new strengths that they can acquire in compensation for those weaknesses that have become apparent. They are, in short, different parties. To speak of the *challenge* to party rather than of its decline or failure, is perhaps to be on surer ground, albeit also fundamentally misconceived. For what we now see in western democracies is less a challenge to party in general, and rather more a challenge, inevitably so, to cartel parties in particular.

6
Popular Legitimacy and Public Privileges: Party Organizations in Civil Society and the State

The study of parties and party systems still constitutes one of the largest and most active subfields within comparative politics (e.g. Janda, 1993). It is also a study which continues to present an immensely varied landscape, ranging from work which explores the relationship of parties to the wider society, through work which is concerned with the role of parties in government, to work which, often at a more theoretical level, deals with the interactions between parties and with the dynamics of party systems. We now know a great deal, for example, about cross-national developments in the ties which bind, or fail to bind, parties to their voters, whether this be expressed in terms of the stability and change of electoral preferences (see, for example, Dalton *et al.*, 1984*b*; Crewe and Denver, 1985; Bartolini and Mair, 1990), or in terms of the sociology of party support (see, for example, Rose 1974; Franklin *et al.*, 1992). We also know increasingly more about parties in office, both in terms of processes of coalition formation (e.g. Pridham, 1986; Laver and Schofield, 1990) and in terms of the role of parties in policy-making and in government more generally (e.g. Castles and Wildenmann, 1986; Katz, 1987; Budge and Keman, 1990; Laver and Budge, 1992). Most recently, comparative analysis has also been addressed to the question of parties as strategic actors and as campaigners (e.g. Bowler and Farrell, 1992; Butler and Ranney, 1992). And to all of this work can be added the more wide-ranging and ever-expanding volume of studies on party families and party systems (see, for example, the now dated bibliography in Mair, 1990*a*: 353–60).

At the same time, however, there are also imbalances, with the ever-growing cumulation of knowledge in some areas contrasting sharply with surprisingly evident lacunae in others, and for some time now one of the most obvious of these lacunae has been the empirically grounded study of parties as *organizations* (see Katz and Mair 1992b). This is notwithstanding the fact that much of the pioneering work in the field of party research, by Michels and Ostrogorski in particular, was focused precisely on this area, and also notwithstanding some more recent theoretical discussions which have speculated on differing models of party and party change (e.g. Panebianco, 1988). Thus, while we now know a great deal about parties and their voters, about parties and their governments, and about parties and their competitors, there continue to be severe limits to the comparative understanding of precisely how party organizations work, about how they change, and about how they adapt.

NEW PERSPECTIVES ON THE DEVELOPMENT OF PARTY ORGANIZATIONS

One of the most obvious symptoms of this long-term neglect of comparative research on the development of party organizations is that much of the thinking on the subject still remains caught within a set of terms of reference which was established almost a generation ago. More specifically, and despite the occasional emphasis on more modern variants, much of this thinking remains predicated on the assumption of 'the mass party' as model (see Chapter 5 above). In this view, party organizations are defined primarily with reference to their relationships with civil society; party organizational strength is measured primarily with reference to the size of the membership and the capacity of the party to close off (often predefined) sectors of the electorate; and party structures are understood and assessed primarily in terms of modes of internal representation and accountability. It follows therefore that the attenuation of any of these elements—such as occurs through the privileging of leadership groups inside the party, through the downgrading of the role of members, or through the development of programmes aimed at the voters at large rather than at the party-attached or even party-incorporated clientele—involves also the attenuation, and decline, of party *per se*.

The problem with this line of reasoning begins when the decline of the mass party is treated as signifying the decline of party more generally. In this sense, the mass party is not only the model for what has gone before, but also remains the model almost in perpetuity, such that parties which may be indifferent to membership, which may emphasize the power of their leadership, and which may develop less self-consciously democratic processes of internal decision-making, are somehow also parties in decline. Kirchheimer (1966), for example, who was one of the first authors to signal the demise of the mass party, and who pointed to the emergence of the newer 'catch-all' party, did so with regret, in that he envisaged the new type of party possibly becoming 'too blunt to serve as a link with the functional powerholders of society' (p. 200). Pizzorno (1981), who also emphasized the passing of the mass party, and who depicted it as the now redundant creature of a specific time, was led to advance a series of hypotheses seeking to explain how parties as such could even survive thereafter. Even Panebianco (1988), who argues that the mass party had been superseded by what he refers to as the 'electoral-professional party', suggests that this may also involve the weakening of the position of party 'in every arena' (p. 269). The period of the mass party can therefore be seen to coincide with 'the golden age' of parties, and since then everything has been downhill. Indeed, it was probably this sense of decline which discouraged empirical research in the field of party organizations during the past twenty years, in that it seemed more useful to devote one's research efforts to those 'emerging alternative organizations', such as new social movements, which were increasingly regarded as threatening to displace parties as the active intermediaries between the citizenry and the state (see, for example, Lawson and Merkl, 1988b).

There are also other problems associated with this mass-party-centred argument. In the first place, much of the speculation about the passing of the mass party and about the imputed decline of party more generally has ensued without much reference to empirical evidence, not least because of the sheer difficulty involved in gathering the sort of data which might bolster or even challenge this thesis (see, for example, Bartolini, 1983b; von Beyme, 1985; Katz, 1990). Second, and notwithstanding the insights which have been provided by much of the more theoretical reasoning, the precise way in which different models of party organization may be distinguished still remains relatively unclear. For while these models are certainly useful when seeking to make quite long-term generalizations about party organizational development, they nevertheless prove very difficult to treat in a more specific way, or as genuinely empirical constructs (e.g. Sjöblom, 1981; Dittrich, 1983; Krouwel, 1993). Third, and not least as a result of the legacy of the mass party model, there still remains a tendency to evaluate party organizations in terms of their relations with civil society. Alternative aspects of party organization, on the other hand, particularly those which relate to the party in parliament (cf. Hecksher, 1953: 149–59; von Beyme, 1983), or to the party in central office, still often tend to be ignored.

In the context of the wider research project on change and adaptation in party organizations, of which the analysis in this chapter forms part (see Katz and Mair, 1992a, 1994), there are two principal strategies which have been adopted in order to deal with these problems. The first, and probably the more important of these strategies, aims at going beyond the classic work of Janda (1980) and at remedying the dearth of empirical evidence about party organizational developments by means of a systematic collection of cross-national data over time on all relevant party organizations in a variety of western democracies. Over and above information concerning the electoral and governmental history of almost eighty parties in the twelve countries included in this project, data were also gathered on the development and structure of party membership; on the numbers and allocation of party staff; on the internal distribution of power and the organization and functions of internal party organs; and on party finance, including information on the provision of state subsidies for parties. These data have since been published in a separate handbook (Katz and Mair, 1992a).

The second strategy involves an attempt to move away from the conception of party as a unitary actor, and especially to move away from the almost exclusive concern with the relationship between parties and civil society, by disaggregating party organizations into at least three different elements or faces, each of which interacts with the others. The first of these faces is the *party in public office*, that is, the party organization in government and in parliament. The second is the *party on the ground*, that is, the membership organization, and also potentially the loyal party voters. The third face is the *party in central office*, which is organizationally distinct from the party in public office, and which, at least in the traditional mass party model, organizes and is usually representative of the party on the ground (see Katz and Mair, 1993).

Both strategies facilitate the adoption of a more differentiated and at the same time more grounded approach to the study of party organizational change and adaptation. Both also allow a more sensitive understanding of the broader question of party decline. The availability of cross-national data, for example, not only allows us to test whether any such decline is real or imagined, but, by distinguishing between the different faces, also allows us to pinpoint more precisely where change is taking place, and to find out whether, say, decline in one of these elements is perhaps countered by growth at other levels of the party. Indeed, a central hypothesis which emerges from this project has been that it is really only the party on the ground which is becoming less important or which is in decline, whereas the resources of the party in central office, and especially those of the party in public office, have in fact been strengthened. In this sense, we argue that the emphasis on party decline *tout court* may be misplaced.

PARTY DEMOCRACIES AND THE PROBLEM OF PARTY DECLINE

Two major waves of democratization have marked the beginning and the end of twentieth-century European political history. In the first twenty years, democratization involved the opening up of the political process to more and more formerly excluded citizens, and the granting of the vote to the property-less and to at least some women. Most recently, and in the last twenty years, beginning with the transformations in Greece and Portugal, we have witnessed the widespread collapse of authoritarian regimes, and their replacement by multi-party democracies. These two experiences were far from identical, of course: in one period, democratization was carried by means of enfranchisement and incorporation; in the other, it was effected by means of regime change, a contrast which has also forced other differences to become apparent, most noticeably in terms of the sheer pace and controllability of the democratization process itself. Thus while the democratization process which took place in most of the European countries in the first twenty years of the century was relatively gradual and managed, the most recent experiences of democratization in southern Europe, and most especially in post-communist Europe, have proved both rapid and abrupt.

But despite these crucial differences, there nevertheless remains one major similarity between both processes: that is, both waves of democratization have emphasized, if not required, the agency of political parties. In the first wave, and in the early part of the century, democratization was accompanied by the development and the essential triumph of the mass party, which, in Pizzorno's terms, 'emerge[d] both to strengthen and control the access of the new masses into the political system' (Pizzorno, 1981: 272). These were parties which, necessarily so, were strongly rooted in civil society; which emphasized engagement and involvement; and which at the same time were hierarchical and disciplined. These were parties which came from and belonged to civil society, and which sought to express and then implement the interests of their constituency within public policy. In the most recent wave of democratization too, the role of party has been central, although now, more than half a century on, there is little to suggest that this emphasis on party will promote the emergence of mass parties as such, in that the parties which are developing both in southern and eastern Europe tend to be typified by loose organizational structures, by small if not non-existent memberships, and by an absence of any pronounced ties to civil society. But although far removed from the styles and structures associated with the traditional mass party, the role of party in building these new democracies has nevertheless proved crucial, with the importance of party being seen even in the manner in which these new democracies are defined; for in situations where democratization has resulted from a change of regime rather than from a process of enfranchisement, we see democracy itself being defined not in terms of the rights of citizens, but rather in terms of the existence of a plurality of parties, which compete against one another in free elections.

In modern democracies, therefore, whether these are long-established democracies or newly created democracies, politics is about party politics; to put it another way, the twentieth century is not only the century of democratization, and hence of democracy, but it is also the century of *party* democracy. As the century closes, however, it has become increasingly clear that many of the long-established party democracies in particular are beginning to show distinctly unhealthy symptoms. For despite or, as I will suggest here, perhaps even *because of* the importance of party in our modern democracies, party democracy itself has become an increasingly troubled form of democracy.

For more than a decade now, a major theme within both academic and journalistic discourse has taken 'the decline of party' as more or less a matter of conventional wisdom. Parties are *passé*, it is often argued, and even if it may have been precipitate to have written them off as a result of the challenge of neo-corporatism, a supposedly enduring phenomenon which appears itself to have experienced an untimely demise, it is now the assault from the ground, in the form of changing citizen preferences, which is finally believed to be the catalyst of change. There are two related elements within this new transformative process. On the one hand, the citizenry is seen to have become fragmented and individualized, and preferences have become 'particularized' (van der Eijk *et al.*, 1992: 406–31) in a manner which is largely anathema to the aggregative instincts of traditional party politics. On the other hand, competing channels of representation have opened up in the form of new social movements and 'alternative organizations' (Lawson and Merkl, 1988a) which are often believed to link citizens to the decision-making process in a manner which is at once more effective and more satisfactory.

Both elements are seen to imply that parties, at least as we know them, are becoming increasingly marginalized and ineffective, with the result that, in time, they may simply wither away. This is not seen as necessarily problematic. Indeed, were parties to decline and then eventually disappear, this might even be seen by some observers as a potentially healthy process, in which an increasingly outdated form of politics, a *Jurassic Park*-style politics, could then be replaced by involvement in other 'political' activities which would be closer to the citizens' interests, and in which these citizens could play a more direct and responsible role. Such a development would therefore imply the development of a more self-sufficient citizenry, and this could only be good for democracy. The decline of parties, in short, could be seen to reflect an inevitable change, a change that is certainly not worse, and is perhaps even better; a change, that is, to a healthier, more participant, and more self-controlled style of democracy.

But although there may be a certain truth in these assumptions about party decline, it is nevertheless only a partial truth, in that parties are viewed from one perspective only; that is, from the perspective of their relations with civil society. As a result, these assumptions tend to overlook the extraordinary capacity of parties to see off challenges and so ensure their own survival (see also Chapter 5 above). Even beyond that, however, the assumption that the declining popular relevance of political parties may eventually lead to their passing in quite an unproblematic way is also very questionable. As I will suggest in this chapter, the difficulty with this latter assumption is that it misses the essential contradiction between an apparent weakening of the role of parties as representative agencies on the one hand, and an apparent strengthening of their role as public office-holders on the other. It is, in this sense, a contradiction between the relevance (or its absence) of parties and their visibility: or, more sharply, between the legitimacy (or its absence) of parties on the one hand, and their privileged position on the other, and it is the existence of this particular contradiction which may well pose much more severe problems than are implied by any simple hypothesis of 'party decline'. Before returning to this question, however, I will first briefly review some of the evidence regarding the role of parties as representative agencies, which includes the position of parties 'on the ground' and their relevance as 'purposive' actors, and some of the evidence regarding their position as public office-holders.

Parties on the ground

The most easy and oft-cited evidence of the erosion of parties in modern European democracies is usually drawn from the perspective of ordinary voters and citizens, with the most obvious symptom of this malaise being seen in the already ample but still growing evidence of popular disenchantment and even distrust of parties and of the political class more generally. Indeed, this sense of disenchantment has become so pervasive and endemic that there is now a whole new terminology in which it can be expressed. Whatever the terms, however, it is an attitude which is more than evident from opinion surveys throughout Europe. It can be seen in Norway, for example, where almost half the respondents to a survey in 1989 agreed that politicians basically didn't know what they were talking about; or in France, where more than two-thirds of respondents to a survey in 1991 felt that politicians were not very interested in their problems; or in Austria, where a survey in 1989 reported that more than two-thirds of respondents were in agreement with the proposition that politicians were essentially 'corrupt and bribable'; or in Germany, where a 1991 survey reported that only a quarter of those questioned expressed confidence in the political parties, and that almost two-thirds believed that politicians lined their own pockets; or in the United Kingdom, where a 1994 survey reported that almost two-thirds of respondents regarded the Conservative party as 'sleazy and disreputable'.[1]

Second, and perhaps unsurprisingly, these sorts of attitudes have sometimes been translated into a loosening sense of party attachment or party identification. It must be emphasized, however, that this particular trend is far from universal, and in some cases the sense of party belonging among voters does not appear to have been eroded. Nevertheless, there are quite a number of countries where a decline is certainly apparent. In Austria, for example, those reporting any sense of identification with political parties, whether this be a strong or a weak identification, fell from some 75 per cent of voters in 1969 to 59 per cent in 1990; in West Germany, a similar measure evidenced a decline from 82 per cent in 1972 to less than 75 per cent in 1987, while in Ireland the proportion fell from just over 72 per cent in 1981 to just 40 per cent in 1989. In Sweden, those reporting a strong sense of party identification fell from 52 of voters in 1960 to 27 per cent in 1988, and in the UK the proportion of those with a strong sense of identification with either Labour or the Conservatives fell from some 22 per cent in 1964 to just 7 per cent in 1987 (Katz and Mair, 1992a: 39, 330, 398, 633–4, 789–90, 846; see also Mair, 1984, and Schmitt, 1989).

The third symptom of this malaise, and that which may perhaps prove most worrying for the parties, is reflected in trends in party

---

[1] The sources are as follows: Andersen and Bjorklund (1990: 203); Ysmal, (1992: 407); Müller (1994: 52); Veen *et al.* (1993: 45); *Daily Telegraph*, 10 October 1994. In the case of the United Kingdom, this sort of critical attitude has also begun to pervade the otherwise rather staid establishment press: thus an editorial in the *Independent* asserted that the ruling Conservatives 'have been profoundly corrupted' (12 January 1994), while even the *Daily Telegraph* was driven to complain of the quality of the contemporary Conservative MPs, arguing that 'in the place of the old knights of the shire is a host of frankly inadequate men and women who, far from entering Parliament in any spirit of public service, are driven solely by the pursuit of self-advancement' (quoted in the *Independent*, 15 January 1994).

membership (see Table 6.1). At one level, the changes here may not seem particularly marked and the sense of decay is not particularly pronounced. Six of the eleven countries for which comparable data from the 1960s onwards are available, for example, record an actual increase in the total numbers of party members between the early 1960s and the beginning of the 1990s (the countries are Belgium, Finland, France, Germany, Norway, and Sweden), with only five recording a decline in the total numbers of members across the same period (Austria, Denmark, Italy, the Netherlands, and the UK).[2] At another level, however, and more crucially, the change is quite marked, in that this period has also witnessed a massive growth in the size of European electorates, and the major problem associated with levels of party membership is that they have failed to keep pace with this expansion. In other words, while the total numbers of members may sometimes have remained the same, or even increased, the *relative* membership/electorate ratio has more often than not declined, thus indicating a reduced organizational presence within the society. In fact, only two of the eleven countries for which comparable data are available, Belgium and Germany, have registered an increase in the share of the electorate who maintain a party membership (increasing from 7.8 per cent to 9.2 per cent of the electorate in the case of Belgium, and from 2.7 per cent to 4.2 per cent in the case of West Germany), while a third country, France, has evinced a more or less stable (albeit low) membership–electorate ratio over time. All other countries, by contrast, have registered a sharp decline in their relative membership levels, ranging from the remarkable Danish fall from more than 21 per cent of the electorate in the early 1960s to just less than 7 per cent of the electorate in the late 1980s, to the more muted fall of less than 1 per cent in Sweden across the same period.

This near universal decline in party membership as a share of the electorate clearly indicates that the parties' relative hold on the electorate is being weakened, and this, together with the other evidence cited above, further reinforces the sense of erosion in the position of the party on the ground, and hence a weakening of the capacity of parties to act as representative agencies. What is striking to note, however, is that this sense of erosion is not really immediately discernible at the level of rates of turnout in national

---

[2] For figures on France, see Ysmal (1989: 163); for figures on all other countries cited see Katz and Mair (1992*a*, 1994).

TABLE 6.1. *Development of Party Membership*

| | Beginning of 1960s | | End of 1980s | |
	No. ('000)	% of electorate	No. ('000)	% of electorate
Austria	1,380.7	26.2	1,311.8	21.8
Belgium	468.8	7.8	654.4	9.2
Denmark	599.1	21.1	260.5	6.5
Finland	513.1	18.9	520.1	12.9
Germany	1,001.9[a]	2.7	1,907.5	4.2
Ireland	n.a.	n.a.	129.3	5.3
Italy	4,332.8	12.7	4,405.2	9.7
Netherlands[b]	648.4	9.4	326.4	2.9
Norway	363.7	15.5	432.0	13.5
Sweden	1,092.1	22.0	1,343.3	21.2
UK	3,258.8	9.4	1,426.3	3.3

Notes: [a] Includes estimate of 50,000 for FDP membership.
[b] Includes estimate of 10,000 for CPN in 1963, and the Green Left in 1989.
Source: Katz and Mair (1992*a*; 1994).

elections, even though, in this particular context, patterns of turnout are difficult to interpret. On the one hand, it might be possible to cite long-term trends in the levels of voting turnout, in the expectation that a weakening of the position of the party on the ground would be reflected in a declining propensity to vote. There is little sign of this in reality, however: levels of turnout at national elections still remain reasonably high, and precisely because the size of the electorate has grown so substantially (see Chapter 4 above), the sheer numbers of those voting has also grown. Indeed, despite a modest decline in average turnout levels from just less than 84 per cent to just less than 80 per cent across most of western Europe between the early 1960s and the early 1990s, the actual numbers of those voting in national elections increased by almost one-third—from some 140 million in the early 1960s to more than 184 million in the early 1990s. These figures therefore offer little or no evidence of disenchantment or malaise. On the other hand, it also seems to be the case that a small but none the less increasing proportion of these voters in a variety of different countries are now expressing a preference for 'new-politics' parties of the left and the right, many of which mobilize as 'anti-party parties' in opposition to the established order (see also below). Thus while an increased vote for these parties might be taken to indicate rising anti-party sentiment, and hence malaise, it may also result in an increase (or, at least, not a decrease) in voter turnout, and this, in turn, may be read as evidence of the maintenance of trust and legitimacy. In this particular context, therefore, it is difficult to reach any hard and fast conclusions about potential disenchantment with parties from turnout figures alone.

Parties as purposive actors

From one perspective, then, it can be argued that parties are increasingly unable to *engage* voters and to win their affective commitment. From another perspective, and especially within the boundaries of traditional politics, it might be argued that they are also increasingly unable to convince voters of their relevance in purposive terms. Part of the problem here lies in the changing international circumstances within which national states, and hence national governments and the parties which occupy these governments, attempt to guide and control domestic policy-making. In one sense, all of the European economies are now open economies, and all are becoming 'semi-sovereign' (for the original reference, see Katzenstein, 1987) in that they are now subject to a set of constraints and persuasions that lie quite outside their own direct control. The freedom of manoeuvre of national states and national governments is therefore severely constricted, and the scope for partisan discretion is correspondingly curtailed. This has two immediate effects on the capacity of parties in government to act as representative agencies. In the first place, the responses of national governments to political and economic problems increasingly tend to be influenced by international as well as local pressures, and hence they cannot always respond to domestic demands in a way which fully satisfies the local interests on which they depend for their legitimacy and authority. Second, and perhaps more important, the increasing complexity of the global economy leads to severe problems for the monitoring and control of the policy-making process, and hence undermines the capacity for effective and authoritative action.[3] The result is that governments, and hence the

---

[3] See Stubbs and Underhill (1994). It should be emphasized that this argument does not necessarily imply that all governments which are subject to these

parties in those governments, often find themselves increasingly unable to cope, and increasingly unable to convince sceptical voters of the merits of their partisan purpose.

Indeed, a partisan purpose is itself more difficult to discern. All 'established' parties in western Europe, with one or two notable exceptions, have now been in government at one time or another in the past fifteen or twenty years; all have had their hands on power—whether exclusively or in concert with others; and all have operated within the limits imposed by the post-1973 international economic environment. Faced with burgeoning economic and social problems, many of which in any case lie outside the control of national governments, none of these parties can now plausibly claim to provide a panacea. Moreover, as Richard Rose (e.g. 1990) has pointed out, since much of contemporary policy-making is simply policy-making by inertia, in which governments tinker at the margins of programmes which they have largely inherited, none of these parties might prove capable of even the plausible promise of something new and different, at least in a purposive sense. Given that some of the most exacting scholarship in political science in the early 1980s found it difficult to determine conclusively whether parties had made a difference (see, for example, Castles, 1982, and Rose, 1984), it would then hardly be surprising to find that ordinary voters might also have despaired of a partisan intent.

Nor is this process likely to be ameliorated by the increasing integration of states into the European Union. Quite the contrary. In the first place, despite the growing evidence of popular scepticism about the benefits of further integration, almost all mainstream parties in almost all western European countries are more or less in agreement on the need to pursue the European project, with the challenge to this overarching consensus coming principally from either fringe parties on the left and right, or from maverick elements within the established parties. Here too, then, differences within the mainstream have been blurred to almost non-existence.

international pressures end up by pursuing more or less the same policies or that they are all converging towards a particular (neo-liberal) consensus. Indeed, this suggestion is already contested by scholars who point to evidence of cross-national *divergence* in policy directions and outcomes (see, for example, Scharpf, 1988, and Garrett, 1995). Rather, the argument is that *within* any given country, and almost regardless of whether or not it is diverging from its neighbours and competitors, the range of policy options is being constrained, with the result that *national* partisan differences become muted and *national* partisan policies converge.

Second, as noted above, the Europeanization of policy-making will further constrict the discretion available to national governments and hence to the parties in those national governments, and will further curtail their room for manoeuvre, thus accentuating the apparent decline in their authority. And finally, precisely because decision-making within Europe itself is not seen to be mediated by party—decisions are taken primarily by either the representatives of national governments acting behind closed doors in the various councils of ministers, or by commissioners who formally eschew a representative role, or even, and more marginally so, by a European Parliament which is organized by parliamentary groups standing at one remote remove from the parties as organized at national level—this is likely to undermine even further the relevance of party in representative terms.

The decline of a partisan purpose and the blurring of differences between traditional parties can also be seen at a variety of other levels. In the first place, and most directly, it can be seen in the

TABLE 6.2. *Distance on a left–right scale between a major party of the left and a major party of the centre right, 1983 and 1993*

Country	Parties	Distance in 1983	Distance in 1993[a]	Percentage change
Austria	SPÖ–ÖVP	2.8	1.7	−39.3
Belgium	PS/SP–PSC/CVP	3.4	2.0	−41.2
Denmark	SD–Con	3.5	3.6	+2.9
Finland	SD–Nat. Coal	4.2	3.3	−21.4
France	PS–RPR	5.6	4.2	−25.0
Germany	SPD–CDU	3.4	2.9	−14.7
Ireland	Lab–FF	2.7	1.9	−29.6
Italy	PCI/PDS–DC	3.8	4.2	+10.5
Netherlands	PvdA–CDA	3.1	2.3	−25.9
Norway	Lab–Con	4.7	4.3	−8.5
Spain	PSOE–PP/AP	4.8	3.9	−18.8
Sweden	SD–Con	4.8	4.7	−2.1
UK	Lab–Con	5.5	3.6	−34.6

Notes: [a] The 1993 figures have been adjusted to allow a comparison between the 1993 index, which is based on a 10-point scale (1–10), and the 1983 index, which is based on an 11-point scale.
Source: 1983: Castles and Mair (1984); 1993: Huber and Inglehart (1995).

declining distance which separates these parties in left–right terms. Within the last ten years or so, for example, as two comparable 'expert' surveys indicate (see Table 6.2), the gap which separates the traditional major party on the centre-left from that on the centre-right has declined in eleven of the thirteen European countries for which comparable data are available. In some cases, the increasing proximity of the traditional opponents is particularly marked, as in Belgium, for example, where the gap has been reduced by more than 41 per cent; Austria, where it has been reduced by almost 40 per cent; and the UK, where it has been reduced by almost 35 per cent. Elsewhere, as in Norway and Sweden, for example, the reduction has proved more muted. It is only in Denmark and Italy (notwithstanding the transformation of the PCI into the PDS), on the other hand, that the relative distances between the traditional protagonists have widened in the last ten years (by 3 per cent and 11 per cent respectively).

Second, and more impressionistically, the blurring of differences between the traditional parties can be seen in the gradual broadening of the range of coalition alternatives, and the development of a pattern of promiscuity in the formation of governments which seems to belie any sense of substantive and enduring inter-party conflicts. In West Germany, for example, over the past thirty years, all possible two-party coalitions between the three main parties have proved possible both in principle and in practice; in the Netherlands, each of the three main parties has by now coalesced with each of the others at various stages during the last ten years, with virtually all possible permutations and combinations of governing parties (including a government without the CDA) coming to office at one stage or another; in Italy, the formerly dominant Christian Democrats proved willing to work with both the PSI and, albeit less formally, the PCI (and the PDS); in Ireland, Labour has now had recent experience of joining governments with both Fianna Fáil and Fine Gael, while, more recently, even Fine Gael itself has proved willing to take on the Democratic Left as a coalition ally; in Austria in the last ten years the SPÖ has formed governments with both the FPÖ and the ÖVP; in Belgium, the Socialists, Liberals, and Christians have all recently worked with one another, and also, on occasion, with the Volksunie and the Rassemblement Walloon; even in Sweden, where a sharp two-bloc pattern of competition has long been established, the run-up to the

1994 election witnessed a lengthy discussion of a possible coalition between the Social Democrats and the Liberals.

Finally, it is possible to add to these factors a variety of different elements which together suggest that individual parties may now find it increasingly difficult to maintain a separate identity. In the past, which, to be sure, may well be a largely mythical past, the dominant image of party was that of a more or less 'closed community'. Parties, in this supposed golden age, enjoyed very distinct identities. Each, to a greater or lesser extent, had its own 'natural' constituency, whether defined in terms of class, religion, occupation, or region, the core of which identified with and belonged to the particular party concerned and would rarely, if ever, consider voting for an alternative. Each party also controlled its own organizational resources, whether these were drawn mainly from ordinary supporters, from registered members, or from particular donors. Each more or less maintained its network of communications, in the form of its own internal party press or a sympathetic but ostensibly autonomous 'public' newspaper. Each had its own distinctive programme and ideology which were geared to the needs of its own specific constituency. And each hoped, at best, to be able to form its own government or, at worst, to form a coalition with another party or parties whose interests either approximated to or at least did not substantially conflict with its own interest.

In contemporary politics, on the other hand, this sense of separateness is less and less apparent, with the situation now being characterized more accurately as one in which all of these aspects are now shared between the different parties (see also Chapter 5 above). One of the factors involved here derives from the familiar arguments concerning the erosion of collective identities within civil society—the blurring or even erosion of traditional boundaries based on class and religion, the changing patterns of social stratification, and the emergence of a greater emphasis on individualistic or particularistic identities—one consequence of which is that parties are losing a distinct electoral profile and are now more likely to find themselves sharing the same electoral market (Franklin *et al.*, 1992). A second element relates to party organizational change, and the marked convergence between party organizational styles both within and across national boundaries, whether this is seen in terms of organizational structures *tout court*, or in terms of the techniques of political communication, or in terms of the nature of organizational resources. Most major parties have now abandoned their own independent means of communication, for example, and now prefer to rely on winning space and attention in the shared national media, whether public or private. In most countries, parties have also come to rely much less heavily on their own distinctive organizational resources, and lean increasingly heavily on their shares of the same fount of resources that is provided in the form of state subventions and public subsidies. Indeed, there is ample evidence to suggest that organizational distinctions between parties are gradually becoming a thing of the past and that shared experiences are now increasingly commonplace, not least as a result of the need to conform to the new party laws which have often accompanied the introduction of public subventions (see also below). The third element, as noted above, is that parties are increasingly constrained by the same set of policy parameters, and, at least within the mainstream, find themselves sharing the same policy priorities, often within the context of increasingly promiscuous coalition cabinets. In this sense also, as was probably already beginning to be the case with the emergence of the catch-all party, substantive programmatic and purposive differences become more difficult to discern.

All of this clearly has implications for the capacity of individual parties to maintain a distinct identity, and hence also a distinct purpose. Differences between (mainstream) parties are less easily discerned, especially by voters, and ostensible protagonists may often be lumped together as constituent elements of a more or less undifferentiated political class (von Beyme, 1993), thus helping to render these traditional parties vulnerable to the sort of 'anti-party system' assault which proved so effective in the recent north American campaigns of Ross Perot and Preston Manning, and which is also often echoed within contemporary European polities (von Beyme, 1993: 195–209; Betz, 1994: 36–67). That said, however vulnerable they might become, neither the blurring of differences nor the waning of partisan purpose would seem sufficient in themselves to generate a sense of resentment against parties and against the so-called political class; indeed, at most, these are likely to lead only to indifference and apathy. Conversely, resentment can play a role when this seeming decline in the relevance of parties on the ground is accompanied by a growth in the status, resources, and privileges of the parties in central office and, above all, of the parties in public office.

PARTIES AND THE STATE

Indeed, it is precisely when we turn to the parties in central office and in public office that the most powerful evidence can be marshalled against the simple thesis of party decline. In the first place, and most obviously, more and more parties are gaining access to public office, and in this sense they are also gaining access to more resources on the one hand, and to alternatives means of legitimation on the other. There are now very few parties which are marginalized in this regard. The Finnish Communists and the German Social Democrats joined their first postwar coalitions in the 1960s, and it was also in the 1960s that the first postwar bourgeois coalition was formed in Norway. By the end of the 1970s, parties such as the Belgian Rassemblement Walloon, Volksunie, and Front Démocratique des Bruxellois Francophones had been admitted to government for the first time, as had the Dutch D66. The 1970s also

TABLE 6.3. *The development of party resources*

	Growth in number of staff employed by parties[a] %	Growth in income of party central offices[b] %
Austria	+61	+286
Denmark	+112	+50
Finland	+55	+6
Germany	+268	+35
Ireland	+330	+123
Italy	+140	−25
Netherlands	+17	+41
Norway	+50	+14
Sweden	+55	−4
UK	+24	+46
USA	n.a.	+145

Notes: [a] The change refers to the difference between the position in the late 1960s or early 1970s and that in the late 1980s; only those parties are included where it proved possible to make a direct comparison over time.
[b] The change refers to the difference between the income (in constant prices) in about 1975 and that in 1989/90; only those parties are included where it proved possible to make a direct comparison over time.
Source: as Table 6.1.

witnessed the first bourgeois coalition in Sweden, and the advent to office, after sixteen years of opposition, of the Fine Gael and Labour parties in Ireland. By the end of the 1980s, the governing ranks of European parties had expanded further to include the then Austrian Freedom Party, the Danish Centre Democrats and Christian People's Party, as well as the Finnish Rural Party (see Katz and Mair, 1992*a*; Woldendorp *et al.*, 1993). Other than many of the recently mobilized 'new politics' parties of the left, and virtually all of the 'new politics' parties of the far right, therefore, the only substantial parties which have long remained outside government at a national level are the British Liberal party, which nevertheless formed a pact with the minority Labour government in the late 1970s; and the Italian Communist Party, the majority of which has now reconstituted itself as the reformed and increasingly coalition-minded Democratic Party of the Left (PDS).[4] Governing, even if only sporadically, is therefore by now a standard experience for most parties, and the resources which this brings now constitute an important means of sustenance.

Second, as can be seen from the summary figures reported in Table 6.3, there has been a near universal growth in the overall resources of the various parties for which comparable data are available. The numbers of party staff have increased everywhere, ranging from the massive 330 per cent increase in Ireland (and almost the same in Germany) to more modest increases in Britain and the Netherlands. In these terms at least, parties now have much greater resources at their disposal than was the case some two decades ago, and even these figures leave aside the countless additional personnel resources which are available through government appointments and through the contractual employment of specialist consultants. The incomes of party central offices have also grown almost everywhere in the last fifteen years or so, increasing by more than 300 per cent in the German case, by more than 200 per cent in the Austrian case, and by more than 100 per cent in the Irish case. Only in Sweden, which registered a marginal decline, and in Italy, where the 'official' but now admittedly highly misleading

---

[4] Indeed, shortly after its formation, in April 1993, the party actually joined Carlo Ciampi's new reformist government, but withdrew twenty-four hours later, following the refusal of the Chamber of Deputies to allow the prosecution of the discredited Socialist leader, Bettino Craxi.

figures reveal a decline of almost 25 per cent, has central office income actually fallen in real terms.

Both aspects are of course related, in that it is often real or potential access to public office which has enhanced the ability of parties to accumulate organizational resources such as staff and money. In this sense, the state, which is often the source of these resources, becomes a means by which parties can help ensure their own persistence and survival. Indeed, if there is one single theme which is to be drawn from the diversity apparent in the analyses which have been conducted within the party organization project (see Katz and Mair, 1994), it is that the understanding of party organizational change and adaptation requires us to pay at least as much attention, if not more so, to the linkage between party and state as it does to the linkage between parties and civil society. At the same time, however, it is also clear that it is precisely this particular linkage which has tended to be either ignored or undervalued in previous assessments of party change and stability, which, as noted above, has tended to focus almost exclusively on party relations with civil society (see, for example, Lawson, 1988, and Sainsbury, 1990; for one notable exception, see Müller, 1993).

What is also clear is that it is in the last decade or two that the relevance of the linkage with the state has tended to become particularly important. In a sense, then, the increasingly top-down style of party organizational life which was emphasized in Kirchheimer's (1966) depiction of the catch-all party, and especially in Panebianco's (1988) depiction of the electoral-professional party, and which implied an erosion of the party–civil society linkage, may also be said to have coincided with correspondingly greater emphasis on the linkage between party and state, with the latter offering the potential to compensate for the former (see Chapter 5 above). The balance of linkage has therefore changed, as have the parties themselves.

The state as intermediary?

Taken to extremes, any such movement might well require us to modify the conventional conception in which parties are seen as intermediaries between civil society and the state, a conception which may perhaps have been better suited to those phases in which the parties either represented the interests of civil society or simply acted as a broker for these interests. Instead, by linking themselves more closely to the state, and especially by relying on the state for their resources, they call to mind a more useful heuristic conception in which the state itself might be seen as the intermediary between the parties and the citizenry. This is, to be sure, an extreme and somewhat abstract conception; none the less, it does help us to get away from the increasingly frustrating and often misleading emphasis on the parties' own links with civil society, and to recognize the importance of their ties with the state. In the Italian case in particular, for instance, as can be seen from Bardi and Morlino's (1994) discussion of *partitocrazia*, a conception of the state as intermediary can also help to illuminate the processes by which parties seek to survive.

There is now little doubt about how the state, as opposed to simply civil society, has become unquestionably important for the survival of political parties, both in terms of the legitimacy which public office confers, as well as in terms of the resources and capacities which are either offered by or regulated by the state itself. There are a number of ways in which this may be illustrated. In the first place, as noted above, there are now few if any parties which still maintain their own partisan channel of communication, be this a party press, a party broadcasting system, or whatever. Rather, they now rely almost exclusively on a combination of independent, usually printed media on the one hand, where the access afforded to an individual party depends on whether it can either buy space or convince editors; and, on the other hand, publicly owned and/or controlled broadcasting networks (television and radio), where access, which is becoming increasingly important, is usually guaranteed by law and strictly regulated. As far as this latter outlet is concerned, the manner in which parties present their message, and the relative frequency with which it can be presented, therefore clearly depend in large part on rules and procedures devised by the state.

The second, and significantly more direct way in which the state helps to ensure the position of political parties can be seen in personnel resources. As noted above, for example (see Table 6.3), the numbers of staff working for parties have expanded substantially in the past two decades, and much of this increase can be accounted for by the growth of parliamentary party staff who are paid largely, if not exclusively, from state funds. Indeed, with the exception of

Italy (and perhaps also of the UK, where comparisons over time are difficult to measure), the growth of parliamentary party staff has consistently outstripped that of central office staff. In a number of cases (e.g. Austria, Finland, Germany, Norway, Sweden), parliamentary staff numbers have actually grown by three to four times as much as those in party central offices; in Denmark, the increase in parliamentary staff has been ten times that in central office staff, while in Ireland the ratio is more than twelve to one.

This is not to suggest, however, that there has been a wholesale shift in personnel from the more 'private' party world of the central offices to the more 'public' party world of the parliaments. On the contrary, while the ratio of parliamentary party staff to central office has increased with time, and while the parliamentary bias is therefore certainly being accentuated, it is nevertheless still only in a minority of countries (Denmark, Germany, Ireland, the Netherlands, and the US) that the overall numbers employed in the parties' parliamentary offices now exceed those employed in the central offices. That said, it must also be emphasized that even central office growth may itself be partially explained by the greater availability of state resources, in that a majority of countries now offer direct (and sometimes indirect) public subventions for party central offices, a system which was introduced either at the same time (Finland, Sweden) or slightly later (Austria, Belgium, Denmark, Germany, Norway) than that for parliamentary party offices. Moreover, the parties can also benefit in staff terms from the generous provisions which are often made available to parties in government, allowing them to appoint partisan advisers and consultants to (temporary) senior positions in the public bureaucracy. In general, therefore, much of the organizational capacity available to the parties in staffing terms can be traced to resources which are increasingly provided, either directly or indirectly, by the state.

Third, and following from this, the state is also increasingly important to the parties in sheer financial terms. In Austria and Denmark, for example, *total* state funding for the parties at the national level more or less matches the amounts which they generate from all other sources of income taken together, while in Finland, Norway, and Sweden, the total state subsidies received by the parties significantly exceed their total recorded incomes from other sources. In Ireland, where state subsidies officially do not exist (except for the so-called *Oireachtas* Grant), the total sums received by the parties from the state in 1989 actually amounted to almost half as much again as that received as a result of their own fund-raising efforts. In the German case, once the subsidies for the various party foundations are included, state subsidies account for a sum which is more than ten times greater than that accounted for by other sources. Indeed, it is only in the Netherlands, the UK, and the US that 'private' sources of party funds (membership fees, members' donations, and so on) still constitute a larger source of revenue than that which comes from the public purse.

Fourth, much of the character of contemporary party organization and party activity is increasingly shaped by state regulations, many of which were adopted in the wake of the granting of state subventions. As Poguntke (1994*a*) emphasizes, the German case is perhaps the paradigmatic case of state regulation of party life, especially since the promulgation of the Party Law in 1967, and the regulation of a variety of principles of intra-party democracy. In Sweden, as Pierre and Widfeldt (1994) argue, the process of organizational convergence which has occurred since the 1970s owes much to the new rules regarding state subventions, while the advent of what Koole (1994) refers to as 'a parliamentary party complex' in the Netherlands also followed from the introduction to state subsidies, which in this case were directed to the parties in parliament. In Norway, long-standing laws which offer state financial support for nomination meetings which are conducted in a particular way have encouraged the parties to adopt a uniform procedure of candidate selection (Svåsand, 1994). In Austria, the constitutional principle of the 'free mandate' effectively prevents any formal attempt to bring the party in public office under the control of the extra-parliamentary party (Müller, 1994). More broadly, the very structure of party organizations is determined at least in part by the structure of the state itself, even to the extent that changes in the number of party basic units (or branches) is sometimes simply a response to a process of municipal reform (as, for example, in Belgium and the Netherlands).

Finally, it also seems to be the case that parties in public office have been increasingly willing to take advantage of public resources in order to reward their supporters. While the evidence here is necessarily sketchy and sometimes nebulous, there is nevertheless a degree of consistency which suggests that party patronage, exercised through the state, is becoming an increasingly prevalent (or at least noticeable) phenomenon. The most obvious illustration is provided by the Italian case, and the widespread party corruption which was uncovered by the *mani pulite* investigations. Other, less compelling evidence of patronage has been cited in the cases of Austria, Germany, Finland, and Belgium; in Ireland, questions have been raised in connection with the government favours to the beef industry, while in Britain concern has been expressed about the partisan nature of the appointments policy of the Conservative government on the one hand, and about the links between the Conservatives and private financiers on the other. In all of these cases, it would seem, support for and/or membership of a party may possibly be translated into the receipt of public honour or publicly funded benefits. At the same time, however, from the perspective of the parties themselves, this is also clearly a risky and potentially costly strategy, which can well provoke an anti-party backlash. The Italian evidence is unequivocal in this regard, as is the evidence of increasing popular disenchantment with the style of the traditional parties, and their *Parteibücher*, in Austria.

The potential exploitation of state resources for patronage purposes also highlights a more general problem with the wider conception of state aid for parties. To be sure, as the above points indicate, the state plays an important role in party survival, and increasingly so. None the less, the fact that parties now place greater reliance on state-regulated channels of communications; that they increasingly staff their organizations on the basis of facilities offered through public office; that state subventions constitute an ever-growing proportion of party income; that party life is increasingly regulated by state laws; and that state patronage may offer an expanding source of selective benefits for party supporters, should not simply be taken to imply that parties have suddenly discovered some sort of external drip-feed from which their otherwise ailing organizations can draw more and more nourishment. In other words, these various developments should not be interpreted simply in terms in which 'the state' itself would be seen as an exogenous factor influencing party life. On the contrary, regardless of whether we are dealing with state regulations, or party laws, or levels of state subventions, we are always dealing with decisions which have been taken by the parliament, and by the political class, and therefore by the parties themselves. Thus, while any one party may regard this regulatory context as an exogenous factor to which it must adapt, it is the parties as a whole, or at least as a majority, which have usually devised and determined the character of these regulations. In this sense, rather than thinking in terms of 'the state' helping the parties, it is perhaps more useful to think of it being the parties which are helping themselves, in that, in working to ensure their own survival, they are regulating themselves, paying themselves, and offering resources to themselves, albeit in the name of the state.

CHANGING PARTIES

Whatever is happening to the party on the ground, therefore, there is little to suggest any sense of decline of the party in public office, and hence there is also little to suggest any sense of party decline *tout court*. What we see instead are *changing* parties, in which the balance between the different faces is shifting, and in which, perhaps, they are also becoming more autonomous from one another. This shift towards an emphasis on the party in public office and its autonomy is also encouraged by systemic features, such as the need to negotiate delicate coalition arrangements in countries such as Belgium (Deschouwer, 1994) and, increasingly so, Sweden (Pierre and Widfeldt, 1994). At the same time, however, this shift in the balance of internal party resources also begs two important questions: First, how does this affect the position of the third face of party organization, the party in central office? Second, where does this leave the membership?

The party in central office

The party in central office was crucial to the conception of the mass party, in that it was seen as the voice or guardian of the party on the ground, and as the means by which the party in public office could be held accountable to the mass membership (see Katz and Mair, 1993). More recently, however, although the evidence is difficult to interpret unequivocally, it would appear that both of these features may be eroding. In the first place, there are quite a number of parties which now reveal an increasing tendency for membership of the central office organs, and particularly the various national executive bodies, to be made up by representatives and/or ex-officio members of the party in public office rather than by representatives of the party on the ground. These include many liberal parties (e.g. in Austria, Belgium, Denmark, and Germany), as well as social democratic parties (e.g. the Irish Labour party) and conservative parties (e.g. the Norwegian Høyre). The evidence here is far from consistent in that the statutes of other parties continue to include strict limits on the number of public office-holders who can become members of party executive bodies; limits which, in certain cases (e.g. the Dutch PvdA, the Danish Socialist People's Party, and the Finnish National Coalition) have actually become stricter over time. In other cases, of course, such limits have been eased, and for many parties there are no such formal restrictions at all. Even then, however, it is often difficult to assess changes in the actual extent and influence of public office representation in internal executive organs. Indeed in Belgium, for example, as Deschouwer (1994) suggests, the inclusion of representatives of the party in public office on the parties' national executives need not be interpreted as a sign of the increasing influence of MPs, but rather as a means by which the party in central office maintains control over its public representatives.

Second, there is evidence to suggest that much of the more important work of the party in central office is increasingly being carried out by professionals and consultants, rather than by traditional party bureaucrats or even party activists. The 'accountability' of such staff would seem to matter less than their expertise, and therefore any attempt to assess the workings of such a professional central office in terms of how well it represents the views of the party on the ground (or even the party in public office) may well be misplaced. In this case also, it is the question of increasing central office autonomy which appears to be the most relevant. That said, this new professionalism certainly appears to indicate a shift from a situation in which much of the activities of central office were directed towards the organization and maintenance of the party on the ground (a key concern in the mass party) towards one in which they are now increasingly directed towards the mobilization of support in the electorate at large (as in Panebianco's electoral-professional party). Moreover, once this shift takes place, it is clear that central office will necessarily orient itself more towards the views and demands of the party leadership and the party in public office than to those of the party on the ground.

In one scenario, therefore, the party in central office becomes simply more autonomous; in a second scenario, it becomes more subject to the control of the party in public office; in yet another scenario, as its resources become transferred across to the offices of the party in parliament, it is simply marginalized. Only rarely, it seems, is there evidence of a reaffirmation or a strengthening of its traditional position as representative or guardian of the party on the ground.

The paradoxical role of party membership

The second question, as to where all of this leaves the membership party, or the party on the ground, is more complex. On the face of it, a strengthening of the position and of the resources of the party in public office, and the marginalization of or greater autonomy afforded to the party in central office, would appear to offer little scope for an enhancement of the position of the party on the ground. In this sense, we might anticipate that party members would themselves be marginalized, being deemed unnecessary, or even ignored (see Katz, 1990; for an alternative view, see Scarrow, 1994a). In practice, however, despite the relative decline in membership levels in most countries (see Table 6.1), the evidence does suggest that many parties still consider membership to be of value.

In the first place, despite the widespread introduction of state subventions, membership fees and donations still constitute an important source of revenue for many parties, and, as Koole (1994) emphasizes in the case of the Netherlands, this is particularly true for what might be defined as the 'modern cadre party'. Even beyond the Netherlands, however, where state subventions remain relatively limited, members also contribute quite substantially to party incomes. In Austria, for example, the most recent figures suggest that membership fees account for an average of some 27 per cent of the head office income of the SPÖ and ÖVP; in Denmark, income from members and branches accounts for an average of almost 45 per cent of the head office income of the SD, RV, SF, and KRF; in Germany, the average for the SPD and CDU is almost 20 per cent, while in Ireland, in the case of Fine Gael, income from members, branches, and constituencies accounts for a very high 80 per cent of income. Thus, even though membership fees may often no longer constitute the main source of party revenue, they nevertheless remain important, and the loss of this income would almost certainly weaken the parties. For this reason alone, membership appears to remain an asset. Indeed, when discussing the balance between income generated from the membership and that generated via public subsidies, it is particularly interesting to note the case of Germany, where some of the reforms of public financing which are currently being discussed include provisions which would base the level of subsidy partly on the size of the party's membership, thus offering parties an additional incentive to boost their position on the ground. That said, in cases such as Norway and Sweden, where state subventions are among the highest in Europe, and where parties such as the DNA (in Norway) and the Social Democrats and Moderates (in Sweden) derive only some 10 per cent of their head office income from their members, the costs of maintaining the membership organization may well exceed the revenue which it generates.

Second, as Sundberg (1994) emphasizes at length in his discussion of the Finnish case, and as Müller (1994) points out in the Austrian case, members are also of value to the parties simply as warm bodies which can occupy official positions inside the party itself as well as in public positions. In the Finnish case, for example, it is estimated that more than 55,000 persons are required by the parties to serve on internal party boards; that more than 60,000 persons are required to stand as party candidates in municipal elections; that more than 31,000 candidates are required to stand for parish council elections; and that upwards of 300,000 persons occupy 'positions of trust' in the local administration, including positions on the various boards and councils. To be sure, Finnish democracy, which is an increasingly organized democracy, may be an extreme case in this regard. None the less, even at a more muted level, this syndrome may be regarded as having a wider validity, and as requiring parties to maintain a membership simply in order to influence public decision-making. Sundberg's conclusion is certainly generalizable beyond Finland: the more a party wishes to influence what goes on in society, and on the ground, the more it will need a mass membership. Warm bodies are important, and are not really substitutable.

Third, members can still prove important for organizational and political purposes. As Pierre and Widfeldt (1994) underline in the Swedish case, for example, the parties continue to rely on their membership levels to maintain at least the *image* of a mass party, and as proof that they are seen as viable channels for political representation. Members in this sense are also legitimizers, and it is such a perspective which clearly helps to explain the thinking behind the proposed reforms in the public financing of the German parties. In a related way, members are also useful in that they may help to mobilize voters. This function is, to be sure, less important than was once the case, in that parties now have at their disposal alternative techniques and networks of communication which can prove at least as effective as anything which is done by the membership. As Müller (1994) notes in the case of the Austrian SPÖ, for example, the leadership has appeared to grow increasingly sceptical about the value of the party organization as a means of communicating to the electorate as a whole. On the other hand, however, there is also the case of the Norwegian Conservatives, who have only recently begun to stress the benefits of membership as a means of electoral mobilization, an argument which is also sustained by Seyd and Whiteley's (1992) comprehensive analysis of British Labour party membership. Either way, whether as legitimizers or as active campaigners, membership can continue to constitute an important resource in the process of inter-party competition, and hence it comes as no surprise to see that a number of parties, as in Britain and Ireland, still emphasize the need for membership drives. For all of these reasons, then, it does not seem likely that parties will willingly shed their members or discourage them from involvement in intra-party decision-making. Members might sometimes prove a nuisance, but they can also bring tangible as well as intangible benefits.

Moreover, as noted above, it also seems that many parties are attempting to give their members more say rather than less, and that they are empowering rather than marginalizing them. Many parties now afford their ordinary members a greater voice in candidate selection than was once the case; in addition, more and more parties now seem willing to allow the ordinary members a voice in the selection of party leaders. The somewhat curious pattern that is developing therefore seems to be one in which the party in public office is afforded more power or more autonomy; in which the party in central office is becoming more professionalized; and in which, at the same time, through enhanced democratization, the ordinary members themselves, albeit sometimes fewer in number, are being afforded a greater role. This pattern would certainly seem to characterize the changes in a variety of parties in countries such as Austria, Denmark, Germany, Ireland, and the Netherlands.

At the same time, however, this pattern is also ostensibly paradoxical, in that it suggests that *both* the party on the ground and the party in public office are growing in importance. Conventional wisdom, on the other hand, would suggest more of a see-saw effect, in which the growth in importance of one necessarily involves a decline in the importance of the other. So how are we to understand this apparent paradox? How can parties democratize while at the same time affording more autonomy and power to the party in public office? How can they pursue these two apparently contradictory paths at one and the same time?

One possible answer is that the parties are actually making a careful and conscious distinction between different elements within the party on the ground, in the sense that the process of intra-party democratization is being extended to the members as individuals rather than to what might be called the *organized* party on the ground. In other words, it is not the party congress or the middle-level élite, or the activists who are being empowered, but rather the 'ordinary' members, who are at once more docile and more likely to endorse the policies (and candidates) proposed by the party leadership and by the party in public office. This is, in fact, one of the most commonly distinct trends we see today: ordinary members, often at home, and via postal ballots, are increasingly being consulted by the party leadership, and are increasingly involved in legitimizing the choices of the party in public office, a process which is facilitated by the increasing use of centralized registers of party members. The more organized membership party, on the other hand, be it represented in congress or even in central office, as in the case of the Austrian parties and the Dutch denominational parties, for example, tends to become less relevant. Thus it is not a question of a simple see-saw, in which the gains of the party in public office must be compensated for by the losses of the party on the ground, or vice versa; rather, both can ostensibly become more important, while the activist layer inside the party, the traditionally more troublesome layer, becomes marginalized. Nor is this necessarily a problem for the party leadership, for, in contrast to the activists, these ordinary and often disaggregated members are not very likely to mount a serious challenge against the positions adopted by the leadership (see, for example, Zielonka-Goei, 1992). It is of course difficult to pin down precise figures on this. Moreover, as can be seen in the evidence of membership pressures on the leadership in the Finnish and Swedish cases (Sundberg, 1994; Pierre and Widfeldt, 1994), it is certainly not a univeral phenomenon, and even the more passive members may well prove willing to challenge their leaders on issues such as membership rights. None the less, as the British Labour party would certainly appear to believe, it may well be the case that a fully democratized party is more susceptible to control by the party in public office than is a party in which the ordinary member (but not the activist) is effectively marginalized (Webb, 1994).

In a related vein, it might also be argued that the process of intraparty democratization is often meaningless and/or illusory. Thus, for example, while ordinary members may be given the right to vote in the leadership selection process, they are nevertheless often offered only a limited or constrained choice. The Dutch D66 now includes with its postal ballot on candidate selection an advisory list with an ordering proposed by the national committee of the party (Koole, 1994). Ordinary members in the British and Irish Labour parties now have a direct vote in choosing between the competing candidates for party leader, but the initial nomination of candidates remains the preserve of the party in public office, and the candidates themselves can be drawn only from within the ranks of the parliamentary parties (Webb, 1994; Farrell, 1994). In Belgium, despite the introduction of direct elections by the PSC, the PRL, and the new VLD, and despite an increase in the number of 'real' leadership elections, the party executive bodies still continue to have the strongest effective decision-making voice (Deschouwer, 1994). In Denmark also, the election of party chairman is usually more managed than open (Bille, 1994). Moreover, at other levels within the parties, the opening up of the candidate selection process to a greater membership role, or even to a wider electoral involvement, as in the case of the occasional new 'primaries', for example, can nevertheless still be accompanied, as is the case in Austria (Müller, 1994), by the effective imposition of strong controls and strong discipline on those candidates who manage to become members of the parliamentary party. Democratization on paper may therefore actually coexist with powerful élite influence in practice.

Finally, as indicated above, the whole question of which face of the party is becoming more powerful and which less powerful may itself be misleading, in that we may actually be witnessing a process of mutual and growing autonomy. In the classic mass party model, the relationship between the different faces was essentially hierarchic, with the party on the ground delegating power to the party congress and thence to the party executive, and with both congress and executive scrutinizing and controlling the activities of the party in public office. Even in the catch-all model, the relationship was hierarchic, albeit in reverse flow, with the party in public office emerging to dominate the party in central office and the party congress, and, in so doing, effectively marginalizing the party on the ground. But while no clear single 'model' of party is apparent from the analyses cited above, there is nevertheless a quite widespread consensus that the relevant relationships are now more *stratarchic* than hierarchic, and that each face of the party is now increasingly autonomous in relation to the others. Thus, for example, while local input into the national party in a more hierarchic model was focused on the party congress and, through that, on the party central office, it now seems increasingly focused on the selection of local candidates who, in turn, will eventually constitute the party in public office and will devise their own autonomous codes of discipline and behaviour. Of course, it may also be the case that mutual autonomy will develop to a degree in which the local party will become essentially unconcerned about any real input into the national party (and vice versa), and will devote itself primarily to politics at the local level.

All of this might suggest that the European parties are drifting towards what might be termed an 'American' model of party, which, as depicted by Katz and Kolodny (1994), is almost wholly decentralized and candidate-centred. This would clearly be misleading; for, despite the arguments about the apparent decline in the 'partyness' of European society, there has certainly been no decline in the 'partyness' of the European state (see also Chapter 1 above). On the contrary: given the extent, indeed the increasing extent, to which parties organize the affairs of state and public decision-making in the European polities, they can in no sense be regarded, like their American counterparts, as 'empty vessels'. American parties matter as governing organizations, but within very severe limits. In Europe, by contrast, where modern government continues to be party government, and where modern democracy continues to be party democracy, the party vessels are far from empty.

PARTIES AND THEIR PRIVILEGES

When the nobles had real power as well as privileges, when they governed and administered, their rights could be at once greater and less open to attack . . . True, the nobles enjoyed invidious privileges and rights that weighed heavily on the commoner, but in return for this they kept order, administered justice, saw to the execution of laws, came to the rescue of the oppressed, and watched over the interests of all. The more these functions passed out of the hands of the nobility, the more uncalled-for did their privileges appear—until at last their mere existence seemed a meaningless anachronism. (Tocqueville, 1966: 60)

From an organizational perspective, at least, it is clear that a conception of party *change* or *adaptation* is much more appropriate than the rather misleading conception of party decline. Parties are in fact changing in two important respects. In the first place, party structures are tending to become increasingly stratarchic in character, with the party on the ground, the party in public office, and possibly even the party in central office each stressing its own freedom of manoeuvre. In this sense, and significantly so, we can also witness the erosion of a sense of linkage even inside party itself. Second, parties, and especially the face of the party in public office, are becoming increasingly state-oriented, and are correspondingly less firmly tied to civil society, a process which is particularly evident in terms of the resources which are used by the parties in order to ensure their own survival and legitimacy. Indeed, as suggested above, this increased dependence of parties on the state can also be interpreted as the increased dependence of parties on themselves, since it is the parties themselves which, to all intents and purposes, are the state, or at least, are those who devise the rules and regulations promulgated by the state, and who inevitably privilege their own position.

The outcome of both of these processes, at least in the short term, is therefore a greater sense of party *self-sufficiency*, especially at leadership level. To be sure, parties still need their voters. In many cases, as we have seen, they also still need their members. Increasingly, however, as the different faces of party become more autonomous of one another, and as the party leaderships increasingly turn towards the state for their resources, the relevance of linkages which are based on trust, accountability, and above all, representation, tends to become eroded, both inside and outside the parties. Thus while the parties may become more privileged, they also become more remote, and it is this particular combination of developments that may well have provided the basis for the increasingly widespread anti-party sentiment which now characterizes mass politics in western democracies. On the ground, and in terms of their representative role, parties appear to be less relevant and to be losing some of their key functions. In public office, on the other hand, and in terms of their linkage to the state, they appear to be more privileged than ever. Indeed, if we think of some of the classic functions of party (e.g. King, 1969: 111–41), then it might be concluded that while some of these functions have been undermined (such as the articulation of interests and the aggregation of demands, and perhaps also the formulation of public policy), other functions have acquired an increased importance and visibility (such as the recruitment of political leaders and, above all, the organization of government).

But this does not necessarily reflect a shift towards a new balance or a new equilibrium; on the contrary, it suggests that there may be an absence of balance and an absence of equilibrium, which, in an extreme case, might well act to undermine the legitimacy of party government itself. To put it another way, what can be seen here, albeit in a very embryonic and often muted form, may be precisely the same imbalance between popular irrelevance and public privilege that was famously cited by Tocqueville as contributing to the downfall of the nobility of the French *ancien régime*, and which is quoted at the beginning of this section. On the one hand, the parties as public office-holders, like Tocqueville's nobles, are clearly privileged—indeed, with time, they tend to have become even more privileged. On the other hand, as was suggested earlier, they now appear to lack real representative weight or purpose, and this too has become more evident with time. In other words, their status has increased while their popular relevance has tended to become eroded.

This is not to suggest, however, that contemporary parties, like Tocqueville's nobles, now risk becoming 'meaningless anachronisms'. On the contrary: given the importance of parties in terms of the recruitment of leaders and the organization of government, it is almost impossible to conceive of a parliamentary polity which can really evade the principle of party. Nevertheless, the problem clearly exists, for whatever the importance of party as an organizing principle in government and in the state, Tocqueville was clearly correct in pointing to the dangers involved in combining (enhanced) *public* privilege on the one hand with declining *popular* purpose or relevance on the other.

It is this particular combination which, I feel, lies at the root of the feelings of popular political distrust which were cited earlier in this chapter. This is also probably one of the most important factors lying behind the emergence, albeit not always on a major scale, of anti-party sentiment and anti-party parties (for some recent discussions, see Ignazi, 1992, 1994; Betz, 1994; Poguntke, 1994*b*, and Scarrow, 1994*b*), with the evidence of public privilege helping to translate potential indifference into potential resentment and hence into even greater vulnerability. The disenchantment with parties and even the resentment against parties should therefore not simply be read as a symptom of party decline *tout court*; indeed, were parties to be wholly in decline, as public office-holders as well as representative agencies, then the sense of discontent might well evaporate. Rather, the problem appears to lie in a set of contradictory developments, in which parties are at once less able but more visible, and at once less relevant but more privileged.

PART IV

Party Systems and Structures of Competition

7

Electoral Markets and Stable States

This chapter begins with three clarifications. First, the markets to which it refers are electoral markets and, within these markets, the pattern of competition with which it is concerned is inter-party competition. As is evident, parties will compete with one another when they have a market in which to compete, that is, when there are voters in competition; and the assumption which underlies this paper, albeit guardedly so, is that the actual extent of inter-party competition, and the competitiveness of parties, is at least in part a function of the relative size of the electoral market. As the market expands, therefore, or as the number of voters in competition increases, parties are likely to become more competitive. As the market contracts, on the other hand, and as the number of voters in competition declines, parties are likely to become less competitive.

This assumption is a guarded one, however, and two qualifications are immediately necessary. The first of these is that it cannot be assumed that the competitiveness of parties is entirely a function of the size of the electoral market. In a perfectly balanced two-party system, for example, in which there are very few voters in competition, but where the shift of just one vote can make the difference between being a majority and being a minority, or between victory and defeat, each of the two parties is likely to prove extremely competitive. Hence intense competition can ensue even in situations of very restricted electoral availability. In contemporary Sweden, for example, the balance between the socialist and non-socialist blocs is so finely drawn that even the relatively small Swedish electoral market can sustain quite pronounced electoral competition.

The second qualification is that it cannot be assumed that competition is inevitable in situations of large-scale electoral markets. In certain circumstances, while large numbers of voters may be in competition, there may be few if any other rewards associated with gains in electoral support, and hence the parties may not expend much effort in trying to win over the voters who are available. In Switzerland, for example, the unique formula whereby all four major parties permanently share government office means that there is little point in their competing with one another for extra votes. Hence, even if the Swiss electoral market were to expand significantly, it is unlikely that party competition would become more intense.

In other words, it is not just the sheer size of the electoral market and the extent of electoral availability which are relevant, but also the degree to which competition itself matters. That said, the emphasis must be on qualifying the initial assumption rather than on its wholesale rejection, for, other things being equal, parties are likely to be more competitive when there are more voters in competition and when the electoral market is more open or available. The existence of an electoral market may therefore be seen as a necessary if not a sufficient condition for there being party competition, in much the same way as D'Alimonte (1989) has argued that democracy itself is a necessary but not sufficient condition for there being competition more generally.

The second clarification is that when parties initially confront an electoral market they have a choice of two not necessarily exclusive strategies. In the first place, they can attempt to restrict or narrow that market and thus engage in primarily defensive electoral strategies, mobilizing existing adherents rather than attempting to win new supporters. Second, they may choose simply to compete on the market and so engage in primarily expansive electoral strategies, constantly searching for new voters and placing relatively little emphasis on the mobilization of existing loyalists. To the extent that the former option prevails, the market will progressively contract, and competition itself will be subdued. In the latter situation, on the other hand, the market is likely to remain quite open and competition will be intense.

That said, it must also be recognized that it is only in exceptional circumstances that parties in a given political system will confront a single electoral market. When competition (or the absence of competition) takes place in a multi-dimensional environment, parties may confront a plurality of markets, each of which may be more or less open, and in each of which they may develop defensive or expansive strategies (Sani and Sartori, 1983; Koole and van Praag, 1990). A religious party, for example, may find that a defensive strategy is appropriate in the electoral market which exists along the religious/secular divide, yet it may opt for an expansive strategy in the market which exists along the left/right divide. Thus while one market or sub-market may become quite narrow and closed, another market within the same system may remain quite open. In Belgium, for example, a relatively open market in left–right terms coincides with a remarkably closed market in linguistic terms. In Northern Ireland, there are few if any voters in competition in terms of the primary conflict between unionism and nationalism, yet electoral availability is pronounced and competition intense inside each of the unionist and nationalist blocs.

The third clarification is that the size of the markets in general, and the degree of electoral availability, is largely a function of the strength and pervasiveness of relevant collective political identities (Bartolini and Mair, 1990). Such collective identities may be ascriptive, and may often predate the emergence of political parties as such, as is the case with linguistic, cultural, ethnic, or even gender identities and, to a lesser extent, with religious identities. In other cases, these collective identities may be based on status derived from occupational or class distinctions, or whatever. In some circumstances, of course, while such identities exist, they may not be politically relevant (Sartori, 1969) and hence their impact on electoral markets may be at best indirect. In the Irish Republic, for example, while class identity is quite pronounced, class does not provide a major focus for electoral alignments. In Britain, on the other hand, class is really the only substantial collective identity which is relevant to politics, with religious and ethnic/sub-national identities playing just a marginal role. Whatever about distinctions in terms of the substance and character of collective identities, however, it can be argued that the degree to which individual voters are integrated into a set of relevant collective political identities will help to determine the extent to which an electoral market exists. Where such identities are pervasive and/or pronounced, as has traditionally been the case in Austria, for example, the market for votes will be sharply restricted; where such identities are either weak or marginal, as in the United States, the market will be relatively open.

DEVELOPMENTS AND CONTRASTS IN WESTERN EUROPE

At the risk of some exaggeration, and at the cost of immense generalization, the history of the development of political parties in western Europe can be read as a history of attempts to narrow the electoral market through the promotion and inculcation of mass political identities. This process was most clearly visible in the rise of the mass integration parties in the late nineteenth and early twentieth century, during the lead-up to and in the immediate wake of the extension of voting rights to the working class and the property-less. These parties, with their dense organizational networks, contrasted sharply with the more élitist, electorally oriented, 'cadre' parties, or parties of individual representation, which had tended to dominate politics in the period prior to mass democracy (see also Chapter 5 above). It was the new workers' parties in particular which offered the most striking examples of the new political strategy. Neumann (1956: 404–5; see also Duverger, 1954; Kirchheimer, 1966) has identified the contrast quite succinctly, and, while not expressed in these terms, his remarks also have a clear bearing on the different notions of party competition and electoral markets:

The first example of such a new party was presented by the continental Socialists. Their organization has been jokingly characterized as extending from the cradle to the grave, from the workers' infant-care association to the atheists' cremation society; yet such a description articulates the intrinsic difference from the liberal party of representation, with its principle of 'free recruitment' among a socially uncommitted, free-floating electorate . . . The [new] party can count on its adherents; it has taken over a good part of their social existence.

That the new denominational mass parties of integration did not offer such a striking example as that provided by the class mass parties was hardly surprising. The religious parties, whether Catholic or Protestant, had less need to develop new autonomous organizational networks, since they could feed off the existing Church organizations and the already strongly defined sense of religious identity. In the case of the workers' parties, however, the constituency which they were seeking to represent was itself a relatively new one, and it was only in certain cases, as in Britain for example, that the new parties were in a position to feed off a pre-existing, trade-union-based organizational network.

Through mobilization, integration, and, in Kirchheimer's (1966: 184) terms, through 'the intellectual and moral *encadrement* of the masses,' the new mass integration parties therefore helped to build up and consolidate a set of collective political identities which, in turn, acted to reduce electoral availability. The result, most crucially, was a 'narrowing of the support market' and a 'freezing' of party systems in western Europe (Lipset and Rokkan, 1967: 50–1). To be sure, this freezing process was neither pervasive throughout Europe nor even throughout individual national electorates *tout court*. Organizational networks and the establishment of enduring partisan identities always remained poorly developed in France (Bartolini, 1981), for example, and the result has been that the electoral market as a whole has remained remarkably open, with elections in France being characterized by particularly pronounced levels of electoral volatility. In yet other cases, such as the Republic of Ireland, for example, the process was very uneven, with strong identities being established on the 'strong nationalist' side of the major political divide, and with weak or non-existent identities developing on the 'weak nationalist' side (Mair, 1987*a*: 86–9). The result here is that, while there has been a relatively restricted electoral market in terms of the competition between Fianna Fáil and all other parties, the electoral market among these other parties themselves has always remained quite open.

In short, electoral markets are more restricted in certain countries than in others, and, even within individual countries, certain sub-markets are more restricted than others. Moreover, since the relative degree of restriction depends, at least in part, on the depth and pervasiveness of collective political identities, and since the degree to which parties are competitive depends, also at least in part, on the openness of the electoral market, it then follows that competitiveness itself can be associated with the degree to which the polity is characterized by the presence or absence of strong collective identities. Other things being equal, polities which are characterized by the presence of strong identities are therefore likely to be less competitive than those in which such strong identities are absent. More precisely, polities which are so characterized will tend to be more consensual—at least in certain circumstances, and most obviously when no single group enjoys a clear overall majority.

ELECTORAL MARKETS AND CONSOCIATIONAL DEMOCRACY

This is not a startling conclusion. Indeed, it reflects the logic which lies behind the very notion of consociational democracy (Lijphart, 1968, 1977), whereby strongly segmented societies (i.e. those characterized by very deeply held and mutually exclusive identities, based largely on language or religion) are seen to develop a stable democratic order by means of élite accommodation and a rejection of competitive behaviour; were such segmented societies to be characterized by competitive behaviour, on the other hand, it is argued that this could result in either the collapse of the polity itself or the adoption of non-democratic means of control.

But while a variety of factors have been seen as being conducive towards the development of consociational or accommodationist solutions in segmented societies—the society should be strongly segmented, and characterized by substantial élite authority; there should be a multiple balance of power between the different segments; the country concerned should be small; there should be at least some degree of overarching loyalty to the system in question; and there should already be a tradition of élite accommodation (see Daalder, 1974; Lijphart, 1977: chapter 3)—surprisingly little emphasis has been placed on what is the major theme of this present chapter, and that is the particular influence exerted by the size of the electoral market itself. Indeed, by taking this particular factor on board, and by recognizing that the 'bondedness' of the electorate may discourage competition and leave parties and élites with little choice but to accommodate to one another, we can then make much more sense of the reasons why élites should prove so 'willing' to abandon competitive strategies.

This has been one of the main elements addressed by Pappalardo (1981) in his extensive criticisms of the consociational theorists, in which he argues that much of the discussion of the preconditions of consociational democracy has mistakenly implied an immense voluntarism on the part of the accommodating élites, thus also implying that these same élites might equally have 'chosen' to be competitive. If, on the other hand, we accept, as Pappalardo does (1981: 367–75), that the restrictions in the electoral market more or less 'oblige' élites to forgo an expansive competitive strategy—the pervasiveness of identities is such that there are few voters in competition and hence few rewards to be gained as a result of electoral competition—then it is not simply a matter of élite choice or élite willingness. Rather, élites and parties accommodate one another because they don't really have any other option. Competition, in effect, is pointless: 'consociational democracy is not so much a pact among minorities in equilibrium or minorities *tout court*, as a pact among minorities who do not want and *are not in a position* to change the existing distribution of power' (Pappalardo, 1981: 369, emphasis added).

Evidence of the existence of relatively restricted electoral markets in the classic consociational democracies in western Europe certainly supports the notion that there would have been few rewards in competition, and that none of the minorities would have been in a position to change the existing balance of power. In the interwar period, for example, at a time when Belgium, the Netherlands, and Switzerland could be regarded as the paradigmatic cases of consociationalism, their mean level of electoral volatility (at 8.4) was just two-thirds of that which prevailed in the non-consociational democracies of western Europe (12.0).[1] Moreover, if we rank-order the thirteen principal west European democracies in the interwar years in terms of their mean levels of volatility, we find that Switzerland, the Netherlands, and Belgium occupy the ninth, tenth, and eleventh positions respectively, with lower levels of volatility being recorded only in Finland and Denmark.

A similar pattern prevails during the first postwar decades, from 1945 to 1965, when the consociational practices also remained robust, and when Austria could be included as a fourth paradigmatic case. During this period the mean level of electoral volatility in the four consociational countries was 5.8, as against a mean level of 8.9 in the remaining non-consociational countries. In terms of the rank-order of countries, however, Belgium figures quite high on the list, coming in fifth position, with Austria in seventh, the Netherlands in eighth, and with Switzerland recording the lowest level of any country. Nevertheless, the overall pattern in both periods is undeniable. The three and later four consociational democracies are characterized by relatively restricted electoral

[1] Mean electoral volatility offers a useful index of the aggregate electoral change from one election to the next, and hence also offers a useful summary indicator of the potential openness of the electoral market. The figures cited in this chapter are drawn from Bartolini and Mair (1990).

markets, and hence discouraged expansive competitive strategies. Here, indeed, the élites appeared to have little option but to cooperate with one another.

To be sure, other, less palatable possibilities might be said to have existed. In Northern Ireland, for example, during the period of the Stormont regime, electoral volatility was also particularly low, the electoral market proved remarkably closed, and little competition ensued. Between 1918 and 1970, for example, almost 40 per cent of parliamentary seats in Northern Ireland remained uncontested (McAllister, 1977: 16), with fewer than 20 per cent of seats being characterized by a direct nationalist versus unionist contest. This was a non-competitive system *par excellence*, in which, as is well known, the response of the dominant unionist élite fell considerably short of accommodationism. Indeed, and unlike the consociational democracies, the absence of competition in Northern Ireland led to exclusion and effective majority tyranny, which eventually brought about the collapse of the regime. But it is here that the other preconditions of consociationalism come into play, for, unlike Northern Ireland, the consociational democracies were *also* characterized by a multiple balance of power, with no one segment enjoying anything approaching the overwhelming majority status of the Northern Irish unionists. Moreover, there also existed an overarching commitment to system maintenance in the consociational democracies, a characteristic which, quite evidently, has always been lacking in Ulster.

SMALL STATES AND LARGE STATES

It is not just the consociational democracies which are relevant here. The logic goes further than this. In principle, what marks the consociational democracies off from the other west European polities is not the existence of restricted electoral markets as such. Nor is it even the fact that this restriction derives from the pervasiveness of strong, collective, and politically relevant identities. Rather, what makes these systems different is that their segmentation results from their being *plural societies*, with the segments or pillars being primarily defined by linguistic or religious divisions. Elsewhere in western Europe, as Almond (1956) originally emphasized and as Lijphart (1968) also appeared to accept, democratic stability, whether accommodationist or not, was associated with the existence of non-plural (or homogeneous) political cultures which, by definition, could not be regarded as segmented. The logic of conso-ciationalism could not be seen to apply to any of these other sys-tems. Hence, most crucially, any accommodationist behaviour, and any practices which more or less approximated to consociational-ism which might be observed in these homogeneous political cultures would have to be explained by *other* factors.

This is precisely the task which Katzenstein (1985) sets for him-self in his justly renowned *Small States in World Markets*. For, in analyzing patterns of industrial policy in western Europe, he finds that small states *in general*, and not just the consociational demo-cracies/plural societies, tend to develop a policy style which is quite distinctive from that developed in the larger states, and which is characterized by accommodation, compromise, and cooperation between different élites and different parties. But while the degree of segmentation and the traditions of consociationalism might prove adequate to account for this pattern in Belgium, the Netherlands, Switzerland, and even Austria, they are clearly inap-propriate in any explanation of the similar patterns which are found in the more homogeneous smaller democracies such as Denmark, Norway, and Sweden.

Hence Katzenstein's search for an alternative, or at least an addi-tional explanation, and hence his primary emphasis on the fact that these small states are particularly vulnerable to the vagaries of the international economy. It is this vulnerability, he argues, and the need to ensure economic survival in a potentially hostile trading environment, which forces these smaller states to adopt a consen-sual rather than an adversarial style of policy-making. The argu-ment is a reasonably convincing one, and Katzenstein builds a strong and largely plausible case in favour of the notion that the openness of a national economy may have an important impact on patterns of domestic politics. Moreover, it is an argument which does not rest exclusively on this single variable, but which also incorporates an appreciation of the influence of certain institutional characteristics (such as proportional electoral formulae), as well as that of the particular patterns of political fragmentation in these homogeneous small states (such as the existence of a weak and divided right).

That said, I would suggest that Katzenstein has actually neglected one other element which is of equally fundamental importance, and that is that the consensual patterns in these other small states derive almost as much from the character of their electoral markets as do the accommodationist patterns in the traditional consociational democracies. In other words, I would suggest that the absence of competitive policy styles in countries such as Denmark, Norway, and Sweden may not just be because they have shared a sense of economic vulnerability with the consociational democracies; rather, or in addition, it may be because they have *also shared a restricted electoral market*. More important, it can be argued that this restriction also derives from the pervasiveness of strong, collective, and politically relevant identities, and from a pattern of effective segmentation. In the case of the 'homogeneous' countries, however, and unlike the consociational democracies, this segmentation obviously does not derive from differences in language or religion; rather, it is based primarily on the cementing of *class* identities.

While the limited scope of this present chapter affords little opportunity to do more than simply assert such a possibility, the limited evidence which currently exists does offer some support for the argument. In the first place, there is no doubt that small states, even when not divided by language and religion, have experienced a more restricted electoral market than is the case with large states. In the interwar years, for example, which was the period which proved most crucial in laying the foundations for the consensual practices which have since proved so characteristic of the small states (Katzenstein 1985: chapter 4), the mean level of electoral volatility in Denmark, Norway, and Sweden was just 7.8. In the larger and more competitive states of France, Germany, and the United Kingdom, on the other hand, the mean level of electoral volatility was 14.1, almost double that in the Scandinavian states. Indeed, if one also includes the few democratic elections which were held in Italy in this period, the mean level in the larger states rises to 16.8, substantially more than double that in the smaller Scandinavian countries.

A similar contrast is evident in the early postwar years; that is, in the period 1945–65. In this case the mean level of electoral volatility in the four larger states was 11.5, which includes a remarkably low figure of just 4.6 for the then appropriately Butskellite British case; without the UK, the mean level in France, West Germany, and Italy, which were the three most volatile elec-

TABLE 7.1. *Mean electoral volatility by type of state*

Period	Consociational democracies[1]	Small homogeneous states	Large states
1918–44	8.4	7.8	16.8 (14.1)[2]
1945–65	5.8	6.2	11.5 (13.8)[3]

Notes: [1] Includes Austria in 1945-65 period; [2] Figure in brackets excludes Italy; [3] Figure in brackets excludes UK.
Source: Bartolini and Mair (1990).

torates in western Europe in this period, comes to 13.8. In Denmark, Norway, and Sweden, by contrast, the mean level was just 6.2. These, and the earlier figures concerning the consociational democracies, are summarized in Table 7.1.

These crude aggregate figures therefore suggest that there were substantially fewer voters in competition in the smaller Scandinavian states than was the case in the larger west European democracies, and hence they indicate that, as in the consociational democracies, there existed quite a restricted electoral market. Other things being equal, it was therefore also likely that the various parties and élites in these smaller states would have perceived that there was relatively little to gain through the adoption of *expansive* competitive strategies: since there were relatively few voters available to be won, there would have been little point in trying to compete for them. Moreover, and unlike Northern Ireland, the prospects for outright victory were also slim, particularly as far as socialist–bourgeois competition was concerned,[2] and hence a strategy of compromise and consensus would have seemed more appealing. In the larger democracies, on the other hand, and particularly in France, Germany, and Italy during both the interwar and early postwar years, intensive competition would have made sense. In these cases, there was a lot to gain.

But how does this relate to the question of segmentation? Quite simply, these smaller and more homogeneous democracies were not only characterized by a restricted electoral market, but also by one

[2] See Bartolini (1983a), and Przeworski and Sprague (1986); note also Katzenstein's (1985) emphasis on the importance of proportional electoral formulae and the political fragmentation of the right.

whose closure appears to have been derived, at least in part, from the existence of dense organizational networks which, in a manner similar to the pattern wrought by linguistic and/or religious *verzuiling* (literally, 'pillarization') in the consociational democracies, bonded voters into a set of strong identities. In the cases of Denmark, Norway, and Sweden, however, and unusually so, it was a pattern of segmentation which was based on *class* organizations and *class* identities.

TABLE 7.2. *Ranking of West European democracies in terms of working class organizational density**

	1918–44**	1945–65
	High density	*High density*
1	Austria	Sweden
2	Denmark	Austria
3	Sweden	Denmark
4	Switzerland	Norway
5	Norway	Italy
6	Belgium	Switzerland
7	Germany	Belgium
8	Netherlands	Ireland
9	United Kingdom	United Kingdom
10	Ireland	Netherlands
11	Finland	Finland
12	France	West Germany
13		France
	Low Density	*Low Density*

Note: * Ranking refers to an index summing trade union density and membership ratio of class left parties; ** Italian data not available.
Source: As Table 7.1.

As can be seen from Table 7.2, the figures here are quite revealing. Employing an index of working-class organizational density which is calculated by summing levels of trade-union density and the membership ratio of class left parties (Bartolini and Mair, 1990: 231–8), it can be seen that the density of class organizational networks in Denmark, Norway, and Sweden have proved particularly pronounced, especially when contrasted with that in the larger democracies. In the interwar period, for example, these three smaller democracies ranked in second, third, and fifth positions in terms of their levels of organizational density, with Germany, the United Kingdom, and France ranking in seventh, ninth, and last positions respectively. The contrast is even more marked in the early postwar period, with Sweden, Denmark, and Norway occupying first, third, and fourth positions respectively, as against the United Kingdom which occupies ninth position, and Germany and France, which occupy the bottom two positions.

The density of class organizational networks therefore not only tends to be much more pronounced in the smaller democracies than in the larger democracies, but also to be particularly pronounced in the more 'homogeneous' of the smaller democracies. This suggests that the class 'subcultures' within these smaller states can play a similar restrictive role in relation to the electoral markets to that played by the primarily linguistic and religious subcultures in the consociational democracies (although it should be emphasized that in the case of Austria and Switzerland class organizational density is also relatively pronounced); and this, in turn, suggests that the segmentally based incentives towards accommodationism which have existed in the consociational democracies may not really be that much different from those which exist in the small and more homogeneous democracies. While the *source* of segmentation in the consociational democracies is certainly distinctive—being derived, as it is, from religion and language rather than or as well as class— the *implications* of that segmentation seem readily comparable.

In other words, just as segmentation along religious and linguistic lines has restricted electoral markets and discouraged expansive competition in the consociational democracies, so too has class segmentation discouraged competitive politics in the more homogeneous small democracies. Indeed, Pappalardo's (1981: 369) depiction of the electoral stalemate which has proved so influential in the consociational democracies could equally well have been applied to the cases of Denmark, Norway, and Sweden, particularly in so far as socialist–bourgeois competition is concerned. Thus:

the movement of votes among the parties is hindered by at least three closely related factors: the heavy social and organizational ties, incompatible beliefs, and the feelings of hostility and mutual diffidence of the opposing subcultural alignments; the internal homogeneity of these alignments, the members of which are seldom, if at all, exposed to crosscutting pressures and so scarcely sensitive to the appeals from other quarters; and, finally, the high level of party identification, which implies long-term loyalty of the voters to their subcultural representatives.

Some concluding remarks and qualifications are necessary in this context. First, it is not my intention to suggest that the factors emphasized by Katzenstein, such as international economic vulnerability, divisions within the political right, and so on, play little or no role in the explanation of consensual political behaviour. Rather, I am simply suggesting that such an explanation neglects the fact that segmentation or *verzuiling* may also derive from class identities; in other words, the concept itself has a potentially much wider application than to the plural societies alone, or only to those divisions which are based only on religion or language (see also Rokkan, 1977).

Second, by taking account of the potential for segmentation on the basis of class alignments in particular, we are then in a better position to understand not only consensual behaviour in homogeneous political cultures, such as Denmark, Norway, and Sweden, but also that in the relatively exceptional Austrian case (see Katzenstein, 1985: 181–9) which, as we have seen in Table 7.2, is not only a consociational country, but also one which is characterized by a particularly pronounced level of class organizational density.

Third, the real test of the validity of this argument, as well as the real test of Katzenstein's own explanations, may best be carried out by a closer examination of some of the cases which are neglected in both analyses. The Italian case is particularly interesting in this regard, for example, since it is a large country which has recently been characterized by quite a restricted electoral market and relatively strong organizational networks (in both class and religious terms). In addition, despite its size, Italy also appears to have been characterized by a certain degree of non-competitive accommodationism, reflected most clearly in the *compromesso storico* strategy of the Italian Communist Party, as well as in the governing agreements of the late 1970s. The Irish and Finnish cases are also particularly interesting. These are small, economically vulnerable states which, quite unusually, are also characterized by relatively low levels of class organizational density (see Table 7.2). But they also have quite contrasting patterns of electoral availability. Finland,

for example, has one of the lowest mean levels of electoral volatility in western Europe, whereas Ireland ranks among the more
volatile countries. Here too, therefore, it would be interesting to test
for the extent to which differential patterns of competitive politics
have prevailed.

Fourth, it must also be emphasized that much of this argument
derives from patterns within cross-national data in both the interwar and early postwar periods, when the electoral markets in both
the homogeneous and consociational states proved particularly
restricted. More recent developments, on the other hand, have not
only suggested a weakening of some of the organizational networks
which have sustained strong identities (as in the Netherlands and
Denmark, for example—see Irwin and van Holsteyn, 1989; Sundberg, 1987), but have also indicated a greater opening-up of electoral markets and an increase in electoral volatility in some of these
countries, which suggest, in turn, that there may now exist greater
incentives towards expansive competition.

Finally, the qualifications with which this chapter began must
also be borne in mind. Competitive behaviour is more likely in a
context of open electoral markets and is less likely in the context of
closed electoral markets. But this is as far as it goes, and there is
no inevitability implied. The stakes are also important. In Switzerland, for example, it is not just the closure of the electoral market
which is relevant, but also the fact that, almost regardless of any
electoral shifts which do occur, none of the four major parties is
likely to be excluded from the governing cartel. In the United
Kingdom, by contrast, even a very closed electoral market can
prove highly competitive, in that even small swings can make the
difference between governmental incumbency and opposition.

SOME IMPLICATIONS FOR THE NEW EAST
EUROPEAN DEMOCRACIES

If this argument can be summarized without qualifications and
caveats, it would run as follows: the prevalence of strong, collective, and politically relevant identities tends to close off electoral
markets; these identities, in turn, tend to be derived from strong
organizational networks and subcultures, whether built around language, religion, or class, which act to isolate their adherents and to

cement political loyalties; in such a situation, competitive expansive electoral strategies prove unrewarding, and, other things being equal (and most particularly if there exists both a multiple balance of power and overarching systemic loyalties), democratic politics will therefore tend to be more accommodating, more consensual, and inevitably, more stable. Finally, this pattern will be reinforced if the stakes are not too large, and if outright victory would not be seen to result in an overwhelming set of rewards.

If this is true, then it does not bode well for the future stabilization of democracy in eastern Europe, at least in the reasonably short term (see also Chapter 8 below). In the first place, the stakes in the new democracies in Eastern Europe are large, with the state, in effect, being up for grabs. Whoever comes to power is not only in a position to determine that most crucial of resources, the rules of the game, but is also in a position to control the new bureaucracies and new government agencies. Given that much will now start from scratch, there are few if any legacies which will need to be accommodated. Party, inevitably, will make a difference.

Second, and even more crucially, the new electoral markets in eastern Europe, as new markets, are particularly open, and the new electorates are almost entirely available. In one sense, of course, this situation can be seen as no different from that which prevailed in much of the rest of Europe in the early part of the century, when the suffrage was extended and when floods of newly enfranchised and largely available voters were incorporated into the national electorates, thus raising levels of electoral volatility quite considerably (Bartolini and Mair, 1990: 147–51). In the case of the new democracies of eastern Europe, however, it must be emphasized that these newly enfranchised voters constitute virtually the entire body of the electorate, and few will have entered with pre-existing partisan loyalties.

Third, precisely because of the all-embracing nature of state power which existed prior to the revolutions of 1989, civil society in eastern Europe has remained largely underdeveloped. This too will enhance the availability of the new electorates, in that there is little in the way of an independent set of organizational networks which could promote and sustain collective identities and thus provide channels for mass integration. Independent trade unions remain largely weak and inchoate. With some notable exceptions, religious organizations, where they exist, are also weak and undeveloped. Mass parties, in effect, are as yet non-existent. And while sub-national identities are more evident and pervasive than is the case in western Europe, their particular impact is more likely to be disintegrative than integrative.

In short, the new electoral markets in eastern Europe are likely to be open, and the electorates likely to be available, to an extent which is almost without parallel in twentieth-century European history. And given that the stakes are so high, and given also the combination of severe economic difficulties and enhanced economic expectations, the result is likely to be an extremely competitive democratic politics which, in turn, may well hamper the stabilization of democracy itself. Indeed, even by the summer of 1990, the signs of such competitiveness had already become apparent: the clashes between miners and students in Romania, and the allegations of corruption and intimidation in the country's first free elections; the sit-ins in Sofia which had been organized in protest against the election of the reconstituted Communist party in Bulgaria; the split in Solidarity in Poland; the threatened break-up of the East German coalition as the constituent parties seek to determine how the East German end of the first all-German elections is to be organized, and so on. The stakes are high, the voters are available, and hence the pressure to accommodate to one's opponents is effectively non-existent. Only time will tell whether the inculcation of stable partisan identities will prove possible, and hence whether a stable democratic order will eventually emerge.

Such few lessons as can be found in western Europe are not wholly positive. In the 1970s, and in a foretaste of the transformation which recently occurred in eastern Europe, Spain, Greece, and Portugal each effected a transition to democracy. In all three cases, the stabilization of that democracy has proved somewhat problematic, and political competition has proved intense. More recently, in Greece, three successive general elections were required in order to find a government which could command a majority. Here too, the campaigns themselves were dominated by allegations of corruption and intimidation. In Spain, the party system has been held together only as the result of the dominance of one single party, initially the UCD, which in the space of just the three years between 1979 and 1982 witnessed its electoral support falling from 35 per cent to just 7 per cent, and later the Socialists. Indeed, until recently, and with the exception of the Socialists, and the various but disintegrative sub-national parties, every other 'party' in Spain was largely just a loose and effectively fragmented coalition of smaller groups, and electoral volatility remains remarkably high. In Portugal also, volatility has been particularly pronounced, with few strongly defined parties and with a recent and possibly temporary stability being achieved only as a result of a massive swing towards the conservative Social Democrats, whose vote shot up from 30 per cent in 1985 to over 50 per cent in 1987.

These new southern European democracies therefore continue to be characterized by very open electoral markets, enhanced electoral availability (even class organizational density remains remarkably low), and intense inter-party competition, all of which inevitably hamper the stabilization of an enduring democratic order. That said, these particular countries have enjoyed two crucial advantages which, at least as yet, do not seem available to the more vulnerable new democracies of eastern Europe. First, and from a more secure base, they have begun to enjoy quite substantial economic growth and increased prosperity, particularly since the mid-1980s. And second, and more important, they have been integrated into the European Community. In contrast, some at least of the new eastern European democracies may well be facing quite a prolonged period of relative poverty and isolation, which, when added to the immensely competitive styles which are likely to characterize their electoral markets, may continue to leave a question mark over their ability to establish and sustain a stable democratic order.

8

What is Different about Post-Communist Party Systems?[1]

This chapter is intended to explore some preliminary thoughts on the specific characteristics of newly emerging party systems, and of newly emerging post-communist party systems in particular. I should add that this is all within a specifically European context, since I would be very hesitant indeed to generalize these remarks to non-European settings. Of course, the very notion of a newly emerging party *system* may well be a contradiction in terms, in that to speak of a system of parties is to ascribe some degree of stability and predictability to the interactions between the parties concerned. And given that the numbers of parties involved in these newly emerging 'party systems' are far from stable, and given that even the individual parties themselves are far from stable—whether in terms of size, structure, or even name—it is clearly somewhat premature to think in terms of the interactions between these parties as being susceptible to any hard and fast definition in systemic terms.

Be that as it may, the purpose of this chapter is to identify the major reasons why these newly emerging post-communist party 'systems' may look and perform differently from established party systems. In brief, I will suggest that differences in the democratization process, in the character of the electorate, and in the context of competition together create formidable obstacles in the path of eventual consolidation, and that these also imply a pattern of party competition which is likely to prove both more conflictual and adversarial than is the case within the established democracies (see also Chapter 7 above). That said, I must also emphasize from

[1] First presented as the Stein Rokkan Memorial Lecture, University of Bergen, 1995.

the very beginning that the reasons which I enumerate and which I discuss briefly in the course of this chapter, are essentially hypothetical. More precisely, rather than being based on any specific conclusions which might have been derived from a close observation of the new post-communist party systems in practice, they are instead constructed on the basis of an extrapolation, an *ex adverso* extrapolation, of the principal characteriztics associated with established or consolidated party systems. In other words, my approach has been to identify the sort of factors which have encouraged the stabilization and institutionalization of established party systems, and then to turn these on their head in order to hypothesize and speculate about the sorts of factors which are likely to be absent from newly emerging party systems, and from post-communist party systems in particular.

NEWLY EMERGING PARTY SYSTEMS

This is, to repeat, a very hypothetical exercise, which is mainly intended to offer some scope for discussion and further speculation. That said, it is also an exercise which, to a greater or lesser extent, may be applicable not only to post-communist democracies, but also to other post-authoritarian democracies in Europe, such as Germany and Italy in the late 1940s and 1950s, or Portugal and Spain in the 1970s and 1980s. It is also potentially applicable to party systems emerging in the wake of national independence, such as, for example, Ireland (and possibly also Finland) in the 1920s, as well as, indeed, albeit probably more loosely, to west European party systems in general as they developed in the wake of full democratization and universal suffrage in the early part of this century.

To be sure, each of these situations will differ in certain important respects, and most notably in terms of their periodization, the differential strategies available for electoral mobilization, the varying nature of the tasks facing those constructing the new democratic regime, and in the extent to which there already existed an autonomous and well-developed civil society. Thus, for example, those parties and party systems which emerged in a context in which there already existed a network of mass communication, and in which it was possible to gain instant access to voters (such as in post-communist Europe), will tend to operate under a very different set of circumstances than those which emerged in earlier periods (e.g. Ireland in the 1920s, or even Germany or Italy in the late 1940s). Equally, party systems which emerged within a context in which civil society was largely undernourished and inchoate (such as, again, post-communist Europe) will have faced different and arguably much greater problems than those which emerged within a context in which there already existed a reasonably well-developed network of interest organizations and collective identities (such as in Portugal and Spain).

In this sense, and given the potential variation which exists in terms of the nature of civil society, the strategies for mobilization, and the requirements for institutional restructuring, one can conceive of at least four separate clusters of European cases in which new parties and party systems emerged and which, being different from one another, also faced quite differing problems of consolidation. First, there are classic cases with which Stein Rokkan was most concerned in his developmental model, and which were those party systems which emerged, and then 'froze' into place, in the wake of 'the establishment of universal and equal electoral democracy' (Rokkan, 1970: 75) in early twentieth-century Europe, and which also include, almost as a separate category, those party systems, such as that in Ireland, which emerged not only in the wake of democratization, but also within the context of the creation of a new, independent, political system. Second, there were the cases of the new or revived party systems, which emerged in continental Europe in the late 1940s following extended periods of authoritarian rule, as in Germany and Italy. Third, and perhaps most comparable to these latter cases, there were the new party systems which emerged from decades of authoritarian rule in Portugal and Spain in the 1970s. Finally, and most recently, there is now the enormous range of cases of newly emerging party systems in post-communist Europe. It is on this last group that I will concentrate, paying particular attention to east central Europe, while at the same time trying to draw some lessons from the experiences of the other clusters of newly emerging party systems (see also Cotta, 1995; Morlino, 1995; Pempel, 1990).[2]

---

[2] The broad themes of this chapter have also been addressed in a number of valuable articles which only recently came to my attention. See, in particular, the very insightful analysis by Geddes (1995), as well as the series of articles included in Waller (1995), and especially that by Rose (1995). Lewis (1996) offers a very

POST-COMMUNIST DEMOCRATIZATION IS DIFFERENT

The first and most obvious difference to emphasize is that the new party systems of post-communist Europe are emerging in the wake of a democratization process which is itself *sui generis*. For example, and at the risk of both over-exaggeration and over-generalization, it can be argued that post-communist Europe represents what is really the first case of European democratization occurring in the effective absence of a real civil society. With few exceptions—and included among these exceptions are both Solidarity and the Catholic Church in Poland, as well as the Evangelical Churches in East Germany—such social organizations as existed prior to the collapse of the long-standing communist regimes enjoyed little or no autonomy from what Michael Waller (1994) has referred to as the 'communist power monopoly'. Nor, with the exception of an occasionally self-standing agrarian interest, did the prevailing economic structure offer much of a base for independent social organization or collective interests. And while marketization, which often began in a limited form even prior to the collapse of the communist regime, did certainly offer the prospect of an eventual crystallization of interests, its sheer acceleration at the end of the 1980s actually led in the short term to what Judy Batt (1991: 50) refers to as 'an unprecedented degree of social destructuring, volatility and fluidity'.

In this sense, the transition in post-communist Europe differed markedly from those which had earlier taken place in southern Europe, and even from those other managed transitions in the wake of World War II. Power in non-democratic regimes may well be indivisible, but the extent of the power monopoly was clearly without precedent in eastern Europe. Indeed, the democratization process itself was without precedent. In post-communist Europe, as Claus Offe (1992: 14) has argued, we are in fact dealing with a 'triple transition', a process which involves not just democratization, but also marketization and wholesale economic transformation, as well as, quite often, state-building itself, at least in so far as the settlement of territorial issues is concerned. We are thus talking

effective review of many of the problems involved in the analysis of party politics in post-communist democracies.

about the more or less simultaneous traversing of three crucial stages of a process which, as Offe points out, 'were mastered over a centuries-long sequence (from the nation state to capitalism, and then to democracy)' in the case of the 'normal' western European countries.

Even beyond the severe strains imposed by such a triple transition, however, there is also a further fundamental difference between what Offe might refer to as the 'normal' European democratization process and that which occurred in post-communist Europe. More precisely, when democratization has occurred as a result of enfranchisement and the introduction of 'universal and equal electoral democracy', as was the case with most of the west European countries almost a century ago, it usually involved little more than the opening-up of an already existing political system. When democratization occurs as a result of the collapse or defeat of a previously non-democratic regime, on the other hand, it requires a wholesale *restructuring* of the system. To put it another way, and following Dahl (1971: 1–16; see also van Biezen, 1995), democratization in early twentieth-century Europe involved the extension of the right to participate in regimes in which the principle of contestation had already been established, whereas the democratization of the former communist regimes has involved establishing the principle of contestation in regimes which were already participant.

This has two important implications. First, consider the developmental model which Rokkan elaborated and which he applied to the established democracies in western Europe: 'the *terminus ad quem*,' he wrote, 'is the establishment of universal and equal electoral democracy and the "freezing" of party alternatives, in most countries during the 1920s and the 1930s, at any rate before World War II' (1970: 75). But what precisely was this the 'terminus' of? What precisely was culminating in this 'frozen' end-point? In essence, as Rokkan (1970: 227) elsewhere elaborated, it was a process marked by four crucial stages: '[first] the formal *incorporation* of strata and categories of residents kept out of the system under the original criteria; [second] the *mobilization* of those enfranchised citizens in electoral contests; [third] their *activation* into direct participation in public life; [fourth] the breakdown of the traditional systems of local rule through the entry of nationally organized parties into municipal elections, what we call the process of *politicization.*' And the end, then, the terminus, was the freezing of the party systems which had emerged during these four stages. But what happens when we apply this lesson to the post-communist systems? Here the pattern is necessarily different, in that here, albeit in a somewhat mutant form, these four stages had actually been traversed *prior* to the emergence of the new party systems. In other words, these new party systems did not result from and through a long-term process of democratization and politicization, but were rather created in the *aftermath* of that process, in that the citizens had already been effectively 'incorporated', 'mobilized', 'activated', and 'politicized' under the previous non-democratic regime.

And the interesting question this then poses is whether, in such a reversed process, there is also an equivalent bias towards the 'freezing' of alternatives. My own inclination is to suggest that no such bias is likely to exist; or, to put it more mildly, any bias which does exist will be substantially weaker than was the case in western Europe at the beginning of this century. As Lipset and Rokkan (1967: 54) pointed out, the democratization process in western Europe tended to result in a 'high level of organizational mobilization of most sectors in the community,' and it was this which 'left very little leeway for a decisive breakthrough of new party alternatives'. What they are referring to here, so to speak, are the mechanics of the freezing process, and there is almost nothing of equivalence to point to in the post-communist transition. It is in this sense that we can anticipate that party systems which emerge after democratization, which is the post-communist experience, may reflect a quite different dynamic to those which emerged during the process of democratization, which was the 'normal' west European experience. In other words, what we see in post-communist Europe is not a terminus but rather a departure point, a beginning. And that certainly makes a difference.

The second, and related, implication of this staging can be stated more briefly, and that is that the constitution-makers in these new democracies now find themselves obliged to restructure the political system and to establish procedures for competition in a context in which mass politics is already established. This is also an important difference, which I will return to later, in that it suggests that the scope for intense competition will be enormously enhanced. In this sense, perhaps, one of the closest west European parallels to the post-communist experience is offered by the Irish case, in that

Ireland had a more or less fully enfranchised electorate in place at the time of gaining independence, and hence was already operating within a context of mass politics when it set out to create new institutional structures. It might also be pointed out that, in this process, Ireland then went on to experience a period of pronounced instability and intense political competition, and here too we may find certain bleak parallels to the post-communist experience.

THE ELECTORATE AND THE PARTIES ARE DIFFERENT

The second important difference to note about these new party systems is that they are confronting a quite different type of electorate, an electorate which, almost by definition, is substantially more open and more available than those of the established democracies.

Generally speaking, the electorates in the established democracies tend to be relatively closed, being characterized by the presence of a structured set of partisan preferences and by a large degree of predictability. Indeed, despite the recent emphases in the literature on the importance of change and instability in electoral alignments (e.g. Franklin, Mackie, Valen *et al.*, 1992), the long-term trends still continue to indicate a striking bias towards continuity and persistence within the established party systems (Bartolini and Mair, 1990; see also Chapter 4 above). Newly democratized electorates, on the other hand, tend to be more open and more available, and hence they also tend to be more volatile and uncertain.

There are two principal reasons for this. First, newly democratizing electorates in general, and post-communist electorates in particular, are less likely to be underpinned by a strong cleavage structure, and in this sense they are less likely to be easily stabilized or frozen. This is not to say that these electorates are wholly homogeneous, or that they lack any differentiation based on social stratification, occupation, ethnicity, religion, or whatever. On the contrary: in some instances it is clear that divisions along some or all of these lines are at least as important as the equivalent divisions in the established democracies, as is testified by the important recent research by Kitschelt (1992, 1995), Tóka (1993), and others (e.g. Evans and Whitfield, 1993; Rose and Makkai, 1995; McAllister and White, 1995). But while at any one point in time it might well be possible to identify social and attitudinal divisions which are more or less distinctly associated with one or more parties in the post-communist democracies, the fluidity of the social structure on the one hand, together with the relative lack of crystallization of identities on the other, suggest that such foundations are, as yet, unlikely to constitute a *stable* pattern of alignments. For while cleavage structures act to stabilize electorates, they tend to do so slowly, with the result that almost regardless of region or timing, the early years of party systems, and the early years of newly democratized electorates, tend to prove the most unstable.

TABLE 8.1. *Electoral Volatility in Newly-Emerging Party Systems*

Countries	Average electoral colatility (no. of elections)	Index value (Western Europe, 1960–89 = 100)
Base Line: Western Europe, 1960–89 (*excluding Greece, Portugal, Spain*)	8.4 *(131)*	*100*
Western Europe, 1918–30	12.3 (21)	146
[Ireland, 1923–32	15.9 (3)	189]
Germany, 1949–61	13.9 (3)	165
Italy, 1945–58	14.1 (3)	168
Greece, 1974–85	18.4 (3)	219
Portugal, 1975–80	8.7 (3)	104
Spain, 1977–86	13.6 (3)	162
Czech Republic, 1990–2	19.9 (1)	237
Hungary, 1990–4	25.0 (1)	298
Poland, 1990–3	27.6 (1)	329
Slovakia, 1990–4	25.9 (2)	308

This was largely true for Germany and Italy in the early postwar years, for example, as it was for Portugal and Spain until the late 1980s, while a more generalized tendency towards marked instability was also characteriztic of most of the other west European party systems in the wake of the expansion of the suffrage and full enfranchisement in the early part of the century (Bartolini and Mair, 1990: 68–95; see also Morlino, 1995: 317–28). The contrast in the patterns in these clusters of newly democratizing countries with those in the established west European party systems is certainly quite striking (see Table 8.1). Average electoral volatility in western Europe between 1960 and 1989, for example, was just 8.4 per cent, indicating that, in net aggregate terms, an average of just one in twelve votes switched between different parties at consecutive elections during this period. In the period 1918 to 1930, by contrast, when most of the European party systems were just emerging into full and equal democracy, volatility averaged 12.3 per cent, half as much again as in the postwar established democracies, reaching, incidentally, almost 16 per cent in the 'doubly' new Irish case. In the newly emerging party systems of both Germany and Italy, volatility was also high, averaging 14 per cent across the first three elections in each case, while in Greece and Spain average volatility reached almost 16 per cent in the first three post-transition elections, although here it must be emphasized that, with less than 9 per cent volatility, the Portuguese case proved unusually stable. However, even these high levels of volatility pale by comparison to those recorded in the first post-communist elections, where an *average* of almost 25 per cent of votes switched between the parties in the first pairs of elections in the Czech Republic, Hungary, Poland, and Slovakia.

In any case, and this is the second and more important point, it can also be argued that the cleavage structures which have proved so important in the stabilization of west European party systems are about more than simply divisions in social strata or ascriptive identities. Rather, they have also involved the mobilization of collective *political* identities and, above all, organizational networks, which, when combined with a strong social underpinning, have effectively segmented many of these electorates into relatively stable, and closed, partisan blocs. And this, in turn, as Sartori (1969) reminds us, is at least in part the result of the independent intervention of political parties and other organizations.

It goes almost without saying that in the post-communist democracies such independent partisan intervention is, to say the least of it, quite minimal. In other words, not only is the electorate different, but the parties which 'organize' that electorate are also different, and, in particular, are less grounded within civil society (see the valuable analysis by Kopecky, 1995, which deals with this aspect at much greater length). There are a number of elements involved here. In the first place, many of the new parties are primarily 'internally created' (Duverger, 1954), top-down parties, which have originated within parliament or at the élite level, rather than having been built up from the ground. And, like all such parties, they are either less likely, or simply less able, to establish a strong organizational network at mass level. In this sense, and almost inevitably so, they are parties which are biased towards an emphasis on 'the party in public office' rather than 'the party on the ground' (Katz and Mair, 1993). This would not be true, of course, of any 'externally created' parties, which, by definition, begin with a mass organization on the ground, and which then use this as a base from which to launch and mandate a party in public office. At first sight, however, post-communist Europe seems to offer few examples of such externally created parties, in that even the most likely exceptions, such as the various post-Solidarity parties in Poland, have since become so fractured and fissiparous that they might now also best be regarded as primarily parliamentary manifestations. Moreover, at least in certain cases, such as the Hungarian Fidesz, for example, in what is perhaps a vain hope to limit the scope of conflict through the 'monopolization of politics' at élite level,[3] the parties which have emerged have sometimes based themselves on a conscious rejection of grass-roots involvement.

In the established democracies, to be sure, many of the now prominent parties also began within parliament, and as 'internal' creations. In these cases, however, such parties rarely enjoyed exclusive control, and were usually challenged by externally created opponents, to which they eventually adapted in a process which Duverger (1954) was to define as the 'contagion from the left', which led to the eventual dominance in western Europe of the mass party model. In other words, there existed competing models of party organization, in which the merits of the mass party model soon became evident in a way which encouraged other types of parties to imitate it (see also Chapter 5 above). In post-communist Europe, on the other hand, and this is arguably also true for many of the parties in Spain if not in Portugal, it seems that little effort is being made, or has been made, to build strong popular organizations which might, as Lipset and Rokkan (1967: 51) put it, 'narrow the support market'. And in such circumstances, it is very unlikely that any contagion effect will occur. In short, the absence of a (successful) challenge from a mass party is likely to favour the

---

[3] See Schattschneider (1960: 16): 'any attempt to monopolize politics is almost by definition an attempt to limit the scope of conflict'.

continued maintenance of élitist party organizations, even in the medium to long term.

It is thus interesting to note that even when we allow for the recent relative decline in many of the west European countries, party membership in the new democracies still ranks substantially below the levels which are now being recorded in the established democracies (see also Morlino, 1995: 330–8). In Portugal and Spain, for example, party membership levels currently amount to less than 5 per cent of the electorate, compared to an average of almost 10 per cent in the long-established European democracies (see Table 8.2). In post-communist Europe, levels are even more muted, with just over 3 per cent in Slovakia, 2.5 per cent in Hungary, and just 1.5 per cent in Poland. Indeed, the only possible exception to this pattern, the Czech Republic, owes its relatively high membership ratio of 6.4 per cent largely to the organizational legacy of the electorally marginal former Communist Party, which, in 1993, accounted for almost two-thirds of the total figure (Kopecky, 1995).[4]

It might of course be argued that any such comparison with the established democracies is invidious, especially in the case of the post-communist democracies, and that there has simply been too little time available to the parties in which to develop mass organizations on the ground. If the parties are different, then, it is only because they are new, and, with time, it is likely that they will develop increasingly strong roots within civil society. As against this, however, can be cited the membership levels of Portugal and Spain, which, despite more than two decades of democracy, still lag significantly behind those of most of the established democracies. Moreover, it is also clear that while a tradition of mass membership is difficult to shrug off, and hence while membership remains important for many of the traditional parties in the established democracies, new parties may well find that gaining a large membership proves more trouble than it's worth. However valuable in some respects, members can prove to be a political and administrative nuisance to party leaders (Katz, 1990; Scarrow, 1994*a*;

---

[4] For party membership figures in the new democracies, see Morlino (1995); Gangas (1994); Marcet and Argelaguet (1994); Kopecky (1995); Urmanič (1994); Ágh (1995); for detailed figures on the established democracies, see Katz and Mair (1992*a*), and Chapter 6 above. Note that the figure for Slovakia excludes the HZDS, for which figures are unavailable.

TABLE 8.2. *Party membership as a percentage of the electorate, c. 1989–1992*

Country	Party Membership (%)
Austria	21.8
Sweden	21.2
Norway	13.5
Finland	12.9
Italy	9.7
Belgium	9.2
Denmark	6.5
Ireland	5.3
Portugal	4.9
Germany	4.2
Spain	4.0
United Kingdom	3.3
Slovakia	3.1*
Netherlands	2.9
Hungary	2.5
Czech Republic	1.8**
France	1.7
Poland	1.5

* Excludes HZDS, for which figures are unavailable.
** Excludes former Communist Party, the addition of which would increase the figure to 6.4%.
Source: See footnote 4, p. 185.

Kopecky, 1995; see also Chapter 6 above), and the financial and campaigning costs of low membership levels can now easily be offset by media access, as well as by state subsidies, the principle of which was quickly established in almost all the recent cases of democratization. Mass membership may well have been a priority in party building in the past; for modern parties, however, and these include the new parties developing in post-communist Europe, its relevance might well be questionable. Hence the incentives to acquire a strong position on the ground might well be marked more by their absence than their presence in many of the new democracies.

In sum, if we can conceive of cleavages as being derived from strong and enduring collective identities, which, in turn, are derived at least in part from the anchoring created by a stable social structure on the one hand, and the organizational intervention of parties and related groups on the other, then it seems plausible to conclude that, at least in the medium term, the post-communist democracies will be unlikely to develop strong cleavage structures. And, *ceteris paribus*, this also means that they are likely to continue to be characterized by markedly open and available electorates, which, moreover, as the turnout figures testify, are not yet even fully participant.

THE CONTEXT OF COMPETITION IS DIFFERENT

The third major difference between established party systems on the one hand, and the newly emerging post-communist party systems in particular on the other, involves the context of competition. Again, there are a number of factors involved.

In the first place, and in contrast to the situation in the established democracies, the emerging political class in almost any new democracy is less likely to be characterized by a stable pattern of organizational behaviour. In other words, the political élites are less likely to be motivated by organizational loyalties and commitments, and are correspondingly more likely to resolve conflicts and/or to make political gains by either seceding and establishing separate parties, or by engaging in short-term mergers and alliances with other parties. As we know, this sort of party splitting and merging is relatively uncommon in the west European democracies—indeed a survey of data across fourteen countries and 147 elections in postwar western Europe revealed just fifty-five recorded cases of fission or fusion between different parties (Mair, 1990*b*); that is, an average of only one case of fission/fusion for almost every three elections. The pattern is clearly likely to differ in new democracies. As is evident, the parties which emerge into electoral competition are, in the main, new parties, which, by definition, lack an established standing, status, and legitimacy within the electorate at large. Moreover, and contrasting with the situation in the established democracies, they are also by definition very non-institutionalized parties, which are unlikely to have acquired the sort of identity which stands over and above that of their first leadership (see also Kopecky, 1995) and which is at once an asset (in that voters may identify with the party regardless of shifts in policy or leadership) and a liability (in that efforts to create a new image for an established party often founder in the face of long-term preconceptions and expectations).

It follows from this that many new parties in new democracies are unlikely to be in a position to exert any real organizational sanction on potential dissidents within their ranks, and that they can do little to discourage fractious élites from setting up on their own. And precisely because the parent organization is unlikely to have any special legitimacy or standing in the eyes of the electorate, the fractious élites themselves would not be conscious of any great costs involved in breaking away. For the same reason, party mergers and electoral alliances would not seem to carry much risk, at least electorally, in that there is likely as yet to be little in the way of an established identity which would be in danger of being submerged. Since almost all of the parties are new on the scene, even those newer parties which result from splits and mergers can begin on a virtually equal footing. The result is therefore likely to be continued flux (and possibly even continued fragmentation) in the format of the newly emerging party systems, and this, in turn, is also likely to have an impact upon the context of competition. During the first three elections in both Portugal and Spain, for example, there occurred at least twenty-two cases of party fission or fusion, a ratio which is just about ten times as great as that recorded in the established democracies during the forty years which elapsed between the mid-1940s to the late 1980s.

Not only is it likely that the borders between the different parties will be crossed and broken by frequent fission and fusion, but it is also likely that there will be a marked blurring of the boundaries between all of these parties on the one hand, and other would-be representative agencies on the other. Again this is, or certainly was, uncommon in the established democracies, where, at least in definitional terms, it has always been seen as possible and necessary to distinguish the concept of party from that of interest group and/or (new) social movement. How precisely this distinction is defined varies from author to author; nevertheless, at bottom, the minimal definition which is used tends to concur with, and is best expressed by, that of Sartori (1976: 64): 'a party is any political group that presents at elections, and is capable of placing through elections, candidates for public office'. This is a simple, effective, and easily applied definition, distinguishing groups which aim to influence government from the outside, and those which aim, or have the potential, to become part of government. Moreover, it also enables us to distinguish the role and function of these different organizations within the political system. At first sight, however, this does not appear to be a very useful distinction when applied to the new democracies, and especially to the post-communist democracies, where something so specific as party is not easily separated from a quite vast array of alternative associations. Thus what we understand in many other senses to be interest groups or (new) social movements turn out also to be competitors for public office; and what we might normally understand to be a party (on the basis of its presenting, through elections, candidates for public office) turns out in many other senses of the term to be an interest group or a (new) social movement. It is in this sense that the boundaries between parties and other associations become blurred, and it is in this sense that the political arena at the élite level is also more open and hence more likely to be in flux, thus further complicating the context of competition.

The second major factor which is relevant here, and which is also likely to impact upon the context of competition and thus to promote electoral uncertainty is the strong presence of what might be referred to as 'institutional incentives towards instability'. In an earlier study of the electorates in western Europe in the period 1885–1985, it was argued that much of the variation in electoral (in)stability across countries and time could be largely and most simply explained as the outcome of two competing pressures (Bartolini and Mair, 1990: 253–308). On the one hand, as noted above, there was the pressure for stability which derived from the strength of cleavage structures. On the other hand, there was also the pressure towards *in*stability which derived from changes in the institutional structure within which the parties competed, as well as from changes in the structure of the party system itself. These latter elements included such features as changes in electoral laws, changes in the franchise, changes in levels of turnout, and changes in the numbers of parties. To the extent that these proved more powerful than the competing cleavage factors, the system proved relatively unstable (France is a typical example). To the extent that the cleavage factors proved more powerful, on the other hand, the system tended to be relatively stable (Sweden is a typical example). In western Europe in general, in fact, changes in the institutional context have proved relatively infrequent, thus helping to allow the cleavage factors to predominate, and thus contributing to the long-term bias towards stability.

In new democracies, by contrast, and especially in the post-communist democracies, the institutional environment is exceptionally and inevitably unstable, with conflicts over the initial establishment and subsequent adaptation of the constitutional rules of the game being one of the most evident features of the process of democratic transition and consolidation (see also below). There is little need to detail this aspect here, since it is already the subject of an extensive literature. What can be emphasized, however, is that the process of institutional structuring is not usually something which is, or can be, rapidly completed. Basic constitutions must be written more or less from scratch, involving choices that are of fundamental importance to the character and functioning of the party system (e.g. Lijphart, 1991), and this in itself is clearly a lengthy process; even when eventually written, these constitutions themselves become subject to frequent amendment, a process which is perhaps especially apparent in the regular revisions of the electoral laws; and finally, even when there is basic agreement on the formal rules, there are nevertheless persistent conflicts over interpretations and competences, as can be seen most clearly in the pervasive tensions between presidential and parliamentary prerogatives which now characterize many of the post-communist democracies. As Jan Zielonka (1994: 87) has noted with particular reference to the recent Russian experience, but as is also more or less true throughout the post-communist region:

the entire institutional framework is . . . in flux, causing chaos, friction, and inefficiency. State institutions are assuming new roles and prerogatives under conditions of intense political struggle, rapid social change, and enormous legal confusion. The core rules of institutional bargaining are constantly being re-articulated and renegotiated. Institutions find it hard to acquire the public support and professional skills (to say nothing of internal coherence and adaptability) that they need to cope with the complex challenges that they face. At the same time, they often clash agonizingly among themselves over prestige, authority, and procedures.

And precisely because this institutional uncertainty is unlikely to disappear, at least in the medium-term future, it also implies that the context of competition will continue to be uncertain. And this in turn, when added to the sheer unpredictability regarding the numbers of parties competing for election in the new democracies (see above), will almost inevitably promote further uncertainty and instability.

The final factor which is relevant here concerns one additional feature which has also played a crucial role in the stabilization of electorates in the established western democracies, and which is also inevitably marked by its absence in new democracies, and that is the existence of a clear *structure of competition*. Although this is considered at greater length in Chapter 9 (below), it is worth noting here that there are two contrasting patterns in the structure of party competition which may be distinguished. On the one hand, a structure of party competition can be relatively *closed*, and hence highly predictable, with little or no change over time in the range of governing alternatives or in the pattern of alternation, for example, and with new parties finding it virtually impossible to break through the threshold of government. Such a closed structure of competition clearly constrains voter preferences, in that it limits the choice of governing options in a way which is similar to the limits on the choice of parties in non-fragmented systems, and by so doing it also enhances party system stability, and, indeed, helps to ensure that party systems generate their own momentum and thus freeze into place (see also Chapter 1 above). On the other hand, a structure of party competition can be relatively *open* and hence quite unpredictable, with differing patterns of government alternation, with frequent shifts in the make-up of the governing alternatives, and with new parties gaining relatively easy access to office. This sort of pattern tends to characterize more fragmented systems, especially where there is no large core party of government, and clearly helps to promote instability by imposing few constraints on voter choice.

What is of particular importance in this particular context, however, is that the closure of a structure of competition necessarily requires the development of stable norms and conventions in the patterns of competition and in the processes of government formation. As such, it is also clearly a function of time. As Sartori (1994: 37) notes, it is only 'when the electorate takes for granted a given set of political routes and alternatives very much as drivers take for granted a given system of highways, [that] a party system has reached the stage of structural consolidation qua system'. This is clearly not something which is easily learned *de novo*, and it is therefore also not something which might be seen to characterize newly emerging party 'systems'. Indeed, and as noted above, what is perhaps most striking about new party systems, such as those which are currently emerging in post-communist Europe, is precisely their lack of closure and hence their lack of *systemness*, with systemness here understood to be what Sartori (1976: 43) refers to as the set of 'patterned interactions' between the parties. For not only is the basic format of these new systems uncertain, in that, as has been emphasized, the parties as organizations are often quite loosely constructed, but so also are the modes of competition and the nature of cross-party alliances and coalitions.[5]

Seen from this perspective, the long-term process by which party systems may eventually become consolidated can also be seen a long-term process by which the structure of competition becomes increasingly closed and predictable, and through which, as Schattschneider (1960) might have put it, conflict becomes eventually 'socialized'. To be sure, it might well be the case that a more closed and predictable structure will develop in a number of the post-communist democracies in the longer-term future. But this is, by definition, a relatively lengthy process, and it is only recently, for example, that a reasonably closed structure of competition has become apparent in the now more experienced Portuguese and Spanish cases.

In sum, all three of the (inter-related) factors which act to shape the context of competition, and all of which are, or at least were, more or less characteristic of many of the established party systems—that is, stable organizational structures, institutional certainties, and relatively closed structures of competition—tend to be marked by their absence in the case of newly emerging party systems in general, and in the case of the post-communist party systems in particular. And it is this very absence, in turn, which is likely to play such a crucial role in encouraging and facilitating electoral instability. At the very least, it is clear that the combination of a weak cleavage structure, an uncertain and volatile institutional environment, and a very open and unpredictable structure of competition cannot enhance the prospect of rapid consolidation.

---

[5] It is interesting to note, for example, that in many cases even the potential structuration afforded by the division between communists and anti-communists (or between defenders and opponents of the old regime) has now been broken down by inter-party alliances which cut across that divide, or even by wholesale reorganization within the former communist parties themselves.

THE PATTERN OF COMPETITION IS DIFFERENT

This, then, leads me to my final, and perhaps most important difference, and one which follows almost as the conclusion to the above: for not only is the context of competition different, as we have seen, but so too is the pattern of competition. More specifically, and given the weight of the factors identified earlier, it is likely that élites in new democracies, and those in the post-communist democracies in particular, will prove substantially more conflictual and adversarial than is usually the case in the established democracies. In other words, and following Lijphart's (1968) terminology, it is likely that élites in the post-communist democracies, at least in the medium term, will opt for conflictual rather than coalescent strategies; or, to adapt Lijphart's (1984) more recent terminology, it is likely that competition will prove more majoritarian, and hence adversarial, than consensual. There are two main arguments which can be advanced here, both of which rely heavily on the sort of *ex adverso* reasoning which was alluded to at the beginning of this chapter.

In the first place, while a variety of reasons have been advanced to account for a tendency towards coalescent and consensual strategies within political systems, including for example, the extent of societal pluralism in a given country (e.g. Lijphart, 1977) or its degree of economic openness and hence international vulnerability (e.g. Katzenstein, 1985), one of the most compelling arguments is that which suggests that cooperation and accommodation will increase to the extent that the protagonists are operating in conditions of 'political certainty'. Or, to put it in another and perhaps more familiar way, it is in situations of political *un*certainty that competition is likely to be more intense.

This, for example, has been one of the most important arguments advanced to explain the tendency towards accommodation in those segmented societies in which no one group commands an overall majority (Pappalardo, 1981; Mair, 1994; see also Chapter 7 above). Rather than being the consequence of anything inherent in social pluralism itself, for example, such as the fear of what might occur were conflictual rather than consensual strategies to be pursued, accommodation is here seen as instead reflecting the awareness that nothing much is to be gained by pursuing victory in situations in which all of the votes are more or less already committed. As Pappalardo (1981: 370–1) puts it: 'conditions of stability [deriving] from segmentation are an incentive to cooperation because once there is no hope of winning alone or of making significant progress at anyone else's expense, it is easier to adapt and come to agreement in order to share in the stakes.' Conversely, as segmentation erodes, and as the market for votes opens up, we witness 'the concomitant appearance of a more or less lively competition' (p. 375). In other words, competition is more likely to be intense in situations in which each of the relevant protagonists can reasonably hope to achieve a victory. Knowing you are likely to be defeated, on the other hand, or at least knowing that you cannot win, is more likely to encourage compromise. In this sense, it is the sheer predictability of the alignments in many of the established party systems which tends to encourage cooperation, and it is thus interesting to note that a more consensual politics tends to be fostered precisely in those political systems in which both strong organizational networks and/or subcultural divisions tend to tie voters down in relatively closed electoral communities. As Pappalardo (1981: 370) notes, citing Lehmbruch (1974: 91), it is because 'a political strategy of maximisation of votes cannot work where "the numerical relations of rival groups are rather inflexible", [that] groups are more likely to adopt a behaviour suited to the politics of accommodation'.

It goes almost without saying that these conditions do not prevail in the post-communist democracies. Indeed, if anything, as we have seen, it is precisely a culture of *un*certainty that prevails, and it is this which will tend to promote more competitive strategies. Civil society is itself unstructured and volatile. The parties as organizations are far from institutionalized. The sheer frequency of party fission and fusion, together with the vagaries induced by unfamiliar electoral thresholds on the one hand, and the lack of a fully mobilized electorate on the other, mean that it is not even clear who exactly are or can be the relevant protagonists. The electoral market itself is both malleable and open, and the newly emerging parties appear either unwilling or unable to narrow it, preferring to rely instead on expansive electoral strategies. As Kitschelt (1992: 9–10) puts it, it is a process involving 'emerging political actors who operate in environments characterized by extreme uncertainty and high strategic interdependence. Actors may still be engaged in exploring what their interests are and how to pursue them. This process is fraught with error and sudden reversals.' More specifically, it is a process which encourages conflict rather than compromise, and a politics of outbidding rather than a politics of integration. In electoral terms, at least, a lot is at stake.

There is also a lot which is at stake in substantive and strategic terms, of course, and this is the second argument which is relevant here. This is, after all, a 'triple transition', which implies not only a process that is without precedent, but also one that entails a remarkably high decision load. More specifically, given the gravity of the situation in which public policy currently has to be determined in post-communist Europe, and given the potential impact of the policy choices on the social and economic environment of ordinary citizens, then it is clear that what is at stake in terms of policy competition between the parties is substantially more important than is normally the case in the established democracies, where shifts in government do not really make much of a difference, and where, apart from the effects on the immediate personal fortunes of the competing élites themselves, there is often little to choose between victory and defeat. In the contemporary post-communist democracies, there still remains a lot to play for. And this, in turn, may well mean that there is little real incentive to pursue a strategy of accommodation.[6]

If, as Schattschneider (1960: 66) suggests, 'the definition of the alternatives is the supreme instrument of power', then it is clear that the struggle for power is likely to be much more intense in situations in which, as is still clearly the case in post-communist Europe, these alternatives have yet to be defined. This new political stage is therefore one which has been left open for a more conflictual and competitive pattern of politics, and one which may well breed a reluctance to accept the legitimacy of the positions adopted by one's opponents.

But there is also even more involved here than the substantive policy questions. Since the beginning of the transition from communist rule, the political élites in eastern Europe have been engaged in what might be described in somewhat sophisticated terms as

---

[6] Note, for example, Offe's (1992: 15) suggestion that 'the lack of a developed complexity in civil society leads to the dominance of themes which, albeit suited to conflict, are not also suited to compromise'.

'constitution-building' or 'system-building', and what in reality is the establishment, from scratch, of the rules of the political game. These rules include questions of how the parties are to be treated by the law and by the state; how the electoral system is to be organized; how legislative and executive powers are to be distributed across different institutions; how the powers and position of the head of state are to be specified; how the role of the constitutional court and the constitution itself is to be defined; how the legacy of the past, and especially those surviving persons who were involved in creating that legacy, are to be treated, and so on.

These are profoundly important issues and involve profoundly important decisions. It is these rules of the game which, in both the short and long term, will help to determine which political actors will succeed and which will fail. There are therefore a lot of interests at stake, particularly when it is the players themselves who, as Offe (1992: 17) points out, 'determine the rules according to which the future game will be played, and with which it will be decided who will be a fellow player. Actors are judges in their own case.' And since ending up on the losing side on these decisions, or even taking a mistaken position, may well prove very costly for the long-term prospects of the actors concerned, this process also offers them little incentive to compromise. In other words, what is at issue is not just winning today, but also winning tomorrow, and the day after that. 'If the fall from power endangers the well-being and, eventually, the very life of a power wielder,' notes Sartori (1987: 42) 'he will not relinquish power. Conversely, if the security of staying well and alive hinges on "having power," then power will be sought ferociously, at all costs and with whatever means. Differently put, the peaceful mode of politics assumes that the stakes of politics are not too high.' In the post-communist case, however, as is evident, the stakes are high; there is still a lot to play for.

As I have suggested, the potential instability at the level of the electorate and within the context of competition already makes for an uncertain and volatile mix, which, even in itself, would seem to exacerbate the potential for conflict between the different élites. If we then add to that mix the fact that, in this triple transition, these élites are playing for very high stakes, both substantively and strategically, then it is difficult to avoid the conclusion that these newly emerging systems will also prove significantly more competitive than is the case in the established party systems—indeed, as far as the latter systems are concerned, what is most striking is the long-term process by which consolidation and institutionalization have tended to erode competitiveness (Bartolini and Mair, 1990; see also Chapter 5 above). The danger, then, is of instability and uncertainty encouraging competition and conflict, which, in turn, encourage even greater instability. And this makes for a very different picture from that in many of the established democracies, where stability and predictability have tended to foster compromise and accommodation, and where compromise and accommodation, in turn, have tended to promote even greater stability, if not complacency.

I will conclude briefly. Few would deny the inherently unstable character of the newly emerging party systems in post-communist Europe. It is, moreover, a pattern of instability which has also been echoed on previous occasions, albeit less dramatically, in other newly emerging European party systems, where uncertainty and conflicts of interest also sometimes fostered a strong sense of competitiveness. The key question which remains, however, is whether these most recent additions to the world of competitive multi-party systems, like their predecessors, will also tend to settle down over time, and whether they will also become consolidated.

On the one hand, we can point to the earlier experiences of democratization in Europe and suggest that consolidation is simply a question of time and experience. Much like Germany and Italy in the postwar decades, and Portugal and Spain in the last twenty years, the post-communist democracies will also eventually assimilate to the pattern set by the established democracies. On the other hand, however, the particularly underdeveloped character of civil society in post-communist Europe, the continuing fractiousness of the political class, and the sheer intensity of political competition, all suggest that the varying obstacles which stand in the way of post-communist consolidation are significantly more pronounced than in any of these earlier clusters of democratizing polities, and it is this which is clearly worrying.

As has been underlined again and again by a variety of leading analysts, including Przeworski, Valenzuela, Di Palma, and Schmitter and O'Donnell, the likelihood of a successful consolidation of democracy depends in large part on the willingness of the protagonists to encourage a culture of compromise and accommodation. Winners should not take all. At the same time, however, as

I have tried to emphasize in this chapter, the sheer strain imposed by the triple transition in post-communist Europe, the fact that there is so much to play for, and the fact that the various electorates, like the political systems themselves, are essentially up for grabs, are all likely to combine in discouraging any such open-handed approach. The problem is evident: 'On the one hand,' notes Jasiewicz (1995: 455), 'there is an urgent need to establish and reinforce democratic institutions and processes, immune—as much as possible—to the particularistic interests and preferences of the participants (groups or individuals) involved. On the other hand, nothing else but these very interests and preferences motivate actors to seek and promote specific institutional [and political, PM] solutions.'

9

Party Systems and
Structures of Competition

The classification and categorization of party systems is by now a long-established art. On the one hand, by noting the number of parties in competition in any given polity, and by taking at least some account of the manner in which these parties interact with one another, it has always been possible to gain a reasonably valuable insight into the ways in which these polities differ from one another. On the other hand, following a more normative imperative, it has also often proved tempting to trace the source of problems of the legitimacy and stability of regimes back to the character of their party systems. For both reasons, an understanding of the nature and character of a country's party system has always been accorded priority in cross-national comparative analysis, even if the criteria by which party systems are compared has often been subject to debate.[1]

This chapter begins with a review of the principal existing approaches to the classification of party systems, pointing to both their limits and possibilities when applied within comparative analysis. It then goes on in the second section to underline the importance of understanding the structure of competition in any given party system, since in many ways the whole notion of a party system is centred on the assumption that there exists a stable structure of competition. Structures of competition can be seen to be either closed (and predictable) or open (and unpredictable), depending on the patterns of alternation in government, the degree of innovation or persistence in processes of government formation, and the range of parties gaining access to government. The emphasis in the third

[1] For an overview of some recent cross-national studies in the field, and in addition to the various comparative and national studies which are cited elsewhere in this chapter, see, for example, Gallagher *et al.* (1995), Lawson and Merkl (1988*b*), Mair and Smith (1990), Randall (1988), Ware (1987, 1996), and Wolinetz (1988).

section is on the need to distinguish between processes of electoral change on the one hand, and changes in party systems and the structures of competition on the other, a distinction which also allows us to conceive of situations in which electoral change is the consequence rather than the cause of party system change.

APPROACHES TO THE CLASSIFICATION OF PARTY SYSTEMS: A REVIEW

The most conventional and frequently adopted criterion for classifying party systems is also the most simple: the number of parties in competition. Moreover, the conventional distinction involved here has also proved appealingly straightforward: that between a two-party system on the one hand, and a multiparty (i.e. more than two) system on the other (see Duverger, 1954). Nor was this just a casual categorization; on the contrary, it was believed to tap into a more fundamental distinction between more or less stable and consensual democracies, which were those normally associated with the two-party type, as opposed to more or less unstable and conflictual democracies, which were those associated with the multiparty type. Thus two-party systems, which were typically characteristic of the United Kingdom and the United States, and which invariably involved single-party government, were assumed to enhance accountability, alternation in government, and moderate, centre-seeking competition. Multiparty systems, on the other hand, which usually required coalition administrations, and which were typically characteristic of countries such as France or Italy, prevented voters from gaining a direct voice in the formation of governments, did not necessarily facilitate alternation in government, and sometimes favoured extremist, ideological confrontations between narrowly based political parties. And although this simple association of party system types and political stability and efficacy was later challenged by research into the experiences of some of the smaller European democracies, which boasted both a multiplicity of parties and a strong commitment to consensual government (e.g. Daalder, 1983) and which thus led some early observers to attempt to elaborate a distinction between 'working' multiparty systems (e.g. the Netherlands or Sweden) and 'non-working' or 'immobilist' multiparty systems (e.g. Italy), the core categorization of two-party versus multiparty has nevertheless continued to command a great deal of support within the literature on comparative politics.[2]

This simple distinction is, of course, far from being the only possible approach, and since Duverger a number of attempts have been made to develop more sensitive and discriminating criteria (see Table 9.1).[3] In the conclusion to his classic *Oppositions* volume, for example, Robert Dahl (1966) sought to move away from an almost exclusive concern with simply the numbers of parties, and built an alternative classification based around the competitive strategy adopted by the opposing parties, distinguishing between competitive, cooperative, and coalescent strategies, and distinguishing further between opposition in the electoral arena and opposition in the parliamentary arena (see also Laver, 1989). This led Dahl to elaborate a fourfold typology, distinguishing between strictly competitive systems, co-operative-competitive systems, coalescent-competitive systems, and strictly coalescent systems. Shortly after this, in what proved subsequently a very influential study, Jean Blondel (1968) developed a typology which took account not only of the numbers of parties in competition, but also their relative size (and, in a later refinement, their 'place on the ideological spectrum'), distinguishing four types: two-party systems, two-and-a-half-party systems, multiparty systems with a dominant party, and multiparty systems without a dominant party. In practice, however, this new approach did little more than improve the traditional two-party versus multiparty distinction by disaggregating the otherwise overloaded multiparty category. Stein Rokkan's (1968) contemporaneous attempt to classify the party systems of the smaller European democracies also did little more than disaggregate the multiparty category, in this case by taking account of the likelihood of single-party majorities (akin to Blondel's dominant party) and the degree to which there was a fragmentation of minority party strengths. Using these criteria, Rokkan developed a threefold distinction involving a 'British–German' type system, in which the system was dominated by the competition between two major parties,

---

[2] See, for example, Almond *et al.* (1993: 117–20), where this traditional distinction is recast as one of 'majoritarian' versus multiparty systems; see also the influential study by Lijphart (1984), where one of the key distinctions between majoritarian and consensus democracies is defined as that between a two-party system and a multiparty system.

[3] The approaches reviewed here are also included among the various reprints included in an earlier reader which I edited—see Mair (1990*a*: 285–349).

TABLE 9.1. *Types of party systems*

Author	Principal criteria for classification	Principal types of party system identified
Duverger (1954)	numbers of parties	two-party systems multiparty systems
Dahl (1966)	competitiveness of opposition	strictly competitive cooperative-competitive coalescent-competitive strictly coalescent
Blondel (1968)	numbers of parties relative size of parties	two-party systems two-and-a-half-party systems multiparty systems with one dominant party multiparty systems without dominant party
Rokkan (1968)	numbers of parties likelihood of single-party majorities distribution of minority party strengths	the British–German '1 vs. 1 + 1' system the Scandinavian '1 vs. 3–4' system even multiparty systems: '1 vs. 1 vs. 1 + 2–3'
Sartori (1976)	numbers of parties ideological distance	two-party systems moderate pluralism polarized pluralism predominant-party systems

with a third, minor party also in contention; a 'Scandinavian'-type system in which one big party regularly confronted a more or less formalized alliance between three or four smaller parties; and an 'even' multiparty system in which competition was dominated by three or more parties of equivalent size.

With the notable exception of Dahl, therefore, these early classifications have all remained closely tied to an emphasis on the numbers of parties, albeit sometimes supplemented by attention to the relative electoral weights of the parties involved. In this sense they can also be related to the importance attached to party numbers—or to the 'format' of the party system—in the more comprehensive typology which was later developed by Sartori (1976: 117–323; for earlier versions of this typology, see Sartori 1966, 1970). But although Sartori's approach emphasized the relevance of party numbers, it also went much beyond this by including a second principal criterion which had previously been largely disregarded, that is, the ideological distance separating the parties in the system. Sartori's typology, which was explicitly concerned with the interactions between the parties in any given system—what Sartori refers to as the 'mechanics' of the system—and which was therefore explicitly concerned with differential patterns of competition, drew on the combination of these two criteria. Party systems could therefore be classified according to the number of parties in the system, in which there was a distinction between formats with two parties, those with up to some five parties (limited pluralism), and those with some six parties or more (extreme pluralism); and according to the ideological distance separating the extreme parties in the system, which would either be small ('moderate') or large ('polarized'). The two criteria were not wholly independent, however, in that Sartori also argued that the format of the system, that is, the number of parties, contained mechanical predispositions (that is, it could affect the degree of polarization) such that extreme pluralism could lead to polarization. The combination of both criteria then yielded three principal types of party system—two-party systems, characterized by an evidently limited format and a small ideological distance (e.g. the United Kingdom); moderate pluralism, characterized by limited pluralism and a relatively small ideological distance (e.g. Denmark); and, which was the most important for the typology, polarized pluralism, characterized by extreme pluralism and a large ideological distance (e.g. Italy in the 1960s and 1970s, and Chile prior to the 1973 coup). In addition, Sartori also allowed for the existence of a 'predominant-party system', a system in which one particular party, such as, most notably, Congress in India or the Liberal Democrats in Japan, consistently (that is, over at least four legislatures) won a winning majority of parliamentary seats.[4]

---

[4] Although the predominant-party system constitutes a useful category, it nevertheless fits rather uneasily into Sartori's framework, since it is defined by wholly different, ad hoc criteria, such that a predominant-party system can by definition coexist with every possible category of party numbers (that is, it can develop within a context of a two-party system, a system of limited pluralism, and a system of extreme pluralism) and, at least theoretically, with every possible spread of the ideological distance.

There are a number of reasons why Sartori's typology can be regarded as the most important of those briefly reviewed here. In the first place, it is the most comprehensive of all the available typologies, both in terms of the care with which it is developed and in terms of the way in which it is applied to empirical cases. Second, notwithstanding the continued appeal of the simple two-party/ multiparty distinction, it has subsequently been employed in a variety of sophisticated national and cross-national studies, yielding a degree of insight into the functioning of party systems which is simply incomparably better than that developed by any of the alternative typologies (e.g. Bartolini, 1984; Bille, 1990). Third, as noted, it is explicitly concerned with patterns of competition and with the interactions between parties, and in this sense it is much more directly concerned with the functioning of the party *system* itself. Finally, it underlines the influence exerted by systemic properties, and by the party system, on electoral behavior and electoral outcomes. Unlike any of the other typologies, it therefore allows the party system to operate as an independent variable, constraining or even directing electoral preferences. This last aspect is particularly important in this context, and I will return to it at a later stage.

At the same time, however, and some twenty years after the publication of Sartori's seminal volume, questions can be raised regarding the continued utility and discriminating capacity of the typology, not least because of what is now a potential overcrowding in the 'moderate pluralism' category and a virtual emptying of the alternative types. For example, and this criticism can also be levelled against the traditional Duverger classification, it is now relatively difficult to find an unequivocal example of a real two-party system. The United States, which is often cited as a classic two-party model, might better be described as a 'four-party' system, in which a presidential two-party system coexists with a separate congressional two-party system, or even as having fifty two-party systems, each functioning separately in each of the fifty states (e.g. Katz and Kolodny, 1994). New Zealand, which also offered a classic example of two-party system, is currently experiencing a strong pressure towards fragmentation, which is likely to be even further accentuated by the recent adoption of a proportional electoral formula. The United Kingdom, which was also always seen as the paramount case of a two-party system, currently, albeit perhaps temporarily, fulfils Sartori's conditions for a predominant-party system. Against this, of course, it might be argued that a number of the Latin American systems, and particularly Costa Rica and Venezuela, are now moving more closely towards a two-party model, which could restore the relevance of the category as a whole.

At the other extreme, and particularly given the recent decline and/or eclipse of traditional communist parties, it has also become difficult to find an unambiguous example of polarized pluralism. Sartori's criteria for this latter system had been very carefully elaborated (1976: 131–73), but depended crucially on there being a 'maximum spread of [ideological] opinion' (p. 135), *bilateral* oppositions (p. 134), and hence, necessarily so, on there being a relevant anti-system party (that is, a party which 'undermines the legitimacy of the regime it opposes' (p. 133)) at *each* end of the political spectrum. It follows from this that should *either* of these anti-system alternatives become irrelevant or disappear, there would then occur an inevitable attenuation of the spread of opinion and thus a reduction in the degree of polarization, so forcing the case out of the category. This is now certainly the case in France, for example, where the fading anti-system party of the left, the Communist Party (PCF), was sufficiently legitimated to be admitted to government office in 1981; and in Italy, where the Communist Party (PCI) divided into the unequivocally moderate Democratic Party of the Left (PDS) and the smaller, more radical, but certainly no longer anti-system alternative of the Communist Refoundation (RC). In addition, with the advent of the National Alliance–Social Movement (AN-MSI) to office in the Berlusconi government of 1994, Italy can also be seen to have shed its anti-system alternative of the right. This is not to suggest that anti-system oppositions have everywhere ceased to exist; on the contrary, despite the eclipse of the traditional anti-system parties of the Communist and Fascist variety, a number of European party systems are now confronted with the rise of new parties, particularly on the right, which might well be seen as anti-system in orientation, such as the National Front in France, the Vlaams Blok in Belgium, and possibly also the now transformed Liberal Party in Austria (Betz, 1994; Ignazi, 1992, 1994; Mudde, 1995). But even if these parties do reflect an extreme of opinion on the right-wing side of the political spectrum, they tend not to be counterbalanced by an equivalent anti-system extreme on the left, and hence, by definition, the poles are no longer 'two poles apart' (Sartori, 1976: 135). In short, if two-party systems

the competition for government be understood? Three related factors are relevant here. First, there is the question of the prevailing pattern of alternation in government in any given party system, and the extent to which this is either wholesale, partial, or even non-existent. Second, there is the question of the stability or consistency of the governing alternatives, and the extent to which innovative formulae are adopted. Finally, there is the simple question of who governs, and the extent to which access to government is either open to a wide range of diverse parties or limited to a smaller subset of parties. Let us now look at each of these factors in turn.

Alternation in government

There are three conceivable patterns of alternation which can be considered here. The first and most obvious pattern might be termed *wholesale alternation*, in which a set of incumbents is wholly displaced by a former opposition. In other words, all of the parties in government at time t are removed from office and are replaced at time $t + 1$ by a new government made up of a party or coalition of parties which were previously in opposition. The British case offers the most obvious example of such wholesale alternation, with a single-party Labour government being replaced by a single-party Conservative government, or vice versa. A similar pattern has been evident in New Zealand, with the alternation between Labour and the National parties. But while the classic two-party model offers the most obvious examples of wholesale alternation, the pattern can also be seen in more fragmented systems. In Norway, for example, wholesale alternation has regularly ensued on the basis of shifts between a single-party Labour government on the one hand, and a multiparty bourgeois coalition on the other, reflecting a pattern of competition similar to that which developed in Costa Rica in the 1960s and 1970s. More unusually, the recent French experience has witnessed wholesale alternation between competing coalitions, with the Socialists and various left-wing allies, including the Communist Party, alternating with a coalition of the Gaullists (RPR) and centre-right (UDF). This latter case is quite exceptional, however, in that even in fragmented systems, as was the case over extended periods of time in Ireland, Norway, and Sweden, and as was also the case in Japan in 1993, wholesale alternation has usually involved at least one single-party alternative.

The second pattern, which is more common in fragmented systems, is *partial alternation*, in which a newly incumbent government includes at least one party which also formed part of the previous government. Germany provides the most obvious example here, in that all of the governments which have held office since 1969 have included the small Liberal Party (FDP) as a junior coalition partner, with the role of senior partner alternating sporadically between the Social Democrats (SPD) and the Christian Democrats (CDU–CSU). The Dutch system also approximates this pattern, with the Christian Democrats (CDA) and, prior to 1977, the Catholic People's Party (KVP), tending to persist in office, albeit with alternating coalition partners.[6] Indeed, the major contrast between the German and Dutch patterns of alternation is simply that, in the Dutch case, it has tended to be the biggest single party that has remained in government, whereas it is usually the smaller partner in the German case. Similar enduring patterns of partial alternation, albeit without involving such pronounced long-term continuity of one particular partner in office, can be seen in Belgium, Finland, and Luxembourg. However, the most striking example of partial alternation was that provided by the Italian case throughout most of the postwar period, with the Christian Democrats (DC) holding office continually from 1946 to 1994, occasionally as a minority single-party government, and more often as the senior partner in a variable multiparty coalition. In this sense the Italian case also approximates to that of the Netherlands, the major difference being that, prior to 1977, and despite its size, the core KVP was more often than not in an overall minority within the governing coalition, as was also the case with the CDA in 1981–2.

The third pattern also borders closely on the Italian experience and is marked by a complete absence of alternation, or by *non-alternation*, in which the same party or parties remain in exclusive control of government over an extended period of time, being displaced neither wholly nor partially. Switzerland offers the clearest example of non-alternation over time, with the same four-party coalition holding office since 1959. A similar pattern of non-alternation clearly also characterizes what Sartori defined as pre-

---

[6] Following the 1994 election, and for the first time since the advent of full democracy, a government was formed in the Netherlands without the Christian Democrats/religious mainstream.

dominant-party systems, as in the case of Japan from 1955 to 1993, with the Liberal Democrats holding office almost consistently alone over this forty-year period; in India, where the Congress party held continuous office until its first defeat in 1977; and in Mexico, where the Revolutionary Party (PRI) has held the dominant position since the 1920s.

Innovation and familiarity

Party systems differ not only in their patterns of alternation, but also in the degree to which the alternative governing formulae are either familiar or innovative—that is, whether or not the party or combination of parties has governed before in that particular format (see also Franklin and Mackie, 1983). In the British case, for example, familiarity is everything, and no new governing formula has been experimented with since the broad coalition which held office during World War II. The formulae were also familiar and hence very predictable over a long period in the Irish case, with governments being made up of either Fianna Fáil on the one hand, or a coalition of all the remaining parties on the other, as well as in Germany, which has experimented with no new formula since the advent to office for the first time of the Social Democrat–Liberal coalition in 1969. Notwithstanding the German case, however, it is in systems of partial alternation that the greatest scope exists for innovation. In Italy, for example, despite the long-term dominance of the Christian Democrats, there has been frequent experimentation with new coalition alliances. In the Netherlands, despite the continuity in office of the Catholic Party and, later, the Christian Democrats, innovation has also been particularly marked, with differing and novel combinations of parties succeeding one another in office with remarkable frequency. It is important to note here that, while innovative formulae are obviously involved when the party or parties concerned have never previously held office, they can also be deemed to occur even when the parties have governed before but never in that particular alliance. In the Irish case, for example, the first ever coalition between Fianna Fáil and Labour, which took office in 1993, can be defined as innovative, even though each of the parties involved had already had long experiences of government; similarly, both the People's Party (ÖVP) and Social Democrats' (SPÖ) single-party governments in

Austria (taking office for the first time in 1966 and 1970 respectively) can be treated as innovative, despite the fact that both parties had previously governed together in coalition.

Which parties govern?

The third factor involved here concerns the range of parties which gain access to government. Although not all possible parties can be expected to win a share of office, even with frequent alternation, party systems can nevertheless be distinguished in terms of the degree to which access to office is widely or narrowly dispersed. In other words, party systems can be distinguished in terms of whether all relevant parties eventually cross the threshold of government, as is more or less the case in the Netherlands, for example, or whether governing remains the privilege of just a limited subset of parties, as was the case in postwar Italy. Knowing the range of parties with access to office therefore allows us to distinguish between these latter cases, which otherwise tend to coincide in terms of both of the other criteria indicated above. That is, while both the Netherlands and Italy are similar in the sense of their pattern of partial alternation, in terms of the longevity in office of a core centre party, and in terms of their resort to innovative formulae, they are nevertheless strikingly dissimilar when it comes to the range of parties gaining access to office, with particular parties being persistently excluded in the Italian case, and with virtually no substantial parties being excluded in the Dutch case.

This distinction may also be related to what Sartori defines as polarized pluralism, which, as noted above, required the presence of anti-system parties at each end of the political spectrum, such parties being defined in part as those which were out of competition for government, thus forcing governments to be formed across the span of the centre. Here also, the concern is with whether certain parties are excluded as unacceptable partners in office. Where this criterion differs from that used in the definition of polarized pluralism, however, is that the question of whether or nor such parties are genuinely and objectively 'anti-system', which has always been a point of dispute in the interpretations and criticisms of Sartori's model, becomes irrelevant. Rather, what matters is whether there are parties which are treated, *in practice*, as 'outsiders', and which are regarded by the other parties in the system as unacceptable allies. In this sense, anti-systemness, like beauty, here lies in the eyes of the beholder. It is difficult, for example, to determine whether the Danish Progress Party is genuinely anti-system; on the other hand, it is relatively easy to see that this party has been regarded by its potential allies as an outsider and, up to now, has always languished in opposition (unlike, say, the more ostensibly 'anti-system' Communist Party in France).

Structures of party competition: closed or open?

The combination of these three criteria yields a fairly broad-brush distinction between two contrasting patterns in the structure of party competition (see Table 9.2). On the one hand, the structure of party competition can be relatively *closed*, and hence highly pre-dictable, with little or no change over time in the range of govern-ing alternatives or in the pattern of alternation, and with new parties and/or 'outsider' parties finding it virtually impossible to break through the threshold of government. The British and New Zealand cases have afforded perhaps the best examples of such closed systems, with each being persistently characterized by whole-sale alternation, by a complete absence of innovative formulae, and by the presence of just two governing and governable parties. On the other hand, the structure of party competition can prove rela-tively *open*, and hence quite unpredictable, with differing patterns of alternation, with frequent shifts in the make-up of the governing alternatives, and with new parties gaining relatively easy access to office. The postwar Dutch pattern comes quite close to this form, in that new parties have been relatively easily incorporated into government (such as Democratic Socialists 70 in 1971 and both Democrats 66 and the Radicals (PPR) in 1973) and in that innov-ative formulae have been adopted in almost half of the new gov-ernments formed since 1951.

Where the Dutch system deviates from a wholly open pattern, however, is in the long-term presence in government of the Catholic Party and, later, the Christian Democrats, and in the fact that alter-nation has always been partial. In this sense, and at least prior to 1994 when the first ever 'secular' government was formed, there was always a certain element of predictability involved, and to this extent the structure of competition was at least partially closed. Denmark in the postwar period also comes quite close to an open

TABLE 9.2. *Closed and open structures of competition*

Closed structure of competition	Open structure of competition
Wholesale alternation in office, or non-alternation in office	Partial alternation, or mix of both partial and wholesale alternation
Familiar governing formulae	Innovative governing formulae
Access to government restricted to a limited number of parties	Access to government open to (almost) all parties
Examples:	*Examples*:
United Kingdom, New Zealand (to mid-1990s), Japan (1955–93), Switzerland, Ireland (1948–89)	Denmark, the Netherlands, newly emerging party systems

pattern, having experiences of both partial and wholesale alternation, having frequently adopted innovative formulae (in the case of almost one-third of all postwar governments), and having also proved to be relatively open to new parties, as in 1982, when the Centre Democrats and the Christian People's Party were first admitted to government. On the other hand, even Denmark can be seen as partially closed and somewhat predictable as a result of the persistent exclusion from office of the Progress Party and the Socialist People's Party.

These examples also underline the extent to which the development of a closed structure of competition owes much to the strategies of the established parties, and, in particular, their unwillingness to experiment with innovative formulae and their reluctance to admit new parties into government (Franklin and Mackie, 1983). In some instances, of course, the parties may feel themselves genuinely constrained in this respect, in that any new governing options might require the bridging of what are believed to be ineluctable divides in policy and/or ideology. The structure of competition may therefore be very predictable, and hence closed, as a result of the distances which separate the relevant parties along any one of a variety of different dimensions of competition. Such arguments might well have been used by Christian Democratic leaders in Italy, for example, in order to justify the persistent exclusion of the Communist Party from office, and might equally be cited by a number of different party leaderships in Denmark in order to justify the persistent exclusion of the Progress Party.

In other instances, however, it is obvious that the maintenance of familiar and closed patterns of competition simply constitutes a strategy of self-preservation on the part of the established parties.[7] In Ireland, for example, the long-term refusal of the dominant Fianna Fáil party to even consider entering a coalition, a refusal which contributed substantially to the closure of competition in Ireland (see below), was clearly designed to maintain its status as the only party capable of offering single-party government, and was thus intended to maintain its electoral credibility. A similar sense of self-preservation can be seen to characterize the long-term reluctance of the two major British parties to consider the possibilities of coalition with the smaller Liberal party, even though Labour did come strikingly close to such a path-breaking option during the Lib-Lab Pact in the late 1970s. To be sure, there are real limits on the capacity and willingness of the established parties to maintain a closed structure of competition. New parties might emerge which have to be taken on board, particular party leaders may have their own agendas and priorities, external crises might develop which force the adoption of new strategies, and so on; none the less, any explanation of the degree of closure of any given structure of competition must necessarily focus particular attention on the strategies of the parties themselves.

Closed structures of competition are clearly characteristic of traditional two-party systems, and, of course, of those systems which have experienced a real absence of alternation over time, such as Japan, the Stormont regime in Northern Ireland, Mexico, Singapore, or Switzerland. Conversely, openness and a lack of predictability tend to characterize more fragmented systems which experience partial alternation, especially where there is no large core party of government. Moreover, since closure necessarily requires the development of stable norms and conventions in the patterns of competition and in the processes of government formation, it is also clearly a function of time, and, most crucially, is not something which can be seen to characterize newly emerging party 'systems'.

Indeed, what is most striking about new party systems, such as those which are currently emerging in post-communist Europe, for

---

[7] It is in this sense that such closure also involves what Schattscheider (1960: 69 and *passim*) has termed 'the mobilization of bias', with the emphasis on particular conflicts and on distinct alternatives acting to preserve the interests of the various protagonists. See also Chapter 1 above.

example, is precisely their lack of closure and hence their lack of *systemness* (see Chapter 8 above), a feature which also continues to characterize even many of the older party systems of Latin America. Seen from this perspective, the long-term process by which party systems may eventually become consolidated can also be seen as a long-term process by which the structure of competition becomes increasingly closed and predictable. Thus, while a more closed and predictable structure might well develop in a number of the post-communist democracies in the next decade or so, this will by definition, necessarily involve a relatively lengthy process. Just such a long-term process of structural consolidation might now be seen to be reaching fruition in the relatively recently democratized Portuguese and Spanish systems, as well as in some of the Latin American systems, with perhaps the most notable examples being seen in the drift towards two-partyism in Costa Rica and Venezuela (McDonald and Ruhl, 1989); in this latter region, however, as in the United States, the frequent combination of a presidential system of government on the one hand, and the presence of largely undisciplined parties (e.g. Mainwaring and Shugart, 1994) on the other, suggests that there remains a significant bias against the development of closed structures of competition, at least in the legislative electoral arena.[8] In short, the degree of closure varies, ranging along a continuum from situations in which it is least pronounced, such as in newly emerging party systems, to those in which it is most pronounced, such as in those established systems in which there is little or no innovation in the processes of government formation, and in which new parties rarely if ever break through the governing threshold.[9]

PARTY SYSTEMS AND ELECTORAL OUTCOMES

The notion of the closure or openness of the structure of competition is also important in that it immediately allows us to move away

[8] See Sartori (1994: 181 n. 7); the lack of structuration is also reflected in the persistently high levels of electoral volatility which are strikingly and substantially higher than those occurring in the relatively structured west European systems (Coppedge, 1992).
[9] As noted, it is also probably least pronounced in the legislative electoral arena in presidential systems, notwithstanding any strong structuration which might be evident in the presidential electoral arena in these same systems.

from the conventional idea that party system change is largely, if not exclusively, a function of, or even a synonym for, electoral change (see also Chapter 3 above). It other words, it affords a conception of party system change which may owe its origin to factors other than simply the flux in voter preferences. For although party system stability and change on the one hand, and electoral stability and change on the other, may certainly be related, they are nevertheless far from being mutually equivalent. Electoral alignments might shift, for example, even in quite a dramatic way, without necessarily impinging significantly on the structure of competition, and hence without necessarily altering the character of the party system itself. Conversely, the structure of party competition and hence the nature of the party system itself might suddenly be transformed, even without any significant prior electoral flux.

In Denmark, for example, the 1973 election witnessed one of the most substantial electoral shifts ever to have occurred in postwar Europe, resulting in an immediate doubling of the number of parties represented in parliament. Prior to 1973, five parties had been represented in the Danish Folketing, together accounting for some 93 per cent of the total vote. As a result of the 1973 election, five new parties won representation, and the total vote won by the previously represented parties fell to less than 65 per cent. This was a massive shift by any standards, and since the new entrants to the parliament included both the long-established Communist Party as well as the newly formed right-wing Progress Party, it also resulted in a major increase in the level of polarization.

In practice, however, it is certainly possible to question whether this change had any real systemic impact in Denmark. To be sure, a new government had to be formed, which, in fact, was a minority, single-party Liberal government, the first to take office since 1945. On the other hand, this innovative government was then succeeded by a Social Democratic minority government, which was precisely the same form of government which had held office prior to the 1973 earthquake election, and then eventually by a centre-right coalition, which was differently composed but otherwise essentially similar to the various other centre-right coalitions which had governed Denmark in the early 1950s and late 1960s. To be sure, the increased fragmentation and the greater degree of polarization made governing more difficult after 1973—prior to the short-lived four-party coalition which took office in January 1993 no post-1973 government had enjoyed majority status in parliament (although such a status had also been quite exceptional even prior to 1973); governments tended to collapse more frequently than before; there was now a greater resort to elections, although this had also been not uncommon prior to 1973; and finally, as noted above, new parties had eventually to be accommodated into government, although the Progress Party has not yet been accorded this particular privilege. But the question still remains as to whether this massive shift in electoral preferences has had any real effect whatsoever on the structure of party competition and on the party system itself. Denmark is now, but always has been, quite innovative in terms of governing formulae; it is now, and always has been, reasonably open to new parties coming into government; and now, as before, it experiences both wholesale and partial alternation in government on a regular basis. Moreover, it had once, and still maintains now, a relatively open structure of competition and hence a relatively unconstraining party system. In these terms at least, it appears that 1973 has not made any significant difference (on the Danish situation see Pedersen, 1987, 1988, and Bille, 1990).

The Italian case in 1994 might also offer a useful example, even though uncertainty still remains as to whether a genuine transformation of the party system is really under way (see especially the analysis by Bartolini and D'Alimonte, 1995). On the face of it, there is no other established Western party system which has undergone such a profound change. At the electoral level, for example, following decades of relative stability, the 1994 contest resulted in a level of volatility of some 37.2 per cent, which is not only the highest figure recorded in Italian history, but, even more strikingly, is substantially higher than that recorded in almost *any* election held in western Europe between 1885 and 1989.[10] In terms of format, the system has also been totally transformed, with the emergence of new parties and the reconstitution of established parties

---

[10] The index of volatility measures the net aggregate shift in votes from one election to the next, and is the equivalent of the total aggregate gains of all winning parties or the total aggregate losses of all losing parties (see Pedersen, 1983). The average volatility in postwar Europe has been less than 9 per cent, and, apart from the 1994 election in Italy, only four other European elections in the past century have exceeded 35 per cent: Germany in 1919 (47.5 per cent), France in 1945 (36.4 per cent), and Greece in 1950 (47.0 per cent) and 1951 (45.1 per cent)—see Bartolini and D'Alimonte (1995: 443–4); on electoral stability and instability in Europe more generally, see Bartolini and Mair (1990).

leading to a situation in which virtually none of the parties currently represented in the new 1994 parliament was represented under the same name or in the same form as recently as 1987. Finally, it can also be argued that there has also been a major change in the level of polarization, as a result of the transformation of the Communist Party into the Democratic Party of the Left on the one hand and, on the other, the transformation of the Social Movement (MSI) into the National Alliance (AN) and its incorporation into government, which, at least in Sartori's sense of the term, leaves Italy now with no relevant 'anti-system' party.

These are certainly profound changes. The most relevant question, however, is whether these changes will have any long-term impact on the structure of competition. The structure of competition in the 'old' party system was certainly clear. Governments were formed out of the centre, were dominated by the Christian Democrats, and involved shifting alliances with partial alternation across the centre-left and centre-right while excluding both the extreme left (PCI) and extreme right (MSI). Any fundamental change in this pattern would therefore now require governments to be formed almost exclusively from the left or from the right (creating the potential for wholesale alternation), would require the incorporation (or disappearance) of the extremes, and, in this new bipolar world, would require the marginalization of the independent position of the centre.

With the formation of the right-wing Berlusconi government in 1994, it certainly seemed possible that just such a pattern might emerge. Perhaps ironically, however, it quickly became clear that the new alliance would be unable to maintain either its coherence or its majority, and that any consolidation of its position would require the approval of, and incorporation of, the now reduced centre, as represented by the successor to the DC, the People's Party (PPI). At the same time, the PPI itself was divided, being particularly reluctant to share power with the successors of the old extreme right, the National Alliance, and with some sections preferring to incorporate, or ally with, the new centre-left, as represented by the Democratic Party of the Left. As of now, of course, it is too soon to suggest what future patterns or alignments might yet emerge, and in this sense the structure of competition might be regarded as quite open and unpredictable, which, at least in the short term, does represent a fundamental change. Moreover, should the centre split into 'left' and 'right', as currently appears to be the pattern, then a wholly new bipolar structure might develop, and this would certainly transform the Italian party system. But should an independent centre reconstitute itself, and should it prove capable of taking full advantage of its pivotal position by playing left off against right in a way which would allow it to construct a broad alliance across the centre, then, despite the different actors and their different weights in the system, it might well recreate more or less the same structure of competition as had prevailed prior to the 1990s (Bartolini and D'Alimonte, 1995). As in Denmark, therefore, but more markedly so, massive shifts at the level of the electorate and at the level of the format of the party system could yet end up in a party system which reflects more continuity than change. The possibility certainly exists.

Question marks also hang over the real extent of change in the Canadian party system, notwithstanding the electoral earthquake of 1993. In this case, as in Italy, the level of volatility rose to an unprecedented high of 42 per cent, almost five times that of the average level of volatility recorded in the 1970s and 1980s. The consequences were also very far-reaching, with the once powerful Conservative party being reduced to just 16 per cent of the vote (its lowest share since 1949) and, even more strikingly, to just two seats (as against 169 in the previous election). In addition, two new parties, the Reform party and Bloc Québécois, won substantial representation in parliament, the first parties outside the mainstream to do so since the effective demise of Social Credit in the mid-1970s (for analyses of recent developments in the Canadian party system, see Bakvis, 1988, 1991; Carty, 1994; and MacIvor, 1995). Moreover, precisely because these two new parties are so evidently regional in character, they may also signal a potentially enduring shift in electoral alignments. This is substantial change by any standard.

At the same time, however, there is also one striking continuity, in that the Liberal party, the traditional opponent of, and alternative to, the Conservatives, is now back in government with a powerful majority, and thus at least for now, and in terms of the patterns of alternation, the degree of innovation, and the extent of access to government of new parties, Canada remains as it has been for decades. At one level, the system has certainly changed: the Liberals now confront two major opposition parties instead of just one, and a regional divide has now erupted onto the federal stage in a manner which clearly damages Canada's prospects of maintaining its familiar, British-style pattern of wholesale alternation in the future. Nevertheless, and much as in the Italian case, it is precisely because this potential for change still remains to be realized that it is, as yet, impossible to speak of any fundamental transformation in the structure of competition.

Finally, and for a completely contrasting example, we can turn to the Irish case (Mair, 1987*a*, 1993). Lacking a strong cleavage structure, and being characterized by quite marked institutional continuity, the party system had been stabilized largely by a very rigid structure of competition, in which the governments taking office for most of the postwar period were formed by either Fianna Fáil on the one hand, or by a sometimes motley coalition of Fianna Fáil's opponents (principally Fine Gael and the Labour party) on the other. Indeed, in the more recent period, these alternatives also replaced one another in office with remarkable regularity, with each election from 1973 to 1987 resulting in a wholesale alternation in office. This enduring structure of competition had two principal effects. In the first place, it provided Fianna Fáil with one of the major foundations for its appeal, in that the party reaped a major electoral advantage from the fact that it was the only party which had the potential to provide single-party government, and for this reason, for example, it deliberately and very publicly eschewed the idea of coalescing with any other party, preferring to go into opposition on those occasions when it could not command a working majority. Second, this structure of competition helped to prevent Labour, the third party in the system, from mobilizing any independent and potentially realigning strategy. Indeed, the party was almost perpetually constrained by the choice of either languishing in opposition or, regardless of the policy problems involved, joining with Fine Gael as the junior partner in a non-Fianna Fáil coalition. No other option was available.

In 1989, however, all of this changed, when, for a variety of reasons, including the short-term ambition of its then party leader, Fianna Fáil performed a volte-face and decided to enter coalition with a recently formed, right-wing liberal party, the Progressive Democrats (Laver and Arkins, 1990). Four years later, following the collapse of that first experiment, the party formed a new coalition, this time with the Labour party. The result of both decisions was an effective transformation of the party system, with Fianna

Fáil's coalition with the Progressive Democrats effectively undermining the foundations on which the postwar party system had been structured, and with its coalition with Labour then more or less destroying those old foundations in their entirety. Prior to 1989, the Irish party system had been structured around a bipolar pattern of competition—Fianna Fáil versus the rest. In entering coalition with a new and ostensibly 'non-aligned' party, Fianna Fáil had damaged the integrity of the first of those two poles. Later, by entering coalition with one of its traditional opponents, with one of 'the rest', it forced the second pole to collapse. There was, in short, nothing which remained of the old order.

But what is perhaps the most striking feature of this transformation was the fact that, at least initially, and in contrast to the Danish, Italian, and Canadian cases, it occurred in a context of relatively minimal electoral change. The level of volatility in the 1989 election was just 7.8 per cent, which was below the postwar average in Ireland (Mair, 1993: 164), with most of this being accounted for by the sharp drop in support for the Progressive Democrats since their first successful outing in 1987. Elsewhere in the system, and among the established parties, support for Labour rose from 6.4 per cent to 9.5 per cent, support for Fine Gael rose from 27.1 per cent to 29.3 per cent, and support for Fianna Fáil remained precisely at 44.1 per cent. Substantial electoral continuities therefore accompanied what was clearly to become a fundamental transformation of the party system.

What we see here, then, is one instance in which substantial electoral change does not appear to have led to significant party system change (Denmark); one instance in which there has been a major change in the party system change notwithstanding prior electoral stability (Ireland); and two instances in which, despite extraordinary electoral flux, question marks still remain as to whether a new type of party system might develop (Canada and Italy). And what is most important here is that each of these instances therefore underlines the need to separate out the notion of party system stability/change on the one hand, and electoral stability/change on the other.

Not only that, however, for what may be most interesting about the separation of these two processes, and about the recognition that change in party systems may be due to factors other than electoral change—factors such as changes in élite behavior, in party strategy, in the patterns of competition, or whatever—is that it also affords the opportunity to *reverse* the conventional chain of influence, and to probe the extent to which *party system stability (or change) may itself lead to electoral stability (or change), rather than simply the other way around.*

Electoral alignments are, of course, stabilized by a variety of factors, of which the cleavage structure is perhaps the most important (Lipset and Rokkan, 1967; Bartolini and Mair, 1990). At the same time, however, the long-term stabilization of electorates should not be seen simply as a function of the ties that bind distinct social groups (Catholics, workers, farmers, and so on) to parties or to blocs of parties. To be sure, social structure has certainly proved to be an important stabilizing element, especially in countries with strong social cleavages or subcultures, such as Italy, the Netherlands, and Sweden. But if social structure were the only freezing agent, then we would certainly have witnessed much greater change in European electoral alignments in the 1970s and 1980s than has actually been the case. The fact is that many of the old traditional parties in Europe remain alive and kicking despite the widespread weakening of religious and class identities, and despite the long-term processes of individualization (see Chapter 4 above).

There are in fact a variety of factors involved here, with party systems and electoral alignments being also frozen by the constraints imposed by institutional structures such as the electoral system, and by the organizational efforts of the parties themselves (Bartolini and Mair, 1990). What is most relevant in this context, however, is that one additional 'freezing' agent may well be the constraints imposed by the structure of party competition and by its relationship to processes of government formation.[11] As noted above (Chapter 8), a closed structure of competition clearly constrains voter preferences, in that it limits the choice of governing options in a way which is similar to the limits on the choice of parties in non-fragmented systems. A closed structure of competition therefore also clearly enhances party system stability, and indeed, helps to ensure that party systems generate their own momentum

[11] The argument here clearly echoes that of Bakvis (1988: 263), who seeks to explain the Canadian paradox of party system stability in the context of weakly anchored electoral alignments by pointing to the existence of 'a more generalized loyalty to the party system as a whole'. The same might be said of Ireland (see above), and perhaps even of the United States. See also the discussion in Chapter 1 above.

and thus freeze into place. In short, the stabilization of party systems is at least partly a function of the consolidation of a given structure of competition.

What this also implies, of course, and perhaps most interestingly, is that a *change* in that structure may then act to *de*stabilize the party system. In Italy, for example, the basis for a wholesale change in electoral preferences in 1992 and 1994 was at least partially laid by the 'legitimation' of the Democratic Party of the Left, which undermined the terms of reference by which Italian party competition had been structured since the late 1940s. Italian voters, as well as the Italian parties themselves, had long been constrained by the belief that there was no alternative to a Christian Democratic-dominated government. And once such an alternative finally did emerge through the transformation of the unacceptable Communist Party into the highly acceptable Democratic Party of the Left, this particular anchor was cut loose, and voters began to shift in relatively great numbers, eventually leading to the virtual disappearance of the once dominant Christian Democratic Party. In Ireland also, following decades in which there had been no major changes in the electoral balance of the party system, the long-term basis for stability was finally undermined in 1989 when the dominant party, Fianna Fáil, decided for the first time ever to enter a coalition with another party. Prior to then, as noted above, party competition had been structured around the opposition between Fianna Fáil on one side, and all of the smaller parties on the other, and this had severely constrained and stabilized voter preferences. From 1989 onwards, however, when these constraints were removed, the potential for change was greatly enhanced, and hence, while the level of volatility prior to Fianna Fáil's first coalition was relatively muted, the subsequent election witnessed a major upsurge in volatility which resulted in a doubling of the Labour vote to the highest level ever recorded—the result, quite simply, of the removal of what had been up to then the most powerful constraint on electoral mobility.

This is perhaps a roundabout way of saying that the structure of competition, and the structure of competition for government in particular, may impose a major constraint on voter choice, and hence may act to stabilize electoral alignments. In this sense, voters are not simply expressing preferences for individual parties; rather, albeit not always to the same degree in different party systems, and this in itself is an important source of cross-national (and cross-institutional) variance, they are also expressing preferences for potential governments. And in much the same way that a shift in the range of parties on offer can act to undermine established preferences,[12] so too can a shift in the range of governing options, and hence a shift in the structure of competition, act to undermine established preferences and promote instability.

Just such a process might now be seen to be developing in many of the established party systems in western Europe, in that the evidence suggests that we are now witnessing a major shift in the traditional patterns of government formation. There are two trends which are relevant here, each of which suggests that formerly closed structures of competition might now begin to open and hence might well promote greater electoral uncertainty in the future. In the first place, as noted elsewhere in this volume, the last two decades have seen the opening-up of government to an increasingly wide range of political parties, with almost every established and substantial party in western Europe winning at least one period in government, and with the result that governing, even if only sporadically, is by now a standard experience for most parties. Second, a related impression of developments at the level of government suggests that party systems are increasingly characterized by a gradual broadening of the range of coalition alternatives, creating the impression of a growing promiscuity in the process of coalition formation, which, in turn, is also likely to impact upon structures of competition within party systems.

Should these trends continue, then it is certainly possible that we might yet witness the progressive destructuration of traditional patterns of party competition, with formerly closed patterns increasingly giving way to a style which is at once more open and less predictable, a development which has already become apparent in the 1990s in both Ireland and Italy. The result is likely to be the removal of one major constraint on voter choice, and the potential, at least, for a significant destabilization of established electoral alignments. Other constraints on electoral mobility still remain, of course, including both institutional inertia and the cleavage structure itself; but should this particular anchor now begin to shift, and should structures of competition begin to open up, then it will certainly enhance the scope of uncertainty.

---

[12] Note, for example, the strong relationship between the number of parties in competition, on the one hand, and the degree of electoral volatility, on the other (Pedersen, 1983: 48–55; Bartolini and Mair, 1990: 130–45).

REFERENCES

Ágh, Attila (1995), 'The East Central European Party Systems: from "movements" to "cartels" ', paper presented to the conference on Political Representation: Parties and Parliamentary Democracy, Budapest.

Alford, Robert R. (1963), *Party and Society: The Anglo-American Democracies* (Chicago).

—— and Friedland, Roger (1974), 'Nations, Parties and Participation: A Critique of Political Sociology', *Theory & Society*, 1/3: 307–28.

Almond, Gabriel A. (1956), 'Comparative Political Systems', *Journal of Politics*, 18/3: 391–409.

—— Powell, G. Bingham, and Mundt, Robert J. (1993), *Comparative Politics: A Theoretical Framework* (New York).

Andersen, Jørgen Goul, and Bjørklund, Tor (1990), 'Structural Changes and New Cleavages: The Progress Parties in Denmark and Norway', *Acta Sociologica*, 33/3: 195–217.

Andeweg, Rudy B. (1982), *Dutch Voters Adrift: On Explanations of Electoral Change, 1963–1977* (Leiden).

Bakvis, Herman (1988), 'The Canadian Paradox: Party System Stability in the Face of a Weakly Aligned Electorate', in Wolinetz (1988), 245–68.

—— (1991) (ed.), *Representation, Integration and Political Parties in Canada* (Toronto).

Bardi, Luciano, and Morlino, Leonardo (1994), 'Italy: Tracing the Roots of the Great Transformation', in Katz and Mair (1994), 242–77.

Bartolini, Stefano (1981), 'Il Mutamento del Sistema Partitico Francese', *Il Mulino*, 30: 169–219.

—— (1983a), 'The European Left Since World War I: Size, Composition and Electoral Development', in Daalder and Mair (1983), 139–76.

—— (1983b), 'The Membership of Mass Parties: the Social-Democratic Experience', in Daalder and Mair (1983), 177–220.

—— (1984), 'Institutional Constraints and Party Competition in the French Party System.' *West European Politics*, 7/4: 103–27.

—— (1986), 'Partiti e Sistemi di Partito', in Gianfranco Pasquino (ed.), *Manuale di Scienza della Politica* (Bologna), 231–80.

—— and Roberto D'Alimonte (1995), 'Il Sistema Partitico: Una Transizione Difficile', in Stefano Bartolini and Roberto D'Alimonte (eds.), *Maggioritario Ma Non Troppo* (Bologna), 427–66.

Bartolini, Stefano and Mair, Peter (1990), *Identity, Competition and Electoral Availability: The Stabilisation of European Electorates, 1885–1985* (Cambridge).

Batt, Judy (1991), *East Central Europe from Reform to Transformation* (London).

Beer, Samuel H. (1969), *Modern British Politics*, 2nd edn. (London).

Betz, Hans-Georg (1994), *Radical Right-Wing Populism in Western Europe* (Basingstoke) 37–67.

Beyme, Klaus von (1983), 'Governments, Parliaments and the Structure of Power in Political Parties', in Daalder and Mair (1983), 341–68.

—— (1985), *Political Parties in Western Democracies* (New York).

—— (1993), *Die politische Klasse im Parteienstaat* (Frankfurt am Main).

Biezen, Ingrid van (1995), 'New Democracies in Europe: The Emergence and Institutionalization of Party Organizations', unpublished paper, Leiden University.

Bille, Lars (1990), 'Denmark: The Oscillating Party System', in Mair and Smith (1990), 42–58.

—— (1994), 'Denmark: The Decline of the Membership Party?' in Katz and Mair (1994), 134–57.

Blondel, Jean (1968), 'Party Systems and Patterns of Government in Western Democracies', *Canadian Journal of Political Science*, 1/2: 180–203.

Bowler, Sean, and Farrell, David (1992) (eds.), *Electoral Strategies and Political Marketing* (Basingstoke).

Budge, Ian, and Farlie, Dennis (1983), *Explaining and Predicting Elections* (London).

—— Hearl, Derek, and Robertson, David (1987) (eds.), *Ideology, Strategy and Party Change Spatial Analyses of Post-War Election Programmes in Nineteen Democracies* (Cambridge).

—— and Keman, Hans (1990), *Parties and Democracy* (Oxford).

—— and Robertson, David (1987), 'Do Parties Differ, and How? Comparative Discriminant and Factor Analyses', in Budge *et al.* (1987), 387–416.

Butler, David, and Ranney, Austin (1992) (eds.), *Electioneering: A Comparative Study of Continuity and Change* (Oxford).

Carroll, Lewis (1982), *The Penguin Complete Lewis Carroll* (London).

Carty, R. K. (1994), 'Canada', *European Journal of Political Research*, 26/3–4: 255–68.

Castles, Francis G. (1982) (ed.), *The Impact of Parties* (London).

—— and Mair, Peter (1984), 'Left-Right Political Scales: Some "Expert" Judgments', *European Journal of Political Research*, 12/1: 73–88.

—— and Wildenmann, Rudolf (1986) (eds.), *Visions and Realities of Party Government* (Berlin).

Coppedge, Michael (1992), '(De)institutionalization of Latin American Party Systems', paper presented to the XVII International Congress of the Latin American Studies Association, Los Angeles, September.

Cotta, Maurizio (1995), 'La strutturazione dei sistemi partitici nelle nuove democrazie', *Rivista Italiana di Scienza Politica*, 25/2: 267–305.

Cox, Gary W., and McCubbins, Mathew D. (1993), *Legislative Leviathan: Party Government in the House* (Berkeley, Calif.).

Crewe, Ivor, and Denver, David (1985) (eds.), *Electoral Change in Western Democracies: Patterns and Sources of Electoral Volatility* (London).

Daalder, Hans (1966), 'Parties, Elites and Political Developments in Western Europe', in Joseph LaPalombara and Myron Weiner (eds.), *Political Parties and Political Development* (Princeton, N.J.), 43–77.

—— (1974), 'The Consociational Democracy Theme', *World Politics*, 26/4: 604–21.

—— (1983), 'The Comparative Study of European Parties and Party Systems: An Overview', in Daalder and Mair (1983), 1–27.

—— (1984), 'In Search of the Centre of European Party Systems', *American Political Science Review*, 78/1: 92–109.

—— (1992), 'A Crisis of Party?' *Scandinavian Political Studies*, 15/4: 269–87.

—— and Mair, Peter (1983) (eds.), *Western European Party Systems: Continuity and Change* (London).

Dahl, Robert A. (1956), *A Preface to Democratic Theory* (Chicago).

—— (1966), 'Patterns of Opposition', in Robert A. Dahl (ed.), *Political Oppositions in Western Democracies* (New Haven, Conn.), 332–47.

—— (1971), *Polyarchy: Participation and Opposition* (New Haven, Conn.).

D'Alimonte, Roberto (1989), 'Democrazia e Competizione', *Rivista Italiana di Scienza Politica*, 19/1: 115–33.

Dalton, Russell J., and Kuechler, Manfred (1990) (eds.), *Challenging the Political Order: New Social and Political Movements in Western Democracies* (New York).

Dalton, Russell J., Flanagan, Scott C., and Beck, Paul Allen (1984*a*) (eds.), *Electoral Change in Advanced Industrial Democracies: Realignment or Dealignment?* (Princeton: Princeton, N.J.).

—— (1984*b*), 'Political Forces and Partisan Change', in Dalton *et al.* (1984*a*), 451–76.

Deschouwer, Kris (1992), 'The Survival of the Fittest: Measuring and Explaining Adaptation and Change of Political Parties', paper presented at the ECPR Joint Sessions, University of Limerick.

—— (1994), 'The Decline of Consociationalism and the Reluctant Modernization of Belgian Mass Parties', in Katz and Mair (1994), 80–108.

Dittrich, Karl (1983), 'Testing the Catch-All Thesis: Some Difficulties and Possibilities', in Daalder and Mair (1983), 257–66.

Dowding, Keith M., and Kimber, Richard (1987), 'Political Stability and the Science of Comparative Politics', *European Journal of Political Research*, 15/1: 103–22.

Downs, Athony (1957), *An Economic Theory of Democracy* (New York).

Duverger, Maurice (1954), *Political Parties: Their Organization and Activities in the Modern State* (London).

Eijk, Cees van der, Franklin, Mark N., Mackie, Tom, and Valen, Henry (1992), 'Cleavages, Conflict Resolution and Democracy', in Franklin *et al.* (1992), 406–31.

—— and Niemoeller, Kees (1983), *Electoral Change in the Netherlands: Empirical Results and Methods of Measurement* (Amsterdam).

—— and Oppenhuis, Erik (1988), 'Ideological Domains and Party Systems in Western Europe', paper presented to the XIVth World Congress of the International Political Science Association, Washington, D.C.

Einhorn, Eric S., and Logue, John (1988), 'Continuity and Change in the Scandinavian Party Systems', in Wolinetz (1988), 159–202.

Epstein, Leon (1986), *Political Parties in the American Mold* (Madison, Wis.).

Ersson, Svante, and Lane, Jan-Erik (1982), 'Democratic Party Systems in Europe: Dimensions, Change and Stability', *Scandinavian Political Studies*, 5/1: 67–96.

Evans, Geoffrey, and Whitfield, Stephen (1993), 'Identifying the Bases of Party Competition in Eastern Europe', *British Journal of Political Science*, 23/4: 521–48.

Farrell, David (1993), *The Contemporary Irish Party: Campaign and Organizational Developments in a Changing Environment* (Ph.D. thesis, European University Institute, Florence).

—— (1994), 'Ireland: Centralization, Professionalization, and Competitive Pressures', in Katz and Mair (1994), 216–41.

Finer, S. E. (1984), 'The Decline of Party?' in Vernon Bogdanor (ed.), *Parties and Democracy in Britain and America* (New York), 1–6.

Fiorina, Maurice (1981), *Retrospective Voting in American National Elections* (New Haven, Conn.).

Flanagan, Scott C., and Dalton, Russell J. (1984), 'Parties Under Stress: Realignment and Dealignment in Advanced Industrial Societies', *West European Politics*, 7/1: 7–23.

Flora, Peter (1986), 'Introduction', in Peter Flora (ed.), *Growth to Limits: The Western European Welfare States Since World War II. Vol. 1: Sweden, Norway, Finland, Denmark* (Berlin), v–xxxvi.

Franklin, Mark N., and Mackie, Thomas T. (1983), 'Familiarity and Inertia in the Formation of Governing Coalitions in Parliamentary Democracies', *British Journal of Political Science*, 13/2: 275–98.

—— Valen, Henry *et al.* (1992), *Electoral Change: Responses to Social and Attitudinal Structures in Western Countries* (Cambridge).

Friedrich, Carl J. (1968), *Constitutional Government and Democracy*: *Theory and Practice in Europe and America*, 4th edn. (Waltham, Mass.).

Gallagher, Michael, Laver, Michael, and Mair, Peter (1995), *Representative Government in Modern Europe*, 2nd edn (New York).

Gangas, Pilar (1994), *El Desarrollo Organizativo de Los Partidos Politicos Españoles de Implementacion Nacional* (Ph.D. thesis, Universitat Autònoma de Madrid).

Garrett, Geoffrey (1995), 'Capital Mobility, Trade and the Domestic Politics of Economic Policy', *International Organizations*, 49/4: 657–87.

Geddes, Barbara (1995), 'A Comparative Perspective on the Leninist Legacy in Eastern Europe', *Comparative Political Studies*, 28/2: 239–74.

Gould, Stephen Jay (1985), *The Flamingo's Smile*: *Reflections in Natural History* (New York).

—— (1991), *Bully for Brontosaurus*: *Further Reflections in Natural History* (London).

Graetz, Brian, and McAllister, Ian (1987), 'Popular Evaluations of Party Leaders in the Anglo-American Democracies', in Harold D. Clarke and Moshe M. Czudnowski (eds.), *Political Elites in Anglo-American Democracies* (Williston, Ill.), 44–63.

Hecksher, Gunnar (1953), *The Study of Comparative Government and Politics* (Westport, Conn.).

Hildebrandt, Kai, and Dalton, Russell J. (1978), 'The New Politics: Political Change or Sunshine Politics?', in Max Kaase and Klaus von Beyme (eds.), *Elections and Parties* (London), 69–96.

Huber, John, and Inglehart, Ronald (1995), 'Expert Interpretations of Party Space and Party Location in 42 Societies', *Party Politics*, 1/1: 73–111.

Ignazi, Piero (1992), 'The Silent Counter-Revolution: Hypotheses on the Emergence of Extreme Right-Wing Parties in Europe', *European Journal of Political Research*, 22/1: 3–34.

—— (1994), *L'Estrema Destra in Europa* (Bologna).

Inglehart, Ronald (1977), *The Silent Revolution*: *Changing Values and Political Styles Among Western Publics* (Princeton, N.J.).

—— (1984), 'The Changing Structure of Political Cleavages in Western Society', in Dalton *et al.* (1984*a*), 25–69.

—— (1987), 'Value Change in Industrial Societies', *American Political Science Review*, 81/4: 1289–303.

Irwin, Galen A., and Holsteyn, J. J. M. van (1989), 'Decline of the Structured Model of Electoral Competition', in Hans Daalder and Galen A Irwin (eds.), *Politics in the Netherlands*: *How Much Change*? (London), 21–41.

Janda, Kenneth (1980), *Political Parties*: *A Cross-National Survey* (New York).

Janda, Kenneth (1993), 'Comparative Political Parties: Research and Theory', in Ada W. Finifter (ed.), *The State of the Discipline II* (Washington, D.C.), 163–92.

Jasiewicz, Krzystof (1995), 'Poland', *European Journal of Political Research*, 28/3–4: 449–57.

Katz, Richard S. (1986), 'Party Government: A Rationalistic Conception,' in Francis G. Castles and Rudolf Wildenmann (eds.), *Visions and Realities of Party Government* (Berlin), 31–71.

—— (1987) (ed.), *Party Governments: European and American Experiences* (Berlin).

—— (1990), 'Party as Linkage: A Vestigial Function?', *European Journal of Political Research*, 18/1: 143–61.

—— and Kolodny, Robin (1994), 'Party Organization as an Empty Vessel: Parties in American Politics', in Katz and Mair (1994), 23–50.

—— and Mair, Peter (1992*a*) (eds.), *Party Organizations: A Data Handbook on Party Organizations in Western Democracies, 1960–90* (London).

—— (1992*b*), 'Introduction: The Cross-National Study of Party Organizations', in Katz and Mair (1992*a*), 1–20.

—— (1993), 'The Evolution of Party Organizations in Europe: Three Faces of Party Organization', in William Crotty (ed.), *Political Parties in a Changing Age*, special issue of the *American Review of Politics*, 14, 593–617.

—— (1994) (eds.), *How Parties Organize: Change and Adaptation in Party Organizations in Western Democracies* (London).

—— *et al.* (1992), 'The Membership of Political Parties in European Democracies, 1960–1990', *European Journal of Political Research*, 22/3: 329–45.

Katzenstein, Peter J. (1985), *Small States in World Markets: Industrial Policy in Europe* (Ithaca, N.Y.).

—— (1987), *Policy and Politics in West Germany: The Growth of a Semi-Sovereign State* (Philadelphia).

King, Anthony (1969), 'Political Parties in Western Democracies: Some Sceptical Reflections', *Polity*, 2/2: 111–41.

Kirchheimer, Otto (1966), 'The Transformation of West European Party Systems', in Joseph LaPalombara and Myron Weiner (eds.), *Political Parties and Political Development* (Princeton, N.J.), 177–200.

Kitschelt, Herbert (1988), 'Left-Libertarian Parties: Explaining Innovation in Competitive Party Systems', *World Politics*, 40/2: 127–54.

—— (1992), 'The Formation of Party Systems in East Central Europe', *Politics and Society*, 20/1: 7–50.

—— (1995), 'Patterns of Competition in East Central European Party Systems', paper presented to the annual meeting of the American Political Science Association.

Kleinnijenhuis, Jan, and Rietberg, Ewald M. (1995), 'Parties, Media, the Public and the Economy: Patterns of Societal Agenda-Setting', *European Journal of Political Research*, 28/1: 95–118.

Koole, Ruud (1994), 'The Vulnerability of the Modern Cadre Party in the Netherlands', in Katz and Mair (1994), 278–303.

—— and Mair, Peter (1992 *et seq.*) (eds.), *Political Data Yearbook, Vol 1*: *1 January 1991–1 January 1992 et seq.* (Dordrecht).

—— and Praag, Philip van (1990), 'Electoral Competition in a Segmented Society: Campaign Strategies and the Importance of Elite Perceptions', *European Journal of Political Research*, 18/1: 51–70.

Kopecký, Petr (1995), 'Developing Party Organizations in East-Central Europe', *Party Politics*, 1/4: 515–34.

Krasner, Stephen D. (1984), 'Approaches to the State: Alternative Conceptions and Historical Dynamics', *Comparative Politics*, 16/2: 223–46.

Krouwel, André (1993), 'The Organizational Dimension of the Catch-All Party', paper presented to the Workshop on Inter-Party Relationships in National and European Parliamentary Arenas, ECPR Joint Sessions, University of Leiden.

Kriesi, Hanspeter, Koopmans, Ruud, Duyvendak, Jan Willem, and Giugni, Mario C. (1995), *New Social Movements in Western Europe*: *A Comparative Analysis* (London).

Lane, Jan-Erik, and Ersson, Svante (1987), *Politics and Society in Western Europe* (London).

Laver, Michael (1976), 'Strategic Campaign Behaviour for Electors and Parties: The Northern Ireland Assembly Elections of 1973', in Ian Budge, Ivor Crewe, and Dennis Farlie (eds.), *Party Identification and Beyond*: *Representations of Voting and Party Competition* (London), 315–44

—— (1989), 'Party Competition and Party System Change', *Journal of Theoretical Politics*, 1/3: 301–24.

—— and Arkins, Audrey (1990), 'Coalition and Fianna Fáil', in Michael Gallagher and Richard Sinnott (eds.), *How Ireland Voted 1989* (Galway), 192–207.

—— and Budge, Ian (1992) (eds.), *Party Policy and Government Coalitions* (Basingstoke).

—— and Elliott, Sydney (1987), 'Northern Ireland 1921–1973: Party Manifestos and Platforms', in Budge *et al.* (1987), 160–77.

—— and Schofield, Norman (1990), *Multiparty Government* (Oxford).

Lawson, Kay (1980) (ed.), *Political Parties and Linkage*: *A Comparative Perspective* (New Haven, Conn.).

—— (1988), 'When Linkage Fails', in Lawson and Merkl (1988*b*), 13–38.

—— and Merkl, Peter H. (1988*a*), 'Alternative Organizations:

Environmental, Supplementary, Communitarian, and Antiauthoritarian', in Lawson and Merkl (1988*b*), 3–12.

Lawson, Kay, and Merkl, Peter (1988*b*) (eds.), *When Parties Fail*: *Emerging Alternative Organizations* (Princeton, N.J.).

Lehmbruch, Gerhard (1974), 'A Non-Competitive Pattern of Conflict Management in Liberal Democracies: The Cases of Switzerland, Austria, and the Lebanon', in Kenneth McRae (ed.), *Consociational Democracy* (Toronto), 90–7.

—— (1977), 'Liberal Corporatism and Party Government', *Comparative Political Studies*, 10/1: 91–126.

Lewis, Paul G. (1996), 'Introduction and Theoretical Overview', in Paul G. Lewis (ed.), *Party Structure and Organization in East-Central Europe* (Cheltenham), 1–19.

Lijphart, Arend (1968), 'Typologies of Democratic Systems', *Comparative Political Studies*, 1/1: 3–44.

—— (1977), *Democracy in Plural Societies*: *A Comparative Exploration* (New Haven, Conn.).

—— (1984), *Democracies*: *Patterns of Majoritarian and Consensus Government in Twenty One Countries* (New Haven, Conn.).

—— (1991), 'Constitutional Choices in New Democracies', *Journal of Theoretical Politics*, 4/2: 72–84.

Lipset, S. M., and Rokkan, Stein (1967), 'Cleavage Structures, Party Systems and Voter Alignments: an Introduction', in S. M. Lipset and Stein Rokkan (eds.), *Party Systems and Voter Alignments* (New York), 1–64.

Lovenduski, Joni, and Outshoorn, Joyce (1986) (eds.), *The New Politics of Abortion* (London).

Lybeck, Johan A. (1985), 'Is The Lipset-Rokkan Hypothesis Testable?', *Scandinavian Political Studies*, 8/1–2: 105–13.

McAllister, Ian (1977), *The Northern Ireland Social Democratic and Labour Party* (London).

—— and White, Stephen (1995), 'Democracy, Political Parties and Party Formation in Post-Communist Russia', *Party Politics*, 1/1: 49–72.

McDonald, Ronald H., and Ruhl, J. Mark (1989), *Party Politics and Elections in Latin America* (Boulder, Colo.).

MacIvor, Heather (1995), 'Do Canadian Parties Form a Cartel?' unpublished manuscript.

Mackie, Thomas T. (1991), 'General Elections in Western Nations During 1989', *European Journal of Political Research*, 19/1: 157–62.

—— (1992), 'General Elections in Western Nations During 1990', *European Journal of Political Research*, 21/3: 317–32.

—— and Rose, Richard (1982 and 1991), *The International Almanac of Electoral History*, 2nd edn. and 3rd edn. (London).

Maguire, Maria (1983), 'Is There Still Persistence? Electoral Change in Western Europe, 1948–1979', in Daalder and Mair (1983), 67–94.

Mainwaring, Scott, and Shugart, Matthew (1994), 'Electoral Rules, Institutional Engineering, and Party Discipline', paper presented to the conference on Political Parties: Changing Roles in Contemporary Democracies, Madrid, December.

Mair, Peter (1983), 'Adaptation and Control: Towards an Understanding of Party and Party System Change', in Daalder and Mair (1983), 405–30.

—— (1984), 'Party Politics in Western Europe: A Challenge to Party?', *West European Politics*, 7/4: 170–84.

—— (1987a), *The Changing Irish Party System*: *Organization, Ideology and Electoral Competition* (London).

—— (1987b), 'Policy Competition', in Michael Laver, Peter Mair, and Richard Sinnott (eds.), *How Ireland Voted*: *the Irish General Election 1987* (Dublin), 30–47.

—— (1987c), 'The Irish Republic and the Anglo-Irish Agreement', in Paul Teague (ed.), *Beyond the Rhetoric*: *Politics, the Economy and Social Policy in Northern Ireland* (London), 81–110.

—— (1990a) (ed.), *The West European Party System* (Oxford).

—— (1990b), 'The Electoral Payoffs of Fission and Fusion', *British Journal of Political Science*, 20/1: 131–42.

—— (1991), 'The Electoral Universe of Small Parties in Postwar Western Europe', in Ferdinand Mueller-Rommel and Geoffrey Pridham (eds.), *Small Parties in Western Europe*: *Comparative and National Perspectives* (London), 41–70.

—— (1993), 'Fianna Fáil, Labour and the Irish Party System', in Michael Gallagher and Michael Laver (eds.), *How Ireland Voted 1992* (Dublin), 162–73.

—— (1994), 'The Correlates of Consensus Democracy and the Puzzle of Dutch Politics', *West European Politics*, 17/4: 97–123.

—— and Smith, Gordon (1990) (eds.), *Understanding Party System Change in Western Europe* (London).

Marcet, Joan, and Argelaguet, Jordi (1994), 'Regionalist Parties in Catalonia', unpublished paper, Universitat Autònoma de Barcelona.

Mayhew, David R. (1974), *Congress*: *The Electoral Connection* (New Haven, Conn.).

Michels, Robert (1962 [1911]), *Political Parties*: *A Sociological Study of the Oligarchical Tendencies of Modern Democracies* (New York).

Morlino, Leonardo (1995), 'Political Parties and Democratic Consolidation in Southern Europe', in Richard Gunther, P. Nikiforos Daimandouros, and Hans-Jürgen Puhle (eds.), *The Politics of Democratic Consolidation*: *Southern Europe in Comparative Perspective* (Cambridge), 315–88.

Mudde, C. E. (1995), 'Right-Wing Extremism Analysed', *European Journal of Political Research*, 27/2: 203–24.

Müller, Wolfgang C. (1993), 'The Relevance of the State for Party System Change', *Journal of Theoretical Politics*, 5/4: 419–54.

—— (1994), 'The Development of Austrian Party Organizations in the Postwar Period', in Katz and Mair (1994), 51–79.

Neumann, Sigmund (1956), 'Towards a Comparative Study of Political Parties', in Sigmund Neumann (ed.), *Modern Political Parties* (Chicago), 395–421.

Offe, Claus (1992), 'Capitalism by Democratic Design? Democratic Theory Facing the Triple Transition in East-Central Europe', in György Lengyl, Claus Offe, and Jochen Tholen (eds.), *Economic Institutions, Actors and Attitudes: East Central Europe in Transition* (Budapest and Bremen), 11–22.

Ostrogorski, M. I. (1902), *Democracy and the Organization of Political Parties* (London).

Panebianco, Angelo (1988), *Political Parties: Organization and Power* (Cambridge).

Pappalardo, Adriano (1981), 'The Conditions for Consociational Democracy: A Logical and Empirical Critique', *European Journal of Political Research*, 9/3: 365–90.

Pedersen, Mogens N. (1979), 'The Dynamics of European Party Systems: Changing Patterns of Electoral Volatility', *European Journal of Political Research*, 7/1: 1–26.

—— (1983), Patterns of Electoral Volatility in European Party Systems: Explorations in Explanation', in Daalder and Mair (1983), 29–66.

—— (1987), 'The Danish "Working Multiparty System": Breakdown or Adaptation?' in Hans Daalder (ed.), *Party Systems in Denmark, Austria, Switzerland, The Netherlands and Belgium* (London), 1–60.

—— (1988), 'The Defeat of All Parties: The Danish Folketing Election of 1973', in Lawson and Merkl (1988*b*), 257–81.

Pellikaan, Huib (1994), *Anarchie, Staat en het Prisoner's Dilemma* (Delft).

Pempel, T. J. (1990), 'Exclusionary Democracies: the Postauthoritarian experience', in Peter Katzenstein, Theodore Lowi, and Sidney Tarrow (eds.), *Comparative Theory and Political Experience: Mario Einaudi and the Liberal Tradition* (Ithaca, N.Y.), 97–118.

Pierre, Jon, and Widfeldt, Anders (1994), 'Party Organizations in Sweden: Colossuses With Feet of Clay or Flexible Pillars of Government?', in Katz and Mair (1994), 332–56.

Pizzorno, Allesandro (1981), 'Interests and Parties in Pluralism', in Suzanne Berger (ed.), *Organizing Interests in Western Europe: Pluralism, Corporatism, and the Transformation of Politics* (Cambridge), 249–84.

Poguntke, Thomas (1987), 'New Politics and Party Systems', *West European Politics*, 10/1: 76–88.

—— (1994*a*), 'Parties in a Legalistic Culture: The Case of Germany', in Katz and Mair (1994), 185–215.

—— (1994*b*), 'Explorations into a Minefield: Anti-Party Sentiment— Conceptual Thoughts and Empirical Evidence', paper presented to the Joint Sessions of the European Consortium for Political Research, Madrid.

—— (1995), 'Parties and Society in Western Democracies', unpublished manuscript.

Pomper, Gerald M. (1992), 'Concepts of Political Parties', *Journal of Theoretical Politics*, 4/2: 143–59.

Pridham, Geoffrey (1986) (ed.), *Coalitional Behaviour in Theory and Practice: An Inductive Model for Western Europe* (Cambridge).

Przeworski, Adam, and Sprague, John (1986), *Paper Stones: A History of Electoral Socialism* (Chicago).

Rae, Douglas (1971), *The Political Consequences of Electoral Laws*, rev. edn. (New Haven, Conn.).

Randall, Vicky, (1988) (ed.), *Political Parties in the Third World* (London).

Ranney, Austin (1962), *The Doctrine of Responsible Party Government* (Urbana, Ill.).

Rokkan, Stein (1968), 'The Growth and Structuring of Mass Politics in Smaller European Democracies', *Comparative Studies in Society and History*, 10/2: 173–210.

—— (1970), *Citizens, Elections, Parties* (Oslo).

—— (1977), 'Towards a Generalized Concept of *Verzuiling*', *Political Studies*, 25/4: 563–70.

Rose, Richard (1974) (ed.), *Electoral Behaviour: A Comparative Handbook* (New York).

—— (1984), *Do Parties Make a Difference?*, 2nd edn. (Chatham, N.J.).

—— (1990), 'Inheritance Before Choice in Public Policy', *Journal of Theoretical Politics*, 2/3: 263–91.

—— (1995), 'Mobilizing Demobilized Voters in Post-Communist Societies', *Party Politics*, 1/4: 549–63.

—— and McAllister, Ian (1986), *Voters Begin to Choose: From Closed-Class to Open Elections in Britain* (London).

—— and Mackie, Thomas T. (1988), 'Do Parties Persist or Fail? The Big Trade-off Facing Organisations', in Lawson and Merkl (1988*b*), 533–58.

—— and Makkai, Toni (1995), 'Consensus or Dissensus About Welfare in Post-Communist Societies', *European Journal of Political Research*, 28/2: 203–44.

—— and Urwin, Derek W. (1970), 'Persistence and Change in Western Party Systems Since 1945', *Political Studies* 18/3: 287–319.

Sainsbury, Diane (1990) (ed.), *Party Strategies and Party-Voter Linkages*, special issue of the *European Journal of Political Research*, 18/1, 1–161.

Sani, Giacomo, and Sartori, Giovanni (1983), 'Polarization, Fragmentation and Competition in Western Democracies', in Daalder and Mair (1983), 307–40.

Sartori, Giovanni (1966), 'European Political Parties: The Case of Polarized Pluralism', in Joseph LaPalombara and Myron Weiner (eds.), *Political Parties and Political Development* (Princeton, N.J.), 137–76.

—— (1968), 'Political Development and Political Engineering', *Public Policy*, 17, 261–98.

—— (1969), 'From the Sociology of Politics to Political Sociology', in S. M. Lipset (ed.), *Politics and the Social Sciences* (New York), 65–100.

—— (1970), 'The Typology of Party Systems: Proposals for Improvement', in Erik Allardt and Stein Rokkan (eds.), *Mass Politics*: *Studies in Political Sociology* (New York), 322–52.

—— (1976), *Parties and Party Systems*: *A Framework for Analysis* (Cambridge).

—— (1986), 'The Influence of Electoral Systems: Faulty Laws or Faulty Method?' in Bernard Grofman and Arend Lijphart (eds.), *Electoral Laws and Their Political Consequences* (New York), 43–68.

—— (1987), *The Theory of Democracy Revisited*, *Part One*: *The Contemporary Debate* (Chatham, N.J.).

—— (1994), *Comparative Constitutional Engineering*: *An Inquiry into Structures, Incentives and Outcomes* (Basingstoke).

Scarrow, Susan E. (1994a), 'The "Paradox of Enrollment": Assessing the Costs and Benefits of Party Memberships', *European Journal of Political Research*, 25/1: 41–60.

—— (1994b), 'The Consequences of Anti-Party Sentiment: Anti-Party Arguments as Instruments of Change', paper presented to the Joint Sessions of the European Consortium for Political Research, Madrid.

Scharpf, Fritz (1988), *Crisis and Choice in European Social Democracy* (Ithaca, N.Y.).

Schattschneider, E. E. (1942), *Party Government* (New York).

—— (1960), *The Semi-Sovereign People* (New York).

Schmitt, Hermann (1989), 'On Party Attachment in Western Europe and the Utility of Eurobarometer Data', *West European Politics*, 12/2: 122–39.

Scholten, Ilya (1987) (ed.), *Political Stability and Neo-Corporatism* (London).

Seiler, Daniel-Louis (1980), *Partis et Familles politiques* (Paris).

Seyd, Patrick, and Whiteley, Paul (1992), *Labour's Grass Roots* (Oxford).

Shaddick, Matthew (1990), 'New Political Parties in West European Party Systems' (BA thesis, University of Manchester).

Shamir, Michal (1984), 'Are Western European Party Systems "Frozen"?' *Comparative Political Studies*, 17/1: 35–79.

Sjöblom, Gunnar (1981), 'Notes on the Notion of Party Adaptation', paper presented to workshop on Party Adaptation, ECPR Joint Sessions, University of Lancaster.

—— (1987), 'The Role of Political Parties in Denmark and Sweden,' in Richard S. Katz (ed.), *Party Government: European and American Experiences* (Berlin), 155–211.

Smith, Gordon (1988), 'A System Perspective on Party System Change', paper presented to the Workshop on Change in Western European Party Systems, ECPR Joint Sessions, Rimini.

—— (1990), 'Core Persistence, System Change and the "People's Party"', in Mair and Smith (1990), 157–68.

Spruyt, Hendrik (1994), *The Sovereign State and Its Competitors: An Analysis of Systems Change* (Princeton, N.J.).

Stubbs, Richard, and Underhill, Geoffrey R. D. (1994), 'Introduction: State Policies and Global Changes', in Richard Stubbs and Geoffrey R. D. Underhill (eds.), *Political Economy and the Changing Global Order* (Basingstoke), 421–4.

Sundberg, Jan (1987), 'Explaining the Basis of Declining Party Membership in Denmark: a Scandinavian Comparison', *Scandinavian Political Studies*, 10/1: 17–38.

—— (1994), 'Finland: Nationalized Parties, Professionalized Organizations', in Katz and Mair (1994), 158–84.

Svåsand, Lars (1994), 'Change and Adaptation in Norwegian Party Organizations', in Katz and Mair (1994), 304–31.

Tocqueville, Alexis de (1966 [1856]), *The Ancien Régime and the French Revolution*, trans. Stuart Gilbert (Glasgow).

Tóka, Gábor (1993), 'Parties and Electoral Choices in East Central Europe', paper presented to the conference on The Emergence of New Party Systems and Transitions to Democracy, University of Bristol.

Truman, David (1951), *The Governmental Process* (New York).

Urmanič, Martin (1994), *Transformácia Politických Strán a Hnutí na Slovenska po Novembri 1989*, MA thesis, Univerzita Komenského Bratislava.

Valen, Henry (1976), 'National Conflict Structures and Foreign Politics: the Impact of the EEC Issue on Perceived Cleavages in Norwegian Politics', *European Journal of Political Research*, 4/1: 47–82

Veen, Hans-Joachim, Lepszy, Norbert, and Mnich, Peter (1993), *The Republikaner Party in Germany: Right-Wing Menace or Protest Catchall?* (Westport, Conn./*Washington Papers* no. 162).

Waller, Michael (1994), *The End of the Communist Power Monopoly* (Manchester).

Waller, Michael (1995) (ed.), *Party Politics in Eastern Europe*, special issue of *Party Politics*, 1/4: 443–618.

Ware, Alan (1987) (ed.), *Political Parties: Electoral Change and Structural Response* (Oxford).

—— (1996), *Political Parties and Party Systems* (Oxford).

Waxman, Chaim I. (1968) (ed.), *The End of Ideology Debate* (New York).

Webb, Paul D. (1994), 'Party Organizational Change in Britain: The Iron Law of Centralization?', in Katz and Mair (1994), 109–33.

Weber, Max (1946), 'Politics as a Vocation', in H. H. Gerth and C. Wright Mills (eds.), *From Max Weber: Essays in Sociology* (New York), 77–128.

Whyte, John H. (1974). 'Ireland: Politics Without Social Bases', in Richard Rose (ed.), *Electoral Behaviour: A Comparative Handbook* (New York), 619–51.

Wildenmann, Rudolf (1986), 'The Problematic of Party Government', in Castles and Wildenmann (1986), 1–30.

Williamson, Peter J. (1989), *Corporatism in Perspective* (London).

Woldendorp, Jaap, Keman, Hans, and Budge, Ian (1993), *Political Data 1945–1990: Party Governments in Twenty Democracies*, special issue of the *European Journal of Political Research*, 24/1, 1–119.

Wolinetz, Steven B. (1979), 'The Transformation of Western European Party Systems Revisited', *West European Politics*, 2/1: 4–28.

—— (1988) (ed.), *Parties and Party Systems in Liberal Democracies* (London).

Ysmal, Colette (1989), *Les Partis politiques sous la Ve République* (Paris).

—— (1992), 'France', *European Journal of Political Research*, 22/4: 401–8.

Zielonka, Jan (1994), 'Institutional Uncertainty in Post-Communist Democracies', *Journal of Democracy*, 5/2: 87–104.

Zielonka-Goei, Mei Lan (1992), 'Members Marginalising Themselves? Intra-Party Participation in the Netherlands', *West European Politics*, 15/2: 93–106.

INDEX